Marx and Burke:
A Revisionist View

Marx and Burke:
A Revisionist View

Ruth A. Bevan

Open Court Publishing Company
La Salle, Illinois

Printed in the Unted States of America

9006637301

ISBN: 0-87548-144-2

Library of Congress Catolog Card Number: 73-79625

Dedication

In loving memory of my father, the Reverend Vernon F. Bevan, Congregational minister, whose steadfastness and courage in the face of adversity were a beacon light to many, and whose understanding and vision provided me with the ongoing substance of life.

Table of Contents

Foreword

by Russell Kirk

As T. S. Eliot wrote, there are no lost causes because there are no gained causes. Ever since 1789, the world has been convulsed by a struggle of political ideas quite as tremendous as the technological innovations of the modern age. In this contest, the mind of Burke and the mind of Marx continue to move men to action; and no one can say which mode of thought, if either, will triumph in the end. The point of Dr. Bevan's book is that if the zealot may take fire from either Burke or Marx, nevertheless the temperate scholar may derive some measure of wisdom from both.

Miss Bevan's examination of these two political intellects is the first detailed comparison of the great conservative and the great revolutionary. These two are burningly "relevant" to our hour because the questions they raised, and the convictions they affirmed, are the questions and the convictions by which our own generation is confronted. Half a century ago, George Santayana wrote that liberalism was a mere evanescent phase, a weakening of the old order, doomed itself to give place to some condition of society distinctly not intended by the liberals of the nineteenth century; many voices echo Santayana's now. Either the successors of Burke or the successors of Marx, it may be, will inherit the earth; or conceivably the civil social order of the future will owe something to both.

At first glance, the champion of prescription and the champion of upheaval seem to have nothing in common. Yet Dr. Bevan, in dispassionate fashion, draws certain parallels. The most important of these parallels—though it might be palatable to neither political thinker—is that both Burke and Marx (both lawyers' sons) perceived the necessity of founding a social order upon a moral order. They knew that community is not a product of convenience merely: that men must be united in belief, or else everything falls apart.

The brilliant Irish rhetorician, the ornament and organizer of a reforming party, saw in the historic experience of man with God and of man with man the source of the inner order and the outer: for Burke, politics was the art of the possible. The obscure exiled toiler in the British Museum, the German intellectual deliberately gnawing at the foundations of society, saw in the vision of perfect equality, and in the resolution of class struggle, a new order which, once established, would endure forever: for Marx, economic science was the means to the ideal. Those rival apprehensions of the human condition, under various forms and labels, strive against each other for mastery in the concluding decades of the twentieth century.

Burke stood for what he called the "moral imagination": that understanding of man's nature, and of society's complexity, which is derived from a knowledge of history, humane letters, philosophy, theology—and experience of the world. Marx stood for the opposed "idyllic imagination": the dream of man regenerate through the sweeping away of a mass of old institutions. Burke defended a society of diversity; Marx prophesied a society of uniformity. Both had the courage of their convictions, and both attested the rising generation.

Some who read this book, doubtless, will not have read either Burke or Marx—and so may be surprised that neither thinker conforms to the image graven on the tablets of liberal political dogma. Both possessed prophetic powers: Burke in his prediction that revolution must end with an absolute master, for instance; Marx in his prediction of the steady consolidation of economic interests, facilitating the revolutionary's seizure of power. Though the hopes of neither have been fulfilled, surely their vaticinations have been justified by events.

Burke was the voice of an inherited culture rooted in family, class, settled community, and church. Marx was the voice of a nascent culture denying all these, but postulated upon equality of condition. Burke's principal contribution to political theory was his exposition of that political tension which must subsist between the claims of order and the claims of freedom; Marx's chief contribution was the dialectic of the classless society. Liberal statists of the nineteenth century now seem feeble by the side of either of these men.

As Manning put it, at bottom all differences of opinion are theological. Reaffirming the doctrine of the imperfectibility of human beings, Burke would have mankind settle for a tolerable society, known through the historic experience of a nation. Proclaiming anew the doctrine of perfectibility, Marx would have mankind make immanent the teachings of the transcendent religion that he repudiated—marching, instead, to an earthly Zion.

Yet both Burke and Marx were historical empiricists, Dr. Bevan points out convincingly: that is, they rejected the abstractions of Rationalism. The skillful observation of social phenomena, both believed, is necessary for the establishment of order; and the individual cannot divorce himself from society. As Miss Bevan writes, "They rejected that kind of universalism which claimed that all men being equal, rational beings, it is possible through 'right' reason to devise and implement the perfect society on a world-wide scale." Circumstances and institutions mold us; impersonal forces and irrational impulses move us; the mass of men perceive events only as in a glass, darkly. Knowing the limits of private rationality, both applied their own powerful intellects to the study of the roots of community.

In a most difficult exercise, Dr. Bevan succeeds: it is not necessary to agree with her upon every point, but any decent student of the history of ideas must recognize in this book of hers the perceptive meeting of theoretical learning with historical consciousness. Burke and Marx were men of different centuries, different origins, different aspirations. Marx detested the Burke of whom he had read, and for Burke Marxism would have been a more terrible Jacobinism. And yet, with a higher objectivity rare in this age of ideological infatuation, Dr. Bevan gives us fresh insights into the power of both minds. (Hers is not the illusory "objectivity" of a "value-free" behavioral science.) Could they have met, Burke and Marx might have learnt much from one another, she concludes; certainly the reader can profit mightily—as I have—from their conjunction (anything but insane) in her pages. "At a time when anarchism flowers in the minds of many," she affirms, "Burke and Marx remind us that we are by nature a social animal. If we defy that nature, we can only lose in the end our moral identity." Amen to that.

History moves inexorably toward a mundane consummation, Marx argued; we are foolish if we set ourselves against the operations of Providence, Burke declared. And yet Burke and Marx themselves tremendously altered the course of events. They are relevant for even the most ardent innovator or neoterist, in our present discontents, because their armed vision works upon the world still, with a power little diminished; though dead, they give laws to peoples and commands to armies.

Whose mind will prevail, no one can tell today; that depends in part upon the disciples whom either happens to win. "A common soldier, a child, a girl at the door of an inn, have changed the face of fortune, and almost of Nature," Burke says in the Fourth Letter of the *Regicide Peace*. The Whig politician worn out in fruitless opposition, the subversive polemicist sourly grubbing in a reading-room—these two seeming failures stand eminent among those dead who, for good or ill, wake us from congenital obsession with the passing moment and from indulgence of the ravenous ego.

Acknowledgements

This is a book about the political ideas of Edmund Burke and Karl Marx and how these ideas pertain to contemporary society. It is not, therefore, purely an analysis of logical strengths and weaknesses. Rather we are dealing with the motivations for and practical applications of specific ideas about political man. In this endeavor it was vital that in addition to traversing the written words of both theorists I experience as closely as possible the environmental context out of which these ideas came. Thus, although the Deutscher Akademischer Austauschdienst (German Academic Exchange Service) did not finance this study *per se*, it did grant me a two year (1962-64) fellowship for graduate study at the University of Freiburg which afforded me the opportunity not only to continue my studies without financial concern but, importantly, to take in the general European and particular German cultural scenes so necessary in building my understanding of Burke and Marx. While I was in England researching the Burke section of the manuscript, the staff of the British Museum Library was most cooperative and helpful in my efforts to locate various materials. I am also indebted to the Relm Foundation which provided me with a summer research grant in 1969 enabling me to investigate the contemporary West European New Left movement and to relate the ideological commitment of the New Left to basic Marxism.

It was during the reading phase on Burke that I came across the invaluable writings of Dr. Russell Kirk, who transmitted to me the primary explanation of Burke and his ideas and who greatly stimulated my own thoughts on this subject. I am most grateful to Dr. Kirk for his gracious willingness to write the Foreword to this book, and I hold this as a distinct privilege. Professor Karl A. Wittfogel assisted me in numerous ways to enrich my research on Marx. Aside from various source suggestions he made, I was fortunate enough to sit on several occasions in discussion with him and thus gained enormously in my critical appreciation for the living dynamics of Marx's thought. Professor Arnold Zurcher read with patience and diligence the completed manuscript and was instrumental in helping me fashion a more cohesive structure and a stronger style. His very practical appreciation of the operational qualities of ideas facilitated greatly the difficult conceptualization phase of the book. Likewise Professor Sidney Hook's reading of the manuscript was an indispensable aid to the logical development of the ideas therein. His notations and questions brought to life a number of hidden strains within the text. My admiration for him developed not only in regard to his significant scholarly contributions but also in regard to his courage in carrying out his commitment to individual and social justice. I have a real sense of personal honor for having been able to work with him.

Above all, however, I want to express my sincere and deep gratitude to Professor Joseph Dunner. It was he who first stimulated my interest in Political Science as I sat in his undergraduate classes. I received my first instruction in Political Theory from him, and the questions he raised and the concepts he analyzed provided me with a firm foundation for my own thinking thereafter. He, too, read this manuscript with the critical powers of an expert, and hence his suggestions were fundamental to its revision and, therefore, its development. It was from him that I learned the practical significance which the ideas of men have in fashioning a tyrannical or a free political existence. And it was from him that I learned that a social scientist possesses a moral responsibility not only to transmit the truth but to act upon it. His personal dedication in this respect has been and remains a source of unending inspiration and courage to me and to others about him. I am thankful not only for his guidance as a teacher and professional colleague but for his friendship.

New York
January, 1973

Marx and Burke:
A Revisionist View

Introduction

It is a matter of common observation and experience that whoever ventures to speak out upon political affairs, no matter what his station in life, subjects himself to possible controversy and opposition. Opposing and even warring points of view appear to be the stuff rather than the exception of life and a good case can be made for the supposition that without this diversity and conflict either all chance of human development would ebb or the very serenity itself would bear witness to millennial existence. If we accept, therefore, the necessity of discussion, vehement and unorthodox though it at times might be, for a dynamic history, then the purpose of this study will become immediately clear, for it proposes to juxtapose the arguments of a historical conservative, Edmund Burke, and a historical revolutionary, Karl Marx, in the effort to understand contemporary politics.

While circumstances change, there is a curious continuity or reapplicability of human thought. Just as no idea is entirely new, so by the same token is no idea entirely obsolete. Yet clearly not all ideas are relevant all the time; the selection guide must be not only the force of circumstances themselves but the particular individuals involved in these circumstances who in their efforts to be effective search for ideational inspiration and precedents. We are, therefore, not forcing the presence of Burke and Marx, rather they have been called upon in a variety of ways and by a variety of individuals to provide a framework for analyzing contemporary society. Our task here is to examine the alleged separate relevance of each thinker to the modern day scene and, most specifically, to ascertain whether there is any theoretical relationship between them.

The responsibility involved in this comparison of two complex minds is great, for each has in his own right been the source material of endless tomes. But, furthermore, in dealing with such highly controversial figures in politics and political theory, we will be compelled to step quite decisively into the "political thicket." The Dublin-born Edmund Burke, spending the bulk of his adult life within the halls of the English House of Commons, is best remembered for the tenacity with which he upheld tradition and "gentility" against social innovation and the uncultured and brutish. In opposing the French Revolution he encountered significant and often vituperative criticism, since it appeared to his critics that Burke had betrayed his own Whig liberalism and joined therewith, at least ideologically, the opposition Tory ranks. Those who supported Burke at this juncture fell into line as the "Old Whigs" (to differentiate them from the "New Whigs" following Charles James Fox) behind the newly-articulated political commitment, Conservatism.

Quite different in tone, Karl Marx, born in the cathedral city of Trier on the Mosel River in Germany, epitomizes the revolutionary. An energetic writer and political organizer, he devoted his life to the social and political cause of the nineteenth century working class. Shouldering historical evidence that all ruling classes eventually collapse, Marx foresaw the day "bourgeois capitalism" would give way as the revolutionized proletariat broke its shackles to build the egalitarian, classless, communist society. As a political agitator, Marx was certainly a nuisance and a threat to existing governments and for this reason was barred from several European states, finding a haven of refuge finally in England. Within the working class movement itself, he made enemies in theoretical disputes and hence the devoted

"Marxists" formed themselves as a corps against "Lassalleans" and other bands of sibling ideological opponents.

In capsulizing the attitudes of Burke and Marx, we can see that they are not only independently controversial but taken together represent seeming political opposites. Burke and Marx are usually interpreted as the "Right" and "Left" of the political spectrum. C. Wright Mills, speaking from his own leftist bias, gives us a good colloquial differentiation between "Right" and "Left" which allows us to see the alleged areas of controversy between the two outlooks: "The Right, among other things, means—what you are doing, celebrating society as it is, a going concern. Left means, or ought to mean, just the opposite. It means structural criticism and reportage and theories of society, which at some point or another are focused politically as demands and programs."[1] Although Burke could obviously not address himself to Marx, we can accept his criticism of the French revolutionaries as a *carte blanche* abnegation of anything smacking of Jacobinism. But Marx did have the opportunity to read Burke's writings, evidenced by the quotations of Burke's *Thoughts and Details on Scarcity* in Volume One of *Das Kapital*. Establishing no real polemic with the Irishman, he did, however, vent his dislike for Burke by describing him as "the celebrated sophist and sycophant" who " . . . in the pay of the English oligarchy, played the romantic *laudator temporis acti* against the French Revolution, just as, in the pay of the North American Colonies, at the beginning of the American troubles, he had played the liberal against the British oligarchy."[2] Marx clearly resented Burke for what he assumed was the typical political opportunism of an "out and out vulgar bourgeois."[3] It is, therefore, probably quite accurate to assume that Burke and Marx would have felt few, if any, sympathies for each other

---

1. C. Wright Mills, "Letter to the New Left" in Priscilla Long (ed.), *The New Left*, (Boston: Porter Sargent Publisher, 1969), p. 19.

2. *Karl Marx, Capital*, trans. Samuel Moore and Edward Aveling from the Third German Edition (Chicago: Encyclopaedia Britannica, Inc., 1952), p. 157.

3. *Ibid.*, p. 377. Actually, Burke is consistent in his appraisals of the French and American revolutions but Marx out of his own prejudices just never desired to think through Burke's essential position.

and each would probably even have regarded the other as a member of an alien and potentially hostile camp.

Although both men influenced the politics of their times and contributed to the development of political theory, Marx has certainly enjoyed a more flamboyant prominence over the years than Burke. The reason for this lies largely in the fact that Marx's name and theory are inseparable from the growth of the socialist and communist movements. Marxist socialism has pertained and appealed to an international, mainly intellectual, constituency. France, particularly its metropolitan center, Paris, has since the nineteenth century been the meeting ground for all genre of socialist intellectuals who in their interchanges at the universities and small sidewalk cafés of the Quartier Latin have fertilized the theoretical evolution of Marxism and hence its practical importance.[4] For whether one agrees with Marx or not, his ideas concerning the historical socialist imperative form one of the most solid springboards for discussion. In line with this it has been vital for the contemporary "New Left" in its effort to differentiate itself from the "Old Left" to read Marx carefully—albeit perhaps for the first time. Carl Oglesby of the Students for a Democratic Society (SDS) writes that " . . . the American New Left at last begins to take up Marx, more than a little fearful that yet another misreading will be required, but hoping to sustain an additive revision."[5]

Burke's influence, though more subdued, has, however, permeated European and American political thought. His writings

---

4. One example of the current appeal in France of philosophical discussions involving Marxism is the December 7, 1961 "confrontation" between the Existentialist, Jean Paul Sartre, and the French Communist Party ideologue, Roger Garaudy, which reportedly drew an academic audience of 6,000. Further data have been given in evidence of French interest in Marx: "In France more than in any other Western country Marx is published and bought: Marx's works appeared from 1945-1967 in about thrity-five separate editions, among which nine were of the main work, *Das Kapital*, and reached altogether a publication of over 200,000 copies. In the Federal Republic of Germany, by contrast, the only newly published selection of Marx's works in seven volumes reached a printing of about 2,000 copies. In France appeared too the only complete edition [*Gesamtausgabe*] of Marx works (54 volumes) in a non-communist land and since 1963 Marx has been canonized as a 'classic' in the famous 'Pleiade' collection of the Parisian publisher Gallimard." (*Der Spiegel*, June 23, 1969,) p. 145. My translation.

5. Carl Oglesby, (ed.), *The New Left Reader*, (N.Y.: Grove Press, 1969), p. 16.

received much attention in Germany during the nineteenth century and, though never acknowledging this, Hegel perhaps imbibed the general outline of his national concept from Burke. (Marx, a student of Hegel, would have thus indirectly absorbed Burkean ideas.) The British Conservative Party considers Burke one of the major sources of its political thinking, Lord Hugh Cecil dating the very origin of the Party at 1790 " . . . when Edmund Burke broke with his Whig friends over their attitude to the French Revolution."[6] Within the United States, Clinton Rossiter presents a sizeable list of noted personalities who in his estimation "have been heard to voice some of the central ideals of the Burkean tradition" since the 1950's.[7] Rather than passing on to his beneficiaries a systematized ideology, Burke is more often recognized as having set the tone for a distinct "mood" in approaching political issues.

Of the two thinkers, it may seem curious upon retrospection that this Burkean "mood" should have survived this long. Since his day, an industrial revolution has taken place, changing the entire manner of living. In the modern state we no longer sustain a landed gentry which Burke esteemed as specially fit for public service. According to George Sabine, even Burke's parliamentary ideas for which he is most renowned were in fact outmoded in his own time: " . . . Burke's theory of the constitution and his conception of parliamentary government was based upon the actual settlement of 1688 . . . by which effective political control passed into the hands of the Whig nobility. His effort to revivify the Whig Party was already reactionary in 1770, because the great Whig houses no longer had the position of undisputed leadership that they enjoyed after the revolution."[8] Burke's ideal of a "national" parliament composed of loose coalitions around notable personalities commonly dedicated to promoting the "national" rather than a "constituency" interest does not anticipate the development of modern pressure group-constituency democracy

6. Peter Goldman, *Some Principles of Conservatism* (London: Conservative Political Centre, 1961), p. 5.

7. Clinton Rossiter, *Conservatism in America* (New York: Random House, 1962), p. 225.

8. George H. Sabine, *A History of Political Theory* (New York: Holt, Rinehart and Winston, Inc., 1961), p. 609.

or, recently, the preeminence of executive government over the legislature in all contemporary democracies.[9]

Living in and writing of the industrial society, Marx does not suffer from these handicaps. But since many of Marx's "predictions" about the development of capitalist society have not come to pass, one could take the position of George Lichtheim and claim that "we are able to understand Marx because we have reached a point where neither his modes of thought nor those of his nineteenth century opponents are altogether adequate to the realities."[10] (Eduard Bernstein took great pains to show where Marx had gone wrong in his economic theories and to set up a revised social democratic evolutionary rather than revolutionary approach to ameliorating working class conditions.) Even the theoretical stuff of Marxism—his dialectical materialism—seems scholastically old-fashioned in the light of sociological, psychological and political group behavior research results.

Yet the persistent attempt to revive Burke and Marx remains today. While Lichtheim takes the edge off the controversial Marx by his historical analysis, Harold Laski challenges this, stating: "In the sixty years that have passed since Marx's death, he has been, I suppose, the subject of more eager and more voluminous funeral orations than any of his contemporaries. There is no element of his work which has not been declared obsolete. . . . Yet it is evident on every hand that at no time in his life has his influence been wider or more living than it is today."[11] In much the same tone Jeffrey Hart characterizes Burke's revival:

> As everyone knows, an enormous revival of interest in Edmund
> Burke has taken place during the past twenty years or so, the

9. James Burnham corroborates this in writing: "On a world scale the fall of the American Congress seems to be correlated with a more general historical transformation toward political and social forms within which the representative assembly—the major political organism of the post-Renaissance western civilization—does not have a primary political function." (James Burnham, *Congress and the American Tradition* Chicago: Henry Regnery Co., 1965 , p. 337.)

10. George Lichtheim, *Marxism: An Historical and Critical Study* (New York: Frederick A. Praeger, 1963), p. xx

11. Harold J. Laski, *Marx and Today* (London: Victor Gollancz, Ltd., 1953), p. 3.

period, roughly, since the end of the Second World War. Scholars, to be sure, have always been interested in him, and he was widely admired for his style, and by some for his 'practical wisdom,' during the nineteenth century. But the point is that in our time he has come to be read not merely as one among a large number of other important figures in the history of political thought, but as a thinker of intense, of special, contemporary relevance. Burke is our contemporary, he is an *issue*, in a way that Locke is not, and Leibnitz is not, and even Mill is not. Burke has not receded into what Lovejoy called the pathos of time, by which he meant that benign and even tender feeling we have for thought that is now completely, forever, a part of the past—and so neither defines us nor menaces us.[12]

Lewis Feuer boldly states that "the person who would understand the modern world must come to terms with Marx's ideas,"[13] while Harold Laski, a vigorous opponent of Burke, opined that " . . . Burke lives on as though he were still a contemporary of ours with thoughts relevant to every aspect of our time."[14] Neither Burke nor Marx can be avoided in the thicket of contemporary politics. They are there, but why?

In both cases intellectual circles have largely stimulated the renewed interest, for, ironically enough, since World War II, important documentary sources of Burke and Marx have become available. In 1949 Burke's correspondence, which had been in the private possession of the Earl of Fitzwilliam, was transferred to the Sheffield Public Library (England) and subsequently published under the general editorship of Thomas Copeland in six volumes, covering the years 1744 to 1791. In addition, H.V.F. Somerset edited *A Notebook of Edmund Burke* in 1957 bringing together poems, essays and notes of the young Burke at Trinity College. Similarly, in 1959 the Marx-Engels Institute in Moscow made available for the first time a complete English translation of the so-called *Economic and Philosophical Manuscripts* written by the young Marx in 1844.[15] With these sources

12. Jeffrey Hart, "Burke and Radical Freedom," *The Review of Politics*, XXIX (April 1967), p. 221.

13. Karl Marx and Friedrich Engels, *Basic Writings on Politics and Philosophy*, ed. Lewis Feuer (New York: Doubleday and Co., Inc. 1959), Introduction, p. ix.

14. Harold J. Laski, *Edmund Burke* (Dublin: Falconer Press, 1947), p. 1.

15. Although the *Manuscripts* had passed to the Institute from the Archives of the Second

scholars have eagerly studied not only the "young" phase of each thinker but have had the opportunity to trace the origins and maturation of ideas.

Scholars have thus done much to change the old, stereotyped images of Burke and Marx, which, it must be stated, had been initially created by scholars anyway. Marx in his *Kapital* description helped along the image of Burke as an unprincipled, corrupt eighteenth century politician. Others, like Sir Lewis Namier in his history of that period[16] entrenched the image, and Harold Laski, conceding that Burke "makes you argue with him and think out afresh the intellectual position you occupy in politics," nevertheless succumbed to the perennial conclusion of the opponent to Burke as someone "with a deep fear of change, a veneration for whatever is old, a prejudice against reason as the dangerous acid which dissolves that passion for order of which he considered himself to be the appointed guardian. . . ."[17] But now a host of contemporary Burke scholars like Francis Canavan, Ross Hoffman, Russell Kirk and Peter Stanlis present a new Burke. Their Burke is very much the liberal Whig conscious of the necessity to preserve the social context in which human freedom and rationality can survive and flourish. Theirs is a dynamic Burke offering rather unsystematically but clearly recognizable principles of liberal (rather than authoritarian) conservatism. The new Burke, exalted as the "father of modern conservatism," provides conservative political groups with an emphasis upon the nation and its traditions, an accent upon the evolutionary approach to political life and a resistance to rapid, historically-unfounded change, an argumentation in behalf of free enterprise, the concept of the stratified (not "leveled" or egalitarian) though free society and a metaphysical system supporting a God-centered universe in which man as a rational being can progress but which he

---

International in 1927, it was not until 1932 that they were published *in toto.* The Second World War precluded any scholarly concentration upon them during that time.

16. cf. Sir Lewis Namier, *The Structure of Politics at the Accession of George III* (London: Macmillan and Co., Ltd., 1960).

17. Laski, *Edmund Burke, op. cit.,* p. 9.

can never wholly conquer. Walter von Wyss claims these Burkean principles are most relevant today since "the power political problems which control the present resemble those which moved the world during the lifetime and influence of Edmund Burke" and hence this "justifies our remembering a great figure of the second half of the eighteenth century. . . . "[18]

The fact that Marxism became proclaimed state doctrine with the 1917 Russian (Bolsheviki) Revolution largely fashioned Marx's stereotyped image. Although some scholars relegate Marx to intellectual history, others place all responsibility for the development of Soviet Communism at his feet. To the latter his ideas are intrinsically totalitarian, a complete denial of the liberalism developing in Europe since about the seventeenth century. The doctrine of historical materialism has created bitter enemies who refuse to accept either the de-spiritualized economic robot which allegedly Marx presents as Man or the amoralistic qualities of Marxist class-bound *Realpolitik*. And many social scientists, acknowledging with Lichtheim that Marx epitomizes nineteenth century revolutionary social currents and intellectual systems-building,[19] do not take seriously the scientific claims of the thinker in view mainly of his one-factor (economic) analysis of social life.

As the *Economic and Philosophical Manuscripts* became available, a new Marx emerged. The old dialectical materialist, the totalitarian, seemed to soften into a generous, beneficent humanist. In the early *Manuscripts* period the youthful Marx dwells considerably on the problem of alienation—the estrangement of the individual from his "true" self and from meaningful social relationships. Marx therewith seemed to come into focus with the best Western humanist tradition and many a Marx scholar was heartened by the discovery. In Western Europe Jean Paul Sartre in his *Critique of Dialectical Reasoning* (1960) spearheaded the rejuvenation of Marxism in France and portrayed Marx of the *Manuscripts* as a revolutionary humanist. Attempting to break all connection between Marxism and Stalinism, Sartre extolled Marx as the igniter of processes for human liberation from alienation,

---

18. Walter von Wyss, *Edmund Burke* (München: Verlag George D W. Callway, 1966), p. 7. My translation.

19. Lichtheim, *op. cit.*, p. xiv.

poverty and oppression.[20] Erich Fromm, editing one English version of the *Manuscripts*, underscores the importance of Marx's alienation concept in the modern industrial world of anonymous living. Against the background of present day totalitarian Communism, East European Marxist intellectuals following in the footsteps of Leszek Kolakowski and George Lukacs emphasize the humanistic Marx in their drive toward "voluntary socialism." Tying alienation to the presence of oppression in social relations as Marx does, it is small wonder that Marxism has been vital to the nationalist movements of former European colonies, that it has been a "magnetic power," in the words of Lewis Feuer, "unparalleled in the history of mankind, which has drawn into its ideological orbit peoples of different continents and races, from China to Burma to Ghana, Moscow to Belgrade and Djakarta."[21]

We can see that Burke and Marx are not only being revived; they are being transformed. By looking at Burke and Marx simultaneously and comparatively against the background of contemporary politics, we shall be participating in both these processes. If Burke and Marx are each considered important today by his adherents, do they have any fundamental points of agreement? Their contemporary presence does not connote any necessary affinity. Radically different patterns of thought can and often do exist side by side in a given period of time. Karl Mannheim would explain this as the partial points of view symptomatic of ideological politics. But Mannheim went on to conclude that an understanding of the whole *Weltanschauung* required piecing together its separate strains. Hopefully we can *learn* something about ourselves by examining Burke and Marx through the same lens.

Let us begin then by setting down the guidelines of our task. To ascertain the relevance of Burke and of Marx to contemporary politics, we must have a conception of modern society *a priori* to our

20. Not all Marxists accept the humanist interpretation which does serve to undermine the kind of social regimentation found in Communist states. The French Communist, Louis Althusser, of the Ecole Normale Supérieure in Paris emphasizes instead the scientific accomplishment of Marx which to him means solely the analysis of economic systems ("structuralism"). For such structuralist interpreters the qualities of humanism figure as non-scientific or ideological conceptions.

21. Marx and Engels, *Basic Writings, op. cit.*, p. ix.

particular subject matter here. Burke and Marx must fit our requirements rather than the other way around. Three primary characteristics stand out boldly in this respect and we can at this point enumerate and briefly describe them: (1) a scientific orientation; (2) an atomistic tendency in society; and (3) fast-paced social change or the prevalence of accelerated history.

The social significance of the technological revolution in the twentieth century is that man, while utilizing natural forces, has freed himself considerably from their once alleged arbitrariness and hence surrounded himself with an environment substantially of his own making. Although the devastation and turmoil wrought by every earthquake still seems to betray this statement, the trend of modern science points unmistakably in the direction of increased human mastery and control of the natural world as dramatically evidenced in space exploration and modern medicine. As the invention of the printing press in the fifteenth century ushered in a major social revolution, so the break-throughs in electronics and atomic energy, in physics, chemistry and biology have created unique possibilities for as well as serious challenges to social existence. Science has impinged upon the life of every individual today and has conditioned not only our social organization but our very mode of thinking.

Living in an environment of applied science, twentieth century man is impatient with purely speculative thought. While some continue to shrink away from the pressures of contemporary life into a self-made, pre-scientific euphoria, responsible social and political leaders know that utopia-building only means shirking today's social challenges. Broadly speaking, we need a "politics of reality" founded upon a political science.

In virtually every democratic state today, *laissez-faire* governmental policies (though never really pure) have been replaced in various degrees by governmental intervention into and supervision of the "private sector" for the purposes of establishing social justice. The industrial revolution of the nineteenth century tended to destroy the cohesiveness of agrarian society and to undermine cherished values. The result was the modern atomistic society with many of its citizens suffering from general anomie. Welfare statism, whether a right or wrong answer, has been almost the universal response of the democratic state attempting to rebuild a sense of community and social integrity. The "politics of reality" must at the same time be socially creative.

This is an enormous and difficult task for any democracy. The presence of "positive" government active in social regulation poses problems in the area of traditional democratic civil and political liberties. Because of its commitment to individual freedom, the democratic state (especially one as heterogeneous as the United States) has a moral responsibility to consider when attempting the consolidation or integration of its social forces. It must seek the most judicious and ethical balance between the rights of the community and those of the individual.[22]

In addition democratic law-making processes are built upon representative deliberation. While this has obvious advantages in preserving popular sovereignty, it also poses severe handicaps. Government policy which goes through exacting deliberation can be obsolete before it is even implemented and this fact accounts largely for the increase in administrative law-making today. The tendency toward "accelerated history" stimulated primarily by technological advances (historical eras are now defined by their technological rather than social or political content, such as the "Nuclear Age") means

22. Robert Paul Wolff in his essay, "Beyond Tolerance," adds a provocative note to this discussion: " . . . The theory of pluralism in all its forms has the effect in American thought and politics of discriminating not only against certain social groups or interests but also against certain sorts of proposals for the solution of social problems. According to pluralist theory, politics is a contest among social groups for control of the power and decision of government. . . . The typical social problem according to pluralism is therefore some instance of distributive injustice. One group is getting too much, another too little, of the available resources. But there are some social ills in America whose causes do not lie in a maldistribution of wealth, and which cannot be cured therefore by the techniques of pluralist politics. For example, America is growing uglier, more dangerous, and less pleasant to live in, as its citizens grow richer. The reason is that natural beauty, public order, the cultivation of the arts, are not the special interest of any identifiable social group. Consequently, evils and inadequacies in those areas cannot be remedied by shifting the distribution of wealth and power among existing social groups. . . . To deal with such problems, there must be some way of constituting the whole society as a genuine group with a group purpose and a conception of the common good. Pluralism rules this out in theory by portraying society as an aggregate of human communities rather than as itself a human community; and it equally rules out a concern for the general good in practice by encouraging a politics of interest group pressures in which there is no mechanism for the discovery and expression of the common good." (Robert Paul Wolff, Barrington Moore, Jr. and Herbert Marcuse, *A Critique of Pure Tolerance* (Boston: Beacon Press, 1969), pp. 49-50.)

that politics is faced with what seems to be a perpetually revolutionary social front. Leon Trotsky once remarked that anyone desiring peace and solitude would have done well not to have been born in the twentieth century. Although Trotsky's ideological aspirations for socio-political change on an international scale have not materialized, ours has been, nevertheless, an epoch of "permanent revolution" in science, politics and society at large. To be effective, governmental policy must anticipate and coordinate change in bringing about social cohesion and justice.

Keeping these characteristics in mind, we must now ask in what ways Burke and Marx are relevant today. Rebelling against speculative Rationalism, they pursue instead a historical-empirical method of social analysis which to them is "scientific" and hence "realistic." In conjunction with this, as historical empiricists, they emphasize the traits and needs of group or social existence, having as their major value social integration and harmony. Conceiving man the maker of his own history within certain limitations, they consider change the prerequisite of human development. In analyzing in depth each of these commitments in the following chapters, the modern relevance of Burke and Marx and their areas of mutual agreement will become clearer and their differences will be concomitantly more understandable.

We do not pretend to exhaust all facets of the respective theoretical sytems of Burke and Marx. In reality there are many Burkes and many Marxs; such is the kaleidoscopic effect of their intellectual interests and capacities.[23] In both cases the intricacies of

---

23. Burke could be treated from various standpoints—as a parliamentarian, journalist, historian, economist, political party member and political theorist. Regarding the different aspects of Marx, Sidney Hook has written: ". . . there are many Marxs. There is Marx the revolutionary fighter against the European Restoration or the system of Metternich, and Marx the historical sociologist and political economist, deriving from a metaphysical theory of value the scientific equations of doom of capitalist society. There is Marx the social and moral prophet denouncing the exploitation of man by man, and Marx the radical historicist for whom all moral ideals—freedom, equality, fraternity, integrity and independence—are deceptive abstractions concealing the economic class interests at their roots. And, to make the matter even more complicated, we must distinguish all these Marxs, embodied in what was published over a period of forty years, from the Ur-Marx, of the so-called *Economic and Philosophical Manuscripts*, who quietly entered the world in 1832, and was discovered almost a century later to be the most effective ally of the Communist opposition to Stalinism." (Sidney Hook, "The Enlightenment and Marxism," *Journal of the History of Ideas*, XXIX January-March, 1968, p. 93.)

argument concerning specific historical events have been pared to systematize and correlate their general approaches and conclusions. Likewise, the details in economic analysis, particularly in Marx, have been trimmed, although the basic principles behind their thinking will be given full weight. To control the inherent difficulties in all generalizations, we have, however, made frequent use of primary sources. Thus to illustrate major points, Burke and Marx will speak for themselves.[24] Although it is usually said that Friedrich Engels and Marx were in full agreement on all important matters, their correspondence shows they were two distinct individuals with different inclinations and, in some cases, different sentiments and ideas. To provide greater authenticity in the over-all comparison of Burke and Marx, the separate writings of Engels will not be used.

---

24. Burke's language is difficult not only because it is eighteenth century English but also because he put his own individual stamp on the way in which he used language. All capital lettered nouns, adjectives and verbs within a sentence have not been changed in any of the quotations used, as they represent the emphasis Burke wanted to express. Similarly, all irregularities in punctuation have been left. Unless otherwise noted, all translations of Marx's works and letters remain the sole responsibility of the present author.

Chapter I
The Weltanschauungen
of Burke and Marx:
The Politics of Commitment

It can be convincingly argued that all systems of thought should stand or fall according to the force of their internal logic without the crutch of explanatory historical or biographical material. Yet, at the same time, all ideas do remain essentially biographical, reflecting the thinker's personality and experience. Compelled perhaps by human gregariousness and curiosity, we do usually feel moved to ask ultimately what manner of individual conceived this or that thought. Concerned as we are here with comparing two sets of ideas appearing to be radically different, it is pertinent to our purposes to begin with Burke and Marx as personalities in the effort to understand the framework in and against which their ideas were formed.

It is important to remember that Burke and Marx had periods in their lives during which they were active politicians. This involvement in practical affairs eschewed what has often been termed ivory tower intellectualism. Ideas about social life were not intellectual frivolities to them but practical necessities. They were concerned with the observable not the abstract man. Marx chides Kant and Fichte for their otherworldliness in a poem composed between 1836 and 1837:

Kant und Fichte gern zum Äther schweifen
suchten dort ein fernes Land.
Doch ich such' nur tüchtig zu begreifen
was ich auf der Strasse fand.[1]

Burke contested the French revolutionary ideologues like Robespierre
who stressed "pure" rather than practical reason. Writing to a young
French friend, M. Charles-Jean-François Depont, in November 1789,
Burke tried to remind him that there are "theories enough concerning
the Rights of Men. It may not be amiss to add a small degree of
attention to their nature and disposition. It is with Man in the
concrete, it's with common human life and human Actions you are to
be concerned."[2] Burke and Marx each exhibited an emotional
involvement in this preoccupation with Empirical Man.

Quite naturally this emotional fervor and practical orientation
were revealed in each one's use of language. More than researching
scholars, they were social communicators, attempting to create
through effective language an emotional receptiveness for an intellectual argument. It is significant that as young university students both
Burke and Marx wrote poetry, of which imagery is an important
attribute. It is, therefore, not surprising to find in their later writings
ideas couched in dramatic, categorical language. Both were also
engaged in journalism; Marx contributed to various papers, including
the *New Rhenish Newspaper* (*Neue Rheinische Zeitung*) and the *New York
Tribune* (for which he was the European correspondent from 1851 to
1860), and Burke submitted articles and reviews to several student

---

1. Quoted in William M. Johnston, "Karl Marx's Verse of 1836-1837 as a Foreshadowing of
his Early Philosophy," *Journal of the History of Ideas*, XXVIII (April-June 1967), p. 261.
("Kant and Fichte, searching for a distant land, liked to wander to grand ethereal heights.
Yet I seek but capably to understand, what I found upon the street."—my translation.)
There is a parallel here to "New Left" thought. Carl Oglesby has written: "The instinct
from the beginning of the radical New Left was to discover the streets, and there was
nothing at all anti-intellectual about this. It embodied rather a refusal to tolerate the further
separation of thought from its consequences: books argued with each other and lied and in
any case did not make much of a difference; only direct experience was incontrovertible."
Oglesby, *op. cit.*, p. 14.

2. *The Correspondence of Edmund Burke*, ed. Alfred Cobban and Robert A. Smith (6 Vols. gen. ed.
Thomas Copeland; Chicago: University of Chicago Press, 1967), VI, p. 46.

publications, foremost among them *The Reformer*, and to the *Annual Register* (founded in 1758). Since journalism requires the efficient use of language in developing a general concept, their writings show this style in the digestion of voluminous materials into terse social maxims. By way of a single example, we need only compare those sections of the *Communist Manifesto* in which Marx denounces the hypocrisies of the bourgeoisie with those sections in Burke's *Reflections on the Revolution in France* describing the fated Marie Antoinette to evidence the calculated impact of language. Desiring to rivet specific political associations to concrete political issues, Burke surrounded the French Revolution with the imagery and emotion of destruction and death as did Marx vis-à-vis bourgeois capitalism.

Well-educated, each had an extensive knowledge of foreign languages, including English, French, German, Latin and Greek.[3] This linguistic ability exposed each to various intellectual circles and traditions and enhanced his appreciation for the idiomatic and pure content of language. Although intellectuals, Burke and Marx were quite prepared for and capable of translating complex arguments and abstractions into the language of the man in the street. To them language, as a distinctly social tool—what Burke called the "cement of society," must be used to express and communicate concrete social realities.[4] Marx put forth this same notion of language in *The German Ideology*: ". . . language is the first really practical consciousness, for others as well as for myself, and language, like consciousness, arises initially from the need, the necessity of intercourse with other men."[5]

The use of social action language, the penchant for concrete facts, for non-speculative or empirical approaches, for the everyday in life

---

3. Considering the nature of the eighteenth century, Burke's acquisition of an M. A. degree in 1751 from Trinity College and an honorary LL.D. in 1791 put him into the intellectual élite of his time. Marx also fits into this category, having secured a Ph. D. in Philosophy from the University of Jena in 1841.

4. Arthur Samuels, *The Early Life, Correspondence and Writings of the Rt. Hon. Edmund Burke LL.D.* (Cambridge: Cambridge University Press, 1923), p. 228. Quotation from the Minute Book of the Academy of Belles Lettres, parent organization of the famous Historical Society of Trinity College, recorded April 21, 1747.

5. Karl Marx and Friedrich Engels, *Die Deutsche Ideologie* (Berlin: Dietz Verlag, 1960), p. 27.

and for action were functional aspects of their political dispositions. To each of them, politics represented the most viable means to direct persons and events. Considering himself throughout his career a dedicated though relatively unsuccessful reformer, Burke entered Parliament to rescue his Irish homeland from its condition of virtual serfdom and eventually devoted most of his parliamentary years to the cause of administrative reform. Renowned—though not always acclaimed—for his lengthy and vibrant oratory in the House of Commons, he used his parliamentary position for political pedagogy, informing and instructing those whom he considered in political error.[6] The lengths to which Burke would go in countering an adversary can be seen in the impeachment trial of Warren Hastings, Colonial Governor of India. The trial lasted from 1788 to 1795 and cost Hastings £ 70,000.[7] Burke had instigated the impeachment, charging Hastings with violating of the universal law of justice in the exercise of his administrative duties in India. When Hastings claimed a paternalistic government accomodated the ancient indigenous traditions of the colonized Indians, Burke, having researched the sources of Indian religious and civil law, retorted that the Indians subscribed to the basic concepts of equity and freedom found in all just societies.[8]

Likewise Marx considered politics the instrumentality by which to accomplish certain broad social goals. Through political organiza-

6. Burke was an eloquent speaker with whom, Boswell claimed, one could never be bored. His conversational abilities won him membership in the Literary Club, attended by such eighteenth century notables as Dr. Samuel Johnson, Boswell, Sir Joshua Reynolds and Oliver Goldsmith. Burke was also friendly with the famous actors, Garrick and Macklin, from whom it has been suggested he acquired an additional flair for oratorical dramatics. Interestingly enough, Marx, too, was prone toward the theatrical world. While a student in Berlin (1837), he wrote a dramatic play (in addition to a humorous novel) and, like Burke, who wrote theatrical reviews for his student publications, Marx contemplated the organization of a Zeitschrift für Theaterkritik.

7. Goldwin Smith, *A History of England* (New York: Charles Scribner's Sons, 1957), p. 514.

8. In this respect Peter Stanlis has written: "To disprove Hastings' contention that morality varied in time and place, Burke read widely in Oriental jurisprudence. He read the *Koran*, the *Shasta*, and the *Hevada*; he quoted Tamerlane's Institutes. . . . ; he used Joseph White's translations of the *Institutes of Timour* . . .and Jean Baptiste Tavernier's *Travels into Persia and the East Indies*." (Peter J. Stanlis, *Edmund Burke and the Natural Law*, Ann Arbor, Michigan: The University of Michigan Press, 1965, p. 64.)

tion, he hoped to unify the working class of the industrializing states and instruct it in the responsibilities of its historical mission and task. Characteristic of the seriousness and even vehemence with which Marx approached this organization is his written *Critique of the Gotha Program*. The Program was drawn up at the 1875 Gotha Congress of the German Socialist Party. In vying for leadership with Ferdinand Lassalle, Marx systematically and impatiently scrutinized all aspects of the Program which seemed to him ideological concessions made to Lassalle. Marx's section by section analysis and revision, his ridicule of what he considered mere rhetorical gimmicks and illogical arguments have been described as the "typically ill-tempered criticism by the Master in London."[9] For Marx, as for Burke, politics was by far too serious an endeavor to indulge in imprecise, amateurish and wishful thinking.

Burke and Marx were both pedants in the kind of political organization they advocated. There was almost a missionary quality in these two men. They were not merely party members and organizers but instructors, visionaries, and leaders filled with personal conviction and determination, admitting no compromise.[10] This rigidity in pursuing social truth in effect transmutes individual perspectives into universal first principles. The position of a philosopher-politician is all-encompassing. No social event or condition can be dislodged from the matrix of his entire system. Political opposition then takes on the overtones not of a simple intellectual contest between two points of view; it becomes a crisis in fundamentals, in personal essences and identification.

The most dramatic example of such a personalized political opposition concerns Burke's friendship with Charles Fox, a friendship nurtured over the long years of their mutual parliamentary careers and Whig Party membership. The indulgent, wealthy Fox, known and enjoyed for his amiable ways and wit, embraced the French Revolution as the dawn of an emancipated age. Debates on the subject, to which Fox and Burke contributed, ensued in the Com-

9. James Joll, *The Second International: 1889-1914* (New York: Harper and Row, 1966), p. 7.

10. From all biographical accounts, similar descriptions are found of Burke and Marx as leaders. They enjoyed leadership not only because of their intellectual abilities and stamina but also on account of the forcefulness of their personalities and their imposing physical appearances.

mons, turning primarily on the security question confronting England by the alleged infiltration of Jacobins and the subsequent establishment in England of scattered Radical Clubs. In a fiery encounter with Fox during one of these debates, Burke, unable to see any area of grey between their stances, publicly resigned his friendship with Fox and dramatically left the Chamber. Over the issue of the French Revolution, Burke was totally prepared to factionalize the Whig Party (and thereby diminish its already anemic political position) and to break the bonds of life-long friendship.[11]

A less pronounced though none the less exemplary case of a personalized political clash is Burke's relationship with Jean-Jacques Rousseau. Despising Rousseau as a *philosophe,* Burke refused any personal contact with him.[12] And, moreover, Burke distrusted Rousseau as a sophist. How is it, Burke questioned, that a man who preaches human brotherhood and freedom can at the same time abandon his own offspring to the orphanage?

Marx's personality was in this sense very much like Burke's. Unable to bridge a compromise with Lassalle, Marx's intellectual contest with him turned into an emotional antipathy which, even after Lassalle's death in a duel in 1863, Marx continued to vent in his letters to Engels.[13] A relationship Marx had with Moses Hess had initially been an intellectual alliance against men like Bruno Bauer, Ludwig Feuerbach, Arnold Ruge and Max Stirner. Although Hess had come to share many of Marx's thoughts, he, nevertheless, did not measure up completely to Marx's attack upon "true socialism" in the *Communist Manifesto.* Sidney Hook has analyzed Marx's attitude

11. In the *Catalogue of Political and Personal Satires,* ed. Mary Dorothy George (10 Vols.; London: Kegan Paul, Trubner and Co. Ltd., 1938) VI (covering the years 1784 to 1792) found in the British Museum Library and compiled from the Museum's Department of Prints and Drawings are caricatures of this parliamentary scene carried by various newspapers of the time. Fox, reported to have wept copiously after Burke's exit, forms the special satirical theme.

12. cf. Annie Marion Osborn, *Rousseau and Burke* (New York: Russell and Russell, 1964.)

13. Marx coined derogatory nicknames for his opponents and used them frequently in his correspondence with Engels. Lassalle, for example, was dubbed "Itzig" and "The Baron" (because of his cavorting with a wealthy, aristocratic woman). Even in *The German Ideology,* Marx uses such names in referring to Bruno Bauer as "the holy Bruno" and Max Stirner as "Saint Max."

toward his political associates, particularly Hess, in the following manner:

> That many of the things he said of Hess were unjustified, Marx's subsequent attitude towards him reveals clearly. But politically, Marx felt it was his revolutionary duty to oppose with all energy those who blocked the possibility of making any gains by the working class, no matter how small, in its struggle for liberation. He did not spare his friends any more than he spared himself. And although he was furious at stupidity, it was not out of intellectual *hauteur* but out of a realization that if correct theories have practical consequences, mistaken theories have no less practical consequences. There were many things he did not see; but he always saw the implications of doctrines, programs and sometimes even the choice of words, for the class struggle.[14]

These few biographical accounts suffice to show that Burke and Marx each tended toward fanaticism in his devotion to political concepts and principles. With an ingenious manipulation of language, each created for his reader and listener the arch-political drama. If we move from Burke's stage to Marx's, we undoubtedly feel not only little continuity of action but indeed an opposition of worlds. The most striking division for us to draw between them would be over political means. Edmund Burke epitomizes the evolutionary, tradition-oriented political approach. His vituperative condemnation of the French Revolution has earned him the title of major apologist for feudal social concepts and arrangements. Upon entering the House of Commons in 1765, Burke—confronting the corruption of eighteenth century politics as well as a developing and often intemperate British Empire—advocated and pursued a political approach designed to preserve the steady growth of national societies toward their historical goals.

The nation with its network of cultural, historical, and religious experiences projects social values and goals and supplies the coordinated energy for their attainment. Each nation for Burke has the historical opportunity to work itself out as a moral unit. In order for the nation to take advantage of history, social change must be moderate, predicated on the foundations of the past. In this way it is

---

14. Sidney Hook, "Marx's Criticism of 'True Socialism,' " *The New International*, II (January 1935), p. 16.

neither innovation nor revolution but the reform of existing defects in social institutions and practice. Revolution was anathema to Burke because it destroys historical continuity and progress. In this sense he considered the policies of the French revolutionaries suicidal, for these policies were based on the belief that a generation can ignore the past and create *de novo* a sound moral existence. (Burke's support of the American Revolution has been interpreted as a basic contradiction in his thinking. Marx, for instance, claimed that Burke was paid by the American colonies for his support. But since the American colonists were striving to maintain their prescribed rights as Englishmen, Burke considered the Revolution a reaffirmation of historical roots and customs.)

Marx, on the other hand, stipulated that revolution is the necessary prod to historical progress. Social change results from the inevitable tension between the "forces of the old" (thesis) and the "forces of the new" (antithesis), abruptly and cataclysmically resolved by synthesis. Historical goals are achieved only by social conflict out of which comes a new qualitative level of human existence.

Conceiving all socio-political life as the "superstructure" of prevailing economic modes, Marx looked at the nation not as a historical cultural complex but primarily as a historically engendered economic unit. Assuming the class struggle endemic to all pre-Communist states, Marx argued that class interests in like economic systems cut across national state boundaries. They are international phenomena. Thus the proletarian class in all industrial states having a shared class interest enjoys an international class historical existence:

> The Communists are distinguished from other working class parties by this only: 1. In the national struggles of the proletarians of the different countries, they point out and bring to the front the common interests of the entire proletariat, independently of all nationality. 2. In the various stages of development which the struggle of the working class against the bourgeoisie has to pass through, they always and everywhere represent the interests of the movement as a whole.[15]

Burkean "evolutionary" versus Marxist "revolutionary" politics involves "nationalism" versus "internationalism." Burke's

15. Karl Marx and Friedrich Engels, *The Communist Manifesto*, ed. Samuel Beer (New York: Appleton-Century-Crofts, 1955), p. 23.

nationalism supported a class structure derived from feudalism. For common defense and sustenance, a graduated land system was established with the principle of tenure bestowing upon individuals corresponding social obligations and rights. Out of this land tenure arrangement came a social system of interlocking, hierarchically-ordered social bonds eventually hardening into class lines from the king (liege lord) to the free and unfree peasant. In Norman and Angevin England, feudalism was a consolidating, nation-building force. Despite the Glorious Revolution of 1688 and the subsequent constitutional revisions, much of the feudal class orientation and all of the major social and political institutions survived in the eighteenth century. The classes form a social balance in England, said Burke, expressed through the Crown, Parliament and Church of England. To destroy the class system would be to throw the entire social organization out of kilter. Yet Burke did not condone a caste system nor the artificial creation of classes. He left it to each nation to define its own niche, urging that social development depends upon a shared historical consciousness, whatever that might be.

Born almost a century later than Burke, Marx lived under drastically changed social conditions. Industrialization had severed the former social bonds attendant to the agrarian way of life. Germany—never securing for itself the national territorial unity and sense of purpose characteristic of insular England—labored under warring principalities and Prussian hegemony. Though post-Napoleonic Europe entered the more stable and peaceful Metternich Era, militarism, religious dogmatism and class antagonism still characterized the time. Marx rebelled against what might be termed the state-established society in the Prussia of Frederick William II (1797-1840) where Hegel had become, *nolens volens*, the philosopher of the civil bureaucracy.[16]

---

16. Frederick William IV (1840-1861) hoped to base the state on monarchical absolutism and Protestant Pietism. Thus the Hegelian "left" (Hegelische Linke), tolerated before 1840 but disappointed in its hope to win the Prussian state for its ideals, went into opposition. Although, in line with Hegel, the Left continued to view the state as the embodiment of reason and morality, it began to decry the monarchy. Among the Leftist (or radical) Hegelians was Ludwig Feuerbach whose critique in *Das Wesen des Christentums* of Hegel's stress on the Idea (*Weltgeist*) as the true reality had a decisive influence on the young Hegel student, Karl Marx.

Marx saw the new industrial classes related through the "cash nexus" of the capitalist system. The tension between the entrepreneurial exploiting class and the increasingly more impoverished and alienated proletariat could be and would be obliterated only through revolution and the creation of the classless, and hence conflictless, society. Marx saw class conflict institutionalized not only in the economic system but necessarily in the entire superstructure of society. While law to Burke integrates and balances a natural class system, law to Marx emanates from and exacerbates class conflict. It supports the domination of one class over another.

Despite the mélange of principles concerning political life operating in Burke's thinking, he did not attempt to shape them systematically into a science of politics, i.e., a theoretical system based upon generalizations concerning political behavior. Those modern scholars who seek to make out of the social sciences a behavioral science similar in procedure and objectives to the physical sciences probably would acknowledge Burke as a man of keen mind and deep intuitive insights, valuable perhaps as a source of operational hypotheses about political behavior. They would not accept him as a social scientist.

Marx, on the other hand, has been considered a forerunner of modern empirical social science. It was Engels himself who propagandized Marx's and his system of historical materialism as "scientific" to distinguish it from those free-floating schools of "utopian" socialists. As Marx claimed, dialectical materialism is based on the actual observation of social behavior and conditions and on historical evidence of those factors influencing social development. In 1933 Sidney Hook analyzed the interest in Marxism as a science rather than a theory of society and described what he called the "orthodox canonization" of Marx, the scientist:

> The theoretical constructions of orthodox Marxism were built out of phrases and propositions drawn from Marx's own words. Indeed, Kautsky, Hilferding and others denied that their orthodoxy constituted an interpretation. In their eyes it was a faithful exposition of the doctrine. Nevertheless, there was a definite shift in the fundamental character of their expositions. Marxism was no longer regarded as essentially the theory and practice of social revolution, but as a *science* of social development.

> The official theoretical emphasis implied that it was not so much a
> method of making history as of understanding it after it had been
> made. It was offered as something *sachlich* and free from value
> judgments, determining action in the same way that a mountain
> slope determines the movement of a glacier. It was objective and
> scientific in the strict sense. It carried authority not only of power
> but of knowledge.[17]

The prediction that socialism would emerge out of the ruination of
capitalism became the heart of Marx's scientism. Insofar as
socialism was part of the inevitable in future history, Marxists began
to consider it "no longer necessary . . . for a Marxist to be a socialist.
Marxism was *Wissenschaft*; socialism *Weltanschauung*. Marxism was the
science which proved that socialism as a state of society would
come."[18] It was this stress on *Wissenschaft* which legitimized Marx
within intellectual-academic circles. It was the prediction of socialism
which fashioned him as the progenitor of many modern mass political
movements.

Around these differences between Burke and Marx various catch
phrases have come into vogue. Marx is "scientific"; Burke is
"intuitive." Marx is promoting history and therefore "progressive";
Burke is saving history and therefore "conservative." Marx is
"modern"; Burke is "feudal." Marx is "relevant" today; Burke is
"passé." These clichés may be convenient classifiers but they leave us
with only the negative comparison. Is there a positive comparison?
The answer is quite definitely, yes.

Conceiving man as a social being, Burke and Marx sought
organic societies in which all members, functionally inter-related,
pursue common ends. The organic society to them was an empirically
verifiable human necessity. Human beings survive and prosper only
through interdependence. They therefore refuted unconditionally the
atomistic society upheld in traditional liberalism as the apex of
human development.

Burke never used the term "alienation" but the concept is
implicit in his argumentation in behalf of historical societies. Marx,

17. Sidney Hook, *Towards the Understanding of Karl Marx* (New York: The John Day Company,
    1933), pp.25-26.

18. *Ibid.*, p. 26.

accepting the Hegelian word and general concept of estrangement, gave alienation a materialistic (economic) causation and expression. To both thinkers the presence of the *homo viator*, the strange wayfarer, in society represents social schism and hence a moral problem. Considering society the crucial environment through which the individual identifies and expresses himself, alienation—separation and strangeness—signifies a moral disharmony between society and the individual. How is such disharmony eradicated? To answer that question Burke and Marx looked for the proper institutional remedies. To Marx this meant the classless society inaugurated by the social ownership of the means of production, while to Burke it meant the class system operating on the basis of the historical constitution. In both cases, however, it is the organic society which produces the historical harmony, the moral identification, of society and the individual. It is the locus of genuine freedom. Social atomism with its stress on the sovereign individual cannot be, for either Burke or Marx, an environment conducive to general well-being or liberty.

The phenomenon of alienation is an acknowledged disease of the modern complex mass society. Some analysts, hearkening to a bygone primitivism, see alienation as the inevitable consequence of the sophisticated technological society man has created but cannot control. They wish to escape the pressures of civilization by a return to primitivism. Yet Burke and Marx contemplated unity and purpose specifically within highly developed societies. They understood history as a civilization-building process, as the ever-increasing convolution in the techniques of human existence and the increasing refinement in the nature of social relations themselves. Burke fulminated against the French Revolutionaries precisely because he believed they did not comprehend the intricate and delicate nature of the social mechanism. They had over-simplified an intricate organization and hence their schemes for reconstructing society were bound to fail. Similarly, Marx extolled bourgeois capitalism for its multitudinous inventions and advancements which had pushed society to that technically complicated phase capable of admitting the proletarian revolution. Socialism could come only out of the highly advanced capitalistic states and communist society would be the epitome of complex integrated social existence. Burke and Marx took for granted that man as a creative worker would continue to refine his environment. They condoned this as a positive function of developmental history. They did not call for a return to a simpler pastoral existence nor did they approach man's inventiveness as his disguised enemy.

Environment is an important conditioner of human perspectives. The emotional feeling which Burke and Marx both had for a meaningful, harmonious social environment had its roots beyond sheer intellectual fancy. It came from concrete personal experience. Who can perceive the personal ramifications of alienation unless he himself to some degree has felt cutoff from a meaningful social existence? Both Burke and Marx lived a somewhat peripheral social existence. Each was born in an area undergoing political turmoil and subjugation. When Burke was born in Dublin in 1729, Ireland constituted one of the most downtrodden dependencies in the British Empire. It was ruled by an English Protestant "Establishment" or "Ascendancy" which denied the Irish Catholic masses any socio-political rights and personality. Similarly, the Rhineland, in whose Romanized city of Trier Marx was born in 1818, had been withdrawn from French jurisdiction in 1815 (having been annexed by France in 1801) and placed under Prussia by the Congress of Vienna. The resentment of the Catholic Rhinelanders toward their Protestant Prussian governors fanned the spirit of revolution in some quarters of the Rhineland. Marx was one of the most notable expressions of that spirit.

Against this broader social milieu is the significant fact that each came from a religiously heterogeneous family.[19] According to the custom concerning religious intermarriage where no conversion occurred, Burke was raised a Protestant in line with his father's faith while his sister followed the mother's Catholic confirmation. Due to the legal and social persecution of Catholics in Ireland, Burke's Protestantism endowed him with certain real benefits since he belonged to that tiny minority in Ireland—socially privileged—who

---

19. Interesting too is that the Burke and Marx families were educated and middle class. Their fathers were lawyers and, as university students, both Burke and Marx had initially intended to pursue legal studies themselves. But each became more interested in philosophy, history and literature.

could buy, sell, and inherit land without hindrances, and serve the state, if such was their pleasure, in both civil and military capacities.[20]

Vis-a-vis the European Jewish community, Marx too could have enjoyed a socially elevated status due to the fact that his mother and father descended from long rabbinical lines. As purveyor of Jewish learning and culture, the rabbi holds in traditional Jewish communities an aristocratic position. But Marx received no formal Jewish education and he did not endeavor to identify himself in any way with his Jewish background. We can even conclude from his relations with other Jews and from his writings that Marx clearly resented his Jewish heritage.[21] It is small wonder however, that he was so estranged. In 1824, when Marx was but six, his family—upon the initiative of the father—converted to Protestantism. Biographers have speculated whether this conversion was done out of conviction or opportunism. In view of the times, the latter would seem the more probable. Nevertheless, judging from the dislike Marx bore for all religions, his

---

20. Stephen E. Graubard, *Burke, Disraeli and Churchill* (Cambridge: Harvard University Press, 1961), p.17.

21. Burke's religious background engendered within him a tolerance for differing faiths and dissenting views. The persecution of the Irish Catholics as well as the English Protestant Dissenters brought him to their defense within Parliament. On the other hand, the precarious existence of the European Jew reaped only scorn from Marx. If his answer to Bruno Bauer in *On the Jewish Question (Zur Judenfrage)* is to be taken seriously, he equated Judaism with part of the bourgeois "money exchange." Rabbi M. Liber, who attributes "self-hate" to Marx, has analyzed the monograph in the following manner: "Le théologien allemand Bruno Bauer avait soutenu que les juifs, ne pouvaient pas obtenir les droits de citoyens dans un état chrétien. Marx lui répond en transportant la question du domaine réligieux dans le domaine économique. . . . Marx ne s'est occupé du judaisme que cette seule fois, provoqué en quelque sorte par Bauer et par le désir d'appliquer au 'cas' juif ses theories sur le rôle du capital-argent dans l'évolution de la société économique. Il ne comprenait rien de l'esprit du judaisme." (M. Liber, "Judaisme et Socialisme," *La Revue de Paris*, IV (Juillet-Août, 1928), pp. 624-25.)

Burke, like Marx, has at times been accused of anti-Seimitism since he referred to the "Jews in Change Alley." There is nothing in Burke's personal like and basic coneptions, however, to indicate that he was an anti-Seimite. It has to be remembered that in the Jewish East End of London there was an Exchange Alley, a fact stemming from centuries long exclusion of the Jews from artisanship, normal commercial pursuits and agriculture. Burke, steeped in the Bible and full of admiration for the Hebraic tradition, certainly did not hold up Exchange Alley as truly representative of all Jews and Judaism. (cf. Edmund Burke, *Reflections*, New Rochelle, New York: Arlington House, 1966), p. 97 and p. 118.)

home environment was evidently one in which institutionalized religion at least played no positive role.

It was in England, the classic historical society, that Burke and Marx lived the major portion of their adult lives. In a sense they remained aliens all their lives. Burke certainly could have stayed in Ireland. But knowing nothing could be accomplished there to ameliorate the depressed conditions, he voluntarily emigrated to England on what he considered a political mission. Within Georgian society, however, his Irish brogue remained a professional and social handicap and was used by his political opponents as a taunting description to set him apart. In addition to this, the Catholic strain in his family background and his religious toleration stimulated vicious stories among those in the upper echelons of English society that Burke was in fact a priest in disguise.

Marx's sojourn to England, by contrast, was necessitated by his expulsion from Germany, France and Belgium on account of his *Aufruf zur Revolution*. Although Marx had several places of residence in London, he spent many of his years in the Soho district, which at that time was filled with immigrants and which is characterized even to this day by its cosmopolitan atmosphere and separateness from the rest of London. G. D. H. Cole wrote about Marx's stay in London:

> Marx . . . had in some degree the characteristic infirmity of the exile—a persistent *malaise* which aggravates the effects of poverty and ill-health. Through all his years of residence in London, and with all his study of English conditions, he never came any nearer to any understanding, much less to an acceptance, of the modes of British thought and action. He came much nearer to understanding the French but not to liking them. He remained a German of the Germans, eternally convinced that German thought was the only really profound thought, and that it was the mission of Germany—of a regenerated, Socialist Germany—to take the lead in the coming Socialist revolution.[22]

Although the picture is often painted of Burke as a smug member of the genteel set, the truth is that he, like Marx, had to be partially supported by a patron all his life. Beginning his parliamentary career

---

22. G. D. H. Cole, *Marxism and Anarchism*: 1850-1890,Vol. II of *A History of Socialist Thought* (London: Macmillan Co., 1965), p. 310.

in 1765, Burke became Secretary to Charles, Second Marquis of Rockingham, who, until his death in 1783, substantially provided for Burke. The bulk of Burke's parliamentary sittings between 1765 and 1794 were patronage positions from the pocket boroughs of Wendover and Malton. (Although this was not especially unusual for that day and age, the only elected seat Burke held was for Bristol from 1774 to 1780 when he was then defeated.) It is well known that the wealthy industrialist Friedrich Engels, whom Marx first met in 1842, supplied Marx at least a modicum of financial security. Their patrons (who were also personal friends and co-workers) were not the sole source of their incomes. Extraneous amounts were earned by each from writings and, in Burke's case, from political office. But neither ever enjoyed sufficient financial security to raise himself out of the abyss of perpetual debt.[23]

Semi-reclusion seemed to be each one's style of life. Aside from families to which they were singularly devoted, each had but scarcely a handful of friends.[24] No doubt their highly selective and demanding personalities helps account for their interest in only limited friendships. And although England was a resting place for them, the fact that each at one time or another entertained hopes of emigrating to America indicates an ulterior search rather than plain adventurousness.

Each one's reaction to his social separateness was unique. Marx rebelled. He professed no sentimentalism for existing mores or

---

23. For one so concerned with practicality, an odd aspect of Burke's personal life was the purchase of a grandoise country estate for which he had to borrow money from Rockingham. Having enough difficulty repaying the Marquis, the maintenance expenses of the mansion indebted him permanently. It was at the Beaconsfield estate, however, that Burke claimed he was his happiest. It allowed him to be together with his family in the country and to engage in the farming he dearly loved and which he prided himself on pursuing scientifically.

24. Burke was devoted to his only child, Richard, who, besides assisting his father as a researcher, shielded Burke from any knowledge of the extensive family debts. Never marrying and dying at a premature age of tuberculosis, Richard's death so shocked Burke that he never recovered from it. He was ridden with guilt feelings that he had ruined Richard's life and abused his devotion by not encouraging him to be more independent. By the same token, Marx, devoted to his wife, Jenny (daughter of a Prussian officer), is said to have suffered such remorse at her death for having subjected her and their children (only three out of seven children survived childhood) to an impoverished, irregular life, that his health, never good in itself, swiftly declined, bringing on his own death shortly thereafter.

institutions. But in view of this it is remarkable to read in his correspondence with Engels his sensitivity to important social routines. A foremost example is the vexation over his daughter's wedding. He wrote to Engels with the following request in December 1867: "Can you do me a favor and ask Ernest Jones how one most appropriately obtains a civil marriage in London, at the Doctor's Commons or where? At the beginning of April Laura should be getting married."[25] A civil marriage not readily accepted socially (the thought of social ostracism burdened his wife, Jenny), Marx related her anxiety to Engels who replied that Jenny should "tell the philistine neighbors that this way was chosen because Laura is protestant while Paul is catholic."[26] Even though Marx rebelled against the society about him, he was fully aware of certain amenities which had to be satisfied, if only for his family's sake.

Burke, however, seems to have thoroughly enjoyed the English way of life and was interested in its preservation and development. But, as Sir Lewis Namier has pointed out, this commitment did not necessarily win him social acceptance. "But if Burke was in a way looked down upon by his associates, this was due not so much to the contempt which the nobly born felt for his origin as to the admiration which he had for theirs. Clearly no one can treat as an equal a man so full of respect and veneration."[27] Namier overestimates Burke's admiration for the aristocracy. It is correct to say that he felt the upper class, as every other class in society, had a particular function to perform. His endeavor to protect the class structure and balance in no way signified he was unduly enamored with a particular class. He had harsh words to say about aristocrats but still viewed them as the source of social leadership. Yet for both Burke and Marx it must be said that whatever leadership positions they held were due to their intellectual skills and forcefulness of personality rather than to their social positions.

The importance of Burke's and Marx's social thought to the twentieth century lies not only in their deep appreciation of

---

25. Karl Marx and Friedrich Engels, *Briefwechsel* (4 Vols.; Berlin: Dietz Verlag, 1950), III, pp. 550-551.

26. *Ibid.*, p. 552. (Laura Marx married Paul Lafargue.)

27. *Namier, op. cit.*, p. 10.

Gemeinschaft (the integrated community) over *Gesellschaft* (mass, anonymous society) but in their understanding of interrelated concrete social processes. Breaking through the static social constructions of traditional liberalism, they introduce society as a composite of processes operating through and under the impact of historical time. To understand society, claimed Burke and Marx, the social critic must expose its nervous sytem. Society is, after all, human activity; it is organized human energy with an inner dynamism and logic. Burke (far from being the strictly intuitional thinker) and Marx offer social philosophies which are supported by empirical investigations and evidence.

Had their social schemes the complexion of utopian apparitions, Burke and Marx would have merited little, if any, attention in the scientific age of the twentieth century. It was this abstractionism in traditional liberalism which could not meet the rigorous demands of scientific propositions. How can we demonstrate "self-evident truths" to those who do not believe in them or "inalienable rights" to those who will fully abuse and negate those rights in others? But then traditional liberalism did not espouse scientific but rather moral knowledge. Reference to the existent world (the *raison d'être* of science) is inconsequential. "Pure" reason attuned to the moral law alone defines the requisites of reality. It can transform man and his environment to meet these requisites. Hence arch-abstractionists like Thomas Paine were convinced that constitutions could be blueprinted ("rationalized") for all societies irrespective of cultural and other social features.[28] Man is man regardless of time or place.

While Burke and Marx are empiricists, they are of the classic Aristotelian vintage. Unlike modern empiricists (i.e., behavioralists), they recognized the special burdens of a social science. Their politics of reality did not preclude evaluations and moral conclusions. Implicit

---

28. It was this type of idealistic faith in the capabilities of rational democracy which pervaded Europe in the opening decades of the twentieth century. The Weimar Constitution of 1918 has often been cited as more the work of professorial intellectuals than practical politicians. The sobering effects of European politics from 1933 to 1945 resulted in the greater concern for national realities, traditions and abilities. Post World War II constitutions in Italy, Germany and France of the Fifth Republic tend to reflect a Burkean commitment to national traditions and practical necessities. The abstractionism of revolutionary democracy has certainly waned.

in this is the belief that history has direction and is, therefore, meaningful. It is developmental, teleological. But the pattern of history is not self-evident; it must be discovered and then facilitated by active choice and work. And for this we need to have the proper intellectual tools. Burke and Marx both thought they could provide us with this equipment for understanding ourselves.

Chapter II
Historical Empiricism:
Its Philosophical Foundations

Empiricism as a conduct of inquiry has ancient roots, having been popularized by Aristotle in his comparative constitutional studies of the Greek city-states. Burke and Marx are, therefore, not pioneers. Empiricism is considered by many in contemporary social science virtually the only scientific means to acquire knowledge about human behavior. And yet probably most such social scientists would discard Marx and certainly Burke for not having attained their allegedly more rigorous standards of scientific analysis. Since Burke and Marx prided themselves on their "practical" and "scientific" approaches, it is important in relating them to contemporary politics to uncover what they understood by empiricism and how it differs from modern empiricism.[1]

This initial task presents us with a real problem. While Marx was geared to the routines and preoccupations of intellectuals, Burke

1. Burke often interchanged the words "practical" and "scientific." In this respect he expressed eighteenth century attitudes, described by Karl Polanyi: "Science, precisely because it became effective within the circumference of human affairs, meant in eighteenth century England invariably a practical art based on empirical knowledge." (Karl Polanyi, *The Great Transformation* New York: Farrar and Rinehart, Inc., 1944 p. 120).

always considered himself first and foremost a parliamentarian. In his scholarly polemic with Hegel and the neo-Hegelians, Marx explicitly set out to distinguish his materialism from Hegelian idealism. Marx consciously developed himself as a philosopher while Burke, although the philosophically-oriented politician, was pushed into the role of the deliberate philosopher more through the force of circumstance.[2] The political issues of his day—the debates over Empire-building, centering particularly on the crisis with the American colonies, and the French revolution—left him, so he claimed, no choice in his conscience but to give full vent to an articulation and appraisal of "first principles." The writing of the *Reflections* took months of preparation and demonstrates that Burke had indeed the intellectual tenacity and capacity to deal philosophically with political issues.

Any discourse on Burke's general method in social analysis must be based upon isolated comments and implicit meanings in his voluminous speeches and writings. In this respect we must be careful not to give Burke an overly scholastic role and remember that any systematization of his generally diffused ideas must make the essence of the prose in which Burke so eloquently expressed himself more formed and direct.

Yet Burke was certainly fully aware of the intellectual currents of his time. During parliamentary speeches he often indulged in tongue-in-cheek remarks about the "learned men" and their speculative theories of government. Indeed on many occasions he sought to test the intellectual styles *en vogue* against the social realities as he un-

---

2. In his younger years Burke did write two exclusively philosophical tracts. He wrote a satirical attack on Bolingbroke in *A Vindication of Natural Society*. (For a refutation of this as Burke's intent at satire, see Murray N. Rothbard, "A Note on Burke's 'Vindication of Natural Society,'" *Journal of the History of Ideas*, XIX January 1958 . Upon the basis of the *Vindication,* Rothbard tries to make out of Burke an anarchist who gave theoretical sustenance to the communist and individualistic wings of anarchism. Although the work may have played this role inadvertently, it must still be viewed as satire, for Burke in his whole philosophy decried anarchism.) Burke also wrote a critique of Locke's epistemology in *On The Sublime and Beautiful* in which he rejected Locke's utilitarian ethics. In their separate writings however Burke and Marx reflect the different emphasis each put on his role in life, Burke speaking primarily from the standpoint of the parliamentarian and Marx as the intellectual. Although Marx involved himself in political activities and organization, his political experiences were, generally speaking, not within the framework of established political processes and structures. Burke and Marx offer us an "inside" and "outside" view of socio-political life and this is an important conditioning factor to remember about each of them.

derstood them. In his opposition to the speculative (i.e., rational) movements of his time, Burke's method of political reasoning becomes clearly discernible.

Empiricism to Burke as to Marx was more than a method or technique. It represented an underlying philosophical commitment. It must be stressed that with their empirical commitments, Burke and Marx moved out of the intellectual style of their times. They rejected much of the Rationalist movement whose tone had been set largely by René Descartes and which continued through the so-called Enlightenment of the eighteenth century and the Idealism, as epitomized by Hegel, of the nineteenth century. Generally speaking, Rationalism derives from Plato and emphasizes the mind (Idea) as the source of knowledge and as ultimate reality itself. By contrast, empiricism, etymologically stemming from the Greek word, "empeiria," meaning "experience," upholds the belief that knowledge of the external world or reality derives from sense perception. It is thus predicated upon the interaction of man and his environment. It assumes the material or physical to be the proper source of knowledge. There exists, claims the empiricist, an external material reality of which man is a part and which he can perceive. Hence knowledge is the sensual perception and mental rationalization of the external order.[2]*

Crucial to empiricism is the assumption that man's relationship with his environment is both *responsive* and *responsible*. Thus the philosophical empiricist contests the viewpoint of the Rationalist like René Descartes that sense perception, far from presenting an understanding of reality, conveys but chaotic, personalized and confused

---

2*. Aristotle writes in relation to this point: "It is also clear that the loss of any one of the senses entails the loss of a corresponding portion of knowledge, and that, since we learn either by induction or by demonstration, this knowledge cannot be acquired. Thus demonstration develops from universals, induction from particulars; but since it is possible to familiarize the pupil with even the so-called mathematical abstractions only through induction—i.e. only because each subject genus possesses, in virtue of a determinate mathematical character, certain properties which can be treated as separate even though they do not exist in isolation—it is consequently impossible to come to grasp universals except through induction. But induction is impossible for those who have not sense-perception. For it is sense-perception alone which is adequate for grasping the particulars: they cannot be objects of scientific knowledge, because neither can universals give us knowledge of them without induction, nor can we get it through induction without sense perception." Aristotle. *Posterior Analytics. Works of Aristotle.* Vol. I (Chicago: Encyclopaedia Britannica Inc., 1952), p. 111.

impressions, that subjective man is excluded from comprehending the objective external world. The empiricist also disqualifies the position of George Berkeley that the material world does not exist *per se* but only as an idea (*esse est precipio*). Nor does he even consider the so-called problem of solipsism in which Cartesian doctrine is carried to its extreme in affirming the "self" as the only object of verifiable knowledge (Descartes' *cogito ergo sum*), all else being but personal illusion. As empiricists, Burke and Marx vehemently attacked the "metaphysicians" and the "utopians" for having lost themselves in what Burke called the "infinite void of the conjectural world."[3]

The significance of their common acceptance of the empirical method is obviously that it leads into what Kant would call shared mental categories. A method of analysis is, after all, a scheme for investigating reality through specified categories and for expressing reality in the logical inter-linking of these categories. Hence an analytical method directs the eye of the investigator and defines the steps and scope of his investigation.

Burke and Marx, in drawing a sharp and uncompromising dichotomy between the empiricists and rationalists (idealists), thereby succumbed to the assumption held by many intellectuals that there exists an undeniable opposition of forces between Aristotelians and Platonists.[4] This alleged antagonism between the two classical Greeks is probably meaningful only within the context of Western civilization. Were the two juxtaposed against non-Western thinkers, their similarities would perhaps overshadow their differences. The tendency to pit Aristotle and his adherents against Plato and his followers tends to bring within each respective fold some curiously diverse thinkers. Hence the philosophical kinship between the conservative Edmund Burke and the revolutionary Karl Marx is linked to the Aristotelian tradition emphasizing inductive reasoning.

3. Burke, Beaconsfield Edition, *op. cit.*, V. p. 234.

4. Crane Brinton suggests the impracticality of establishing a rigid line of demarcation between empiricists (Aristotelians) and rationalists (Platonists), asserting that such a cleavage "actually *accepts* the terminology and point of view of the Cartesian dualism" between the body and the mind, matter and ideas. He claims that both, despite clear divergences in approach, accept that "the world makes sense—mathematical sense, at bottom." Crane Brinton, *The Shaping of Modern Thought* (Englewood Cliffs, New Jersey: Prentice Hall, Inc., 1963), p. 96.

While differing on method, empiricists and rationalists do commonly subscribe to the important notion that the world is knowable. This commitment betrays a Western outlook, especially as embodied in the Judaic and Christian traditions.[5] Judaism, and with it Christianity, assert the single source of all creation and thus the basic unity of existence despite the plurality of existential forms. Crucial to both religious outlooks is the special position of man himself. This faith in man, his worth and potential abilities, has formed a cornerstone of Western social values. Thus even those who withdraw themselves from or have never been directly exposed to religious education generally imbibe this commitment from operating social mores and legal stipulations. Marx, the revolutionary, was also a product of this value system. In a rather moving passage in his article, "The British Rule in India," written for the *New York Tribune* of June 25, 1853, he expresses his contempt for the village communities in Hindustan, claiming:

> . . . They subjected man to external circumstances instead of elevating man to the sovereign of circumstances, . . . they transformed a self-developing social state into never changing natural destiny, and thus brought about a brutalizing worship of nature, exhibiting its degradation in the fact that man, the sovereign of nature, fell down on his knees in adoration of Hanuman, the monkey, and Sabbala, the cow.[6]

The "sovereign of nature," a Biblical-sounding concept, can comprehend and largely control the flow of events about him because he lives within a structured universe rather than an arbitrary and chaotic one.

This conception of the universe as an ordered whole has stimulated the development of science. Through research and experimentation, the scientist attempts to discover that order and,

---

5. The ancient Greeks, not a part of this tradition, fell more into the Oriental *Weltanschauung* with its concept of fatalism than into the Western historical perspective of linear progression. Yet many Greek ideas filtered into Western thought and mores. It must be remembered, for example, that classical Greek philosophers were revived by the medieval Roman Catholic Church and a rapprochement effected between theology and rational thought (e.g., St. Thomas of Aquinas). Similarly, early Greek translations of the Christian Bible culminated in a certain Hellenization of original Hebraic concepts.

6. Marx, "The British Rule in India," *Basic Writings, op. cit.* p. 480.

ultimately, in so doing to increase man's control over natural forces. Since empiricism emphasizes the material world as the proper subject of knowledge, it has been closely identified with science and scientific knowledge.

The word "science," as derived from the Latin noun "scientia," means simply "knowledge" (the verb "scio" being "to know".) The connection between science as knowledge and empiricism as the means to knowledge would seem clear-cut. But an epistemological problem arises from the fact that not all empirical undertakings culminate in scientific knowledge. If, for example, we observe people walking down the street, we comprehend or experience the nature of moving objects but, we may well not notice finer details about those objects such as the number of individuals or the manner in which they walk. The well-known Japanese film, *Rashomon*, skillfully brought out several different and even conflicting eye-witness accounts of a murder. Obviously the claims to knowledge in this situation are tenuous indeed. Similarly, a child must learn to differentiate a scurrying city crowd from a parade or a riot. We might excuse a child for confusing Molotov cocktails with the firecrackers he knew were part of celebrations like the Fourth of July, and we shall expect his powers of observation and integration to become sufficiently trained as he grows to allow him social adjustment. The majority of children will not, however, go beyond this kind of normal, everyday social knowledge. But the scientist must. The essence of science is then the differentiation and relation of observed phenomena on the highest level.

To attain this level the modern meaning of science has become more specialized, designating only those facts obtained through a carefully controlled method. The scientific method, as worked out by Francis Bacon, prescribes the standards by which perception might be verified as knowledge through rigorous experimentation. Empiricism, in concentrating upon the inductive approach to the study of the material world, thereby has become a highly particularized element of the scientific method as used in the natural and physical sciences.

In what way do Burke and Marx attempt to use the empirical method within the social world? Although we might conceive of order within the organic and inorganic aspects of the natural world, do the multifarious relations conducted by "sovereign man" reflect a commensurate order? Burke and Marx answer in the affirmative. Social problems to them are neither totally spontaneous nor self-engendered eruptions. Society is rather a historically-produced process of events rooted in previously established conditions and necessarily interrelated. The task of the social scientist is to uncover the root causes of socio-political problems in order to understand their effects.

Underlying all complex social relations, according to Burke and Marx, are primary causes or motivating forces which operate as such consistently through history. To penetrate these forces one must cut away what both considered the "secondary features" or effects as readily observed within society. Burke, for example, expressed this, stating: "Wise men will apply their remedies . . . to the causes of evil, which are permanent, not to the occasional organs by which they act, and the transitory modes in which they appear. Otherwise you will be wise historically, a fool in practice."[7] Similarly, Marx in his Preface to the second edition of the first volume of *Capital* differentiates his method on this basis from that of Hegel:

> The mystification which the dialectic suffers in Hegel's hands in no way hinders the fact that he has first demonstrated its general form of movement in a comprehensive and conscious manner. The dialectic stands on its head in Hegel. One must turn it upside down in order to discover the rational core in the mystical cover.[8]

Burke and Marx accept virtually axiomatically that society, composed as it is of human beings, is a natural phenomenon responding to the laws of the natural world. This idea reconfirms the existence quite literally of a "uni-verse" rather than a "multi-verse." The human and the non-human are united through the same scheme of order. Rather than particularism or segregation in the sense of different rules and regulations, there is universalism or integration governed by law prescribing the conditions within which the physical moves and develops. Not determined by human will, the universal law is at bottom what Engels once called a "kingdom of necessity" in

7. Burke, *Reflections*, Beaconsfield Edition, *op. cit.*, p. 419.

8. Karl Marx, *Das Kapital* (Hamburg: Otto Meissners Verlag, 1922), p. xviii.

which everything, to use Burke's terminology, acts out of its given "nature" or "constitution."[9]

Marx does not speculate as to the origins of this universal order. He does not raise the question, "What effects the law?" His empirico-scientific preoccupation led him only to affirm through observation and analysis the existence of such order in the natural and social world. He considered the discovery of the dialectic operating through economic modes of production to be his genuine contribution to social science.

Burke, on the other hand, attributed the basis of such order to the Divine. Although he was a member of the Anglican Church and favored the state establishment of the Church, his religious ideas seem to approximate more a deistic than theistic concept. Since God is identical with nature, natural events cannot be explained by supernatural or transcendent causes. While he certainly thought and spoke in moral categories, he seems to have looked soberly upon religion as a social force. Unlike Marx, Burke considered religion a social bond and hence valuable. And, as Peter Stanlis points out, he appreciated the civilizing influence of the Church and its role, especially under Catholicism, as a unifier of Europe.[10]

Burke was quick to employ Christian tenets and personalities in his speeches and writings; this is particularly the case in the *Reflections* whose poetic prose, however, as previously mentioned, was designed for its emotive effect. Thus he relates, for example, how "mandates for deposing sovereigns were sealed with the signet of 'the Fisherman.' "[11] This was obvious sarcasm on Burke's part. Alluding occasionally to revelation, at times in a somewhat cryptic fashion, it does not appear that he accepted this in its most orthodox sense. It would seem rather

---

9. Friedrich Engels, *Socialism: Utopian and Scientific*, trans. Edward Aveling (New York: International Publishers, 1935), p. 73. With the social ownership of the means of production, Engels claimed that man will finally make the ascent from "the kingdom of necessity to the kingdom of freedom."

10. Stanlis, *op. cit.*, p. 196. Stanlis writes: "In his view of the grand sweep of European history, from the gradual fall of the Roman Empire to the French Revolution, Burke was acutely conscious of the enormous social task the Church had assumed and carried successfully for almost eighteen hundred years."

11. Burke, *Reflections*, Arlington House, *op. cit.*, p. 41.

that Burke looked upon the Biblical events more with a historical perspective. While he undoubtedly subscribed to the ethical content of religion, he was certainly not a fundamentalist, interpreting literally Biblical concepts and events.

Much of the religious terminology used by Burke was the colloquial phraseology of the eighteenth century. As a politician, he wanted to express himself in the language of his contemporaries. Thus Burke's linguistic mannerisms *per se* cannot be considered at face value as evidence of his religious orientation. Interesting is the fact that Marx too often indulged in religious imagery and verbiage in his correspondence with Engels. But here again it must be stated that the use of such language, rooted as it was in the idiomatic and colloquial, did not signify Marx's own religious outlook. His references, therefore, to the "devil," "sin" and "punishment" are but informal expressions.

While supporting the state establishment of religion, Burke insisted upon the separation of church and state in terms of policy making. In his polemic with the Dissenting minister, Dr. Price, who supported the liberal ideology of the French revolutionaries, Burke argued that "politics and the pulpit are terms that have little agreement."[12] He did not believe that theologians should concern themselves with the affairs of state about which they have no knowledge. Although Burke wanted the Church to be protected by the state, he did not sanction its entry into political matters.

Burke supported toleration of diverse religions on the basis that "there is a reasonable worship in them all."[13] His religious outlook, supplying as it did the major premise of his commitment to an ordered universe, would appear, as expressed through his writings, to have been highly intellectualized, non-anthropomorphic and even de-personalized. Burke rebelled against all dogmatism in any area. Indeed in his *Notebook* in an essay entitled, "Religion," he implies a connection between natural inclinations and religious sentiments:

> Metaphysical or physical speculations neither are, or ought to be,
> the Grounds of our Duties; because we can arrive at no certainty in

12. *Ibid.*, p.23.

13. Burke, *"Speech on Bill for Relief of Protestant Dissenters,"* Beaconsfield Edition, *op. cit.*, VII, p. 36.

them. They have a weight when they concur with our own natural
feelings; very little when against them.[14]

Burke considered religious feelings, regardless of the forms in which
they are expressed, to be "natural" to the human being; they
represent the affinity man enjoys with the natural order about him.

Despite their differences regarding the origin of the universal law,
Burke and Marx both accept it as "immutable" in itself, though the
generator of change. Although their mutual attitudes toward change
will be discussed in Chapter V, it is important to mention here that
Burke and Marx accepted change as one of the fundamental tenets of
the universal law. To them the universe, of which human society is an
intimate part, is ordered activity.

In line with this both conceived not only of social but natural
evolution. Grounded in classical Greek thinking, Burke and Marx had
absorbed the ancient idea of "development." Aristotle systematically
refined the concept of developmental change: all organic existence has
the energy and the "logical" potential to fulfill its own essential
existence. Given no obstruction, the acorn matures into the oak tree.
The family merges with other family units to form clans, then villages
and finally the polis. Growth or development is activity conducted
purposely, i.e., toward a "pre-determined" or built-in objective
(*télos*).[14*] Aristotle stipulated that the *telos* or purpose of a thing is the
motive power behind the development of the thing.

Hampered by cyclical conceptions of change, stemming most
likely from the observation of recurrent seasons, the ancient Greeks
did not expand the notion of social and natural development into

---

14. *A Notebook of Edmund Burke*, ed. H.V.F. Somerset (Cambridge: Cambridge University Press,
    1957), p. 71.

14*. Aristotle writes in the *Physics*: "The necessary in nature, then, is plainly what we call by the
    name of matter, and the changes in it. Both causes must be stated by the physicist, but
    especially the end; for that is the cause of the matter, not *vice versa*; and the end is 'that for
    the sake of which,' and the beginning starts from the definition or essence; as in artificial
    products, since a house is of such-and-such a kind, certain things must *necessarily* come to be
    or be there already, or since health is this, these things must necessarily come to be or be
    there already. Similarly if man is this, then these; if these, then those." Aristotle. *Physics*.
    Works of Aristotle. op. cit., p. 277.

evolution.[14]** The Greeks looked upon development as the particularized stages of birth, maturation, decay and death in each living organism. They did not broaden this idea into a concept of a universal *telos*, namely, the gradual but continuous integrating and harmonizing of everything in the universe. This latter notion is the distinct contribution of the ancient Hebrews who with their messianic vision committed themselves to a progressive, linear history, the *telos* of which is the reconciliation of the forces of antagonism in an ever-changing universe. Symbolically, Isaiah prophesied that the coming messianic age would be a time in which the "wolf also shall dwell with the lamb, and the leopard shall lie down with the kid."[15]

As Westerners, Burke and Marx had absorbed these ideas of development and evolution. They constituted the core around which their respective historical perspectives were formed. Thus Burke claimed that each nation possesses in its successive generations the seeds for its own development, the fulfillment of its particular "essence." Likewise Marx asserted that each historical period, "determined" by the prevailing modes of economic production, exerts itself toward its logical end. And each carried over the moral

---

14**. In his *On Generation and Corruption*, Aristotle asserts: "It follows that the coming-to-be of anything, if it is absolutely necessary, must be cyclical—i.e. must return upon itself. For coming-to-be must either be limited or not limited: and if not limited, it must be either rectilinear or cyclical. But the first of these last two alternatives is impossible if coming-to-be is to be eternal, because there could not be any 'originative source' whatever in an infinite rectilinear sequence, whether its members be taken 'downwards' (as future events) or 'upwards' (as past events). Yet coming-to-be must have an 'originative source' (if it is to be necessary and therefore eternal), nor can it be eternal if it is limited. Consequently it must be cyclical. . . . The result we have reached is logically concordant with the eternity of circular motion, i.e. the eternity of the revolution of the heavens (a fact which approved itself on other and independent evidence), since precisely those movements which belong to, and depend upon, this eternal revolution 'come-to-be' of necessity, and of necessity 'will be.' For since the revolving body is always setting something else in motion, the movement of the things it moves must also be circular. Thus, from the being of the 'upper revolution' it follows that the sun revolves in this determinate manner; and since the sun revolves thus, the seasons in consequence come-to-be in a cycle, i.e. return upon themselves; and since they come-to-be cyclically, so in their turn do the things whose coming-to-be the seasons initiate." Aristotle, *On Generation and Corruption* in *Works of Aristotle, op. cit.*, p. 440.

15. Isa. 12:6.

connotations of the Hebraic evolutionary concept of history in ascribing to each successive step in this growth the attainment of ever higher levels of social moral existence.

In actuality both Burke and Marx are attempting to account for civilization-building. Marx, though he would reject paralleling his historiography with that of the Bible, implicitly accepted the latter's format. In "predicting" the establishment of the coming communist society—the social unity created in place of all previous social antagonisms—he was more literally Hebraic than Burke.

Without identifying Marx too closely with Judaic concepts, since he was not an identified Jew or religionist of any sort it is, nevertheless, impressive that there exists a real correlation of historical forms in the two sets of ideas. Sidney Hook has commented on this relationship:

> Despite his refusal to appeal to ethical principles, Marx had a passionate sense of social injustice which burns fiercely in everything he wrote. He would have scoffed at the idea that he was in line with the Hebrew prophets, but he sometimes spoke of the laws of history as if they were the decrees of Jehovah punishing a wicked society, and of the socialist revolution as if it were the catastrophic prelude to a new dispensation.[16]

Taken with caution and reservation, it might be held that Marx's revolutionary approach emanates at least partially from the concept of history put forth by the Hebrews. Hebraic historicism is revolutionary not only because it substitutes active human volition and merit for the Greek concept of the fated individual imprisoned in pre-ordained, unchanging circumstances. It is revolutionary because it also posits a final, complete, universal transformation. Too cautious to deal with any millennium and perhaps too exposed to the Christian additions to the Hebraic theology, Burke was more attuned to the "fallibility" of the historical process.[17] This undoubtedly is one of the sources of his basic conservatism. Burke felt that the Good and valuable attained in history should be consciously protected and

---

16. Sidney Hook, *Marx and the Marxists* (Princeton: D. Van Nostrand Co., Inc., 1955), p. 48.

17. The Christian emphasis upon the Original Sin of man and the necessity of a second coming of the Messiah complicated the original Hebraic concepts and in a sense "de-revolutionized" them.

promoted. Reserved though he was about the millennium, Burke too admitted the possibility of progress in the universe. He rejected out of hand those philosophies of history hearkening back to Greek cyclicalism. In this respect he wrote:

> I am not quite of the mind of those speculators who seemed assured that necessarily, and by the constitutions of things, all states have the same periods of infancy, manhood and decrepitude that are found in the individuals who compose them. Parallels of this sort rather furnish similarities to illustrate or to adorn than supply analogies from whence to reason.[18]

The belief at least in the possibility of human social development and evolution is plausible. It can be argued from the standpoint of the special rational capacities of the human being which permit memory, invention and volition. The human being can conceive of himself in generational terms and hence accumulate knowledge and experience, make new discoveries and act upon them willfully. Human progress is feasible.

Yet both Burke and Marx seem to project the idea of progress into the natural universe as well. It was perhaps easier for Marx, considering the intellectual milieu in which he lived, to supplement the Greek natural and the Hebraic moral *telos* with an overall change in the make-up of the universe. Marx, after all, knew Darwin, who, he said, "amused" him and refers to him several times in his correspondence with Engels. He seems, however, to have rejected the social implications of Darwin's thinking, considering them a justification or support of the bourgeois class and its dominating role in nineteenth century society:

> It [Darwin's theory] is Hobbes' *bellum omnium contra omnes*, and it is reminiscent of Hegel in the Phenomenology, where bourgeois society figures as a spiritual animal kingdom, while for Darwin the animal kingdom figures as bourgeois society.[19]

To Marx, Darwin's "struggle for survival," if applied to social relations, tended to uphold the exploits of the upstart bourgeoisie. He

---

18. Burke, "Letter Addressed to a Member of the Present Parliament on the Proposals for Peace with the Regicide Directory of France," Beaconsfield Edition, *op. cit.*, V, p. 234.

19. Marx and Engels, *Briefwechsel, op. cit.*, III, p. 95. (Letter of June 18, 1862).

thus leaned away from the supposition that society must always be divided against itself.

Despite this disagreement with Darwin, Marx was interested in the physical interaction of the organism with his environment as depicted by Darwin and was very receptive to the idea that such interaction engenders over time physical adjustments and changes. He was, however, more fascinated with the work of the Frenchman, P. Trémaux, who in 1865 published in Paris his *Origine et Transformations de l'Homme et des autres Etres.* The following reason which Marx gives to Engels (who was not impressed by Trémaux) for preferring Trémaux to Darwin is significant for what it conveys about Marx's own philosophical orientation:

> Cross-breeding does not produce, as one believes, the difference, but on the contrary the typical unity of the species. The earth's formation *differentiates* against it (not alone but as the main basis). Progress, which is for Darwin purely accidental, is here necessary on the basis of the development periods of the earth, the degeneration, which Darwin cannot explain, is here simple; ditto the fast extinction of mere transition forms compared with the slowness of the development of the species type, so that the paleontological gaps, which disturbed Darwin, are here necessary. Ditto, therefore, the law of necessity develops the fixity (apart from individual etc. variations) of the formerly constituted species. The difficulties in hybridization in Darwin here on the contrary support the system, as has been demonstrated, as soon as the crossing with others ceases to be fruitful or possible etc.[20]

Crucial ideas to which Marx responded in Trémaux are those of necessity, differentiation and unity of the species explained chiefly through the material forces of the earth's formation. Although Engels tried to downgrade Trémaux, Marx considered the historical and political application of his findings "more important and richer than Darwin's."[21]

---

20. *Ibid.*, p. 424. (Letter of August 7, 1866) Since Marx was writing a letter to Engels, he did not bother to put all his thoughts into complete sentences and hence his style here is rough and staccato.

21. *Ibid.* For Engels' reaction to Trémaux, see his letter of October 5, 1866 to Marx in which he stated that he sees "no reason to follow the man so far, in fact there are many objections against it." (*Ibid.*, p. 433). Engels described, however, "modern materialism" as having

To what extent and in what way did Burke agree with a historical natural universe? If, as Stanlis stipulates, Burke, in spite of his Anglican membership, was "essentially Catholic," his religious indoctrination would have quite definitely militated against the notion of physical evolution.[22] Catholics and Protestants in the eighteenth century accepted the instantaneous and fully-developed creation described in Genesis. Scientific discoveries had as yet produced no challenge to this orthodoxy. And yet in a passage from the *Reflections*, rich in its implications for the discussion at hand, Burke made the following "philosophic analogy":

> Our political system is placed in a just correspondence and symmetry with the order of the world, and with the mode of existence decreed to a permanent body composed of transitory parts,—wherein, by the disposition of a stupendous wisdom, moulding together the great mysterious incorporation of the human race, the whole, at one time, is never old or middle-aged or young, but, in a condition of unchangeable constancy moves on through the varied tenor of perpetual decay, fall, renovation and progression. Thus by preserving the method of nature in the conduct of the state, in what we retain we are never wholly obsolete. By adhering in this manner and on those principles to

absorbed the "more recent discoveries of natural science, according to which nature also has its history in time, the celestial bodies, like the organic species that, under favourable conditions, people them, being born and perishing. And even if nature, as a whole, must still be said to move in recurrent cycles, these cycles assume infinitely larger dimensions." Thus while "old materialism looked upon all previous history as a crude heap of irrationality and violence; modern materialism sees in it the process of evolution of humanity, and aims at discovering the laws thereof." (Friedrich Engels, *Socialism: Utopian and Scientific, op. cit.*, p. 50).

22. Stanlis, *op. cit.*, p. 202. Under Henry VIII the English Church achieved its separation from Rome for political reasons. It was not really until the time of Henry's daughter, Elizabeth I, that the Anglican Church became defined in doctrine and was established as a national church. Compromising with the Catholics in the realm, Elizabeth maintained within the liturgy of the new Church many Catholic features and forms. The Anglican Church became, therefore, somewhat of a hybrid. It would have been possible for a member of the Church to identify himself more with either the Catholic or non-Catholic elements in the doctrinal base of the new Church. Burke never specified any partiality, although he did feel that the differences between the Catholics and Protestants were not very significant. Because he took this viewpoint, he considered religious persecution and segregation anathema. His interest in protecting Catholics was closely related to his concern for Ireland. This fact, which has been construed as evidence for Burke's own Catholic predisposition, more probably reflects his broader political perspective regarding religious toleration.

our forefathers, we are guided, not by the superstitions of antiquarians but by the spirit of philosophic analogy.[23]

Burke hints here at the progressive movement in the physical universe such as is to be found in human society. The analogy between the universe and society is valid for Burke because both are governed at the same time by the natural law. While change is an inherent part of the law (as well as order), it is effected in some degree through the interaction of man and his environment. Human society is thereby in "correspondence and symmetry" with the natural world.

It would seem, judging from his own private life, that Burke assumed man played no minor part in stimulating progressive change within the natural as well as in the human world. He, for example, prided himself on his scientific farming and animal breeding at Gregories, his mansion in Beaconsfield. From this personal experience it might be deduced that he understood that there existed possibilities for improving nature. In his university *Notebook* are scattered references in which he shows his fascination with the production of entirely new properties and substances in chemical experimentation. He was sufficiently initiated into the realm of physical science to understand the dynamism of the universe which could create new and improved physical characteristics. In this vein the young Burke raises the question whether it may ". . . not be that a Different Co-aptation of Parts, and a different Operation of them one on another and perhaps by that means on other Bodies, may increase their gravity, as by such a Diversity of Positions or Motions they acquire other Qualities which they had not before, or have them increased or changed according to the nature of the Cause?"[24]

The word "co-aptation" which Burke uses here is important. It connotes the mutual activity, adjustment and joining together of parts. It was in this manner that he seems to have contemplated the relationship between man and nature. Rather than man adapting to a routinous natural world, there is in reality a two-way impact and process of harmonization. In this respect Burke was very much in the tradition of Montesquieu who emphasized the physical environs,

23. Burke, *Reflections*, Beaconsfield Edition, *op. cit.*, p. 275.

24. Somerset, *op. cit., p. 94.*

such as climate, soil, location, as conditioning factors upon the social life of a people. To understand the different types of state existence, it is accordingly necessary to analyze the geophysical context of the various states. Interesting is the fact that Montesquieu, who influenced Burke heavily, approached the scientific categories of Trémaux, whom Marx held in such esteem.

Burke and Marx responded to material (or physical) explanations of similarities and dissimilarities in human social existence. Thus, although there exists a universal order, observable differences in the human and non-human world verify the operation of a particularizing process of "co-aptation." Different physical conditions bring forth varying life-styles and forms. It is perhaps for this reason that Burke and Marx, while certainly recognizing the national differences among Europeans, emphasized Europe as a "natural" civilizational unit. They thought the localized differences of far less significance than the basic similarities of all Europeans. And they definitely considered them less important than the differences between Europe as a whole and other cultures and civilizations, such as the Orient.

Burke was not as explicit as Marx and Engels were to be on the idea of a historical natural world. Yet insofar as Burke linked change with conservation as well as development in the universe and related this universe to man as a biological entity, he was subscribing to the concept of natural history. In describing the "method of nature," he clearly asserts a dynamic and even "rational" natural process. "We must all obey," he wrote, "the great law of change. It is the most powerful law of Nature."[25] And what is nature? It is "wisdom without reflection, and above it."[26]

Important in the concept of nature held by Burke and Marx is their disqualification of a mechanical universe. According to the mechanist, nature operates analogously to a clock. Every part has its own function which is performed in harmony with all other functions in the entire mechanism. The natural mechanism is supposed to have

---

25. Burke,*"Letter to Sir Hercules Langrische, M..P., on the Subject of the Roman Catholics of Ireland and the Propriety of Admitting them to the Elective Franchise, consistently with the Principles of the Constitution as Established at the Revolution."* Beaconsfield Edition, *op. cit.,* IV, p. 301.

26. Burke, *Reflections*, Beaconsfield Edition, *op. cit.*, p. 274.

been created at one time but left thereafter to its own internal momentum to operate independently. Nature is thereby "objective" existence, unconscious or "lifeless." It exists apart from the "subjective" human world. The static mechanical universe is thus one from which man is totally estranged. By contrast, Burke and Marx posit a changeable yet ordered ("rational") universe of which man is a vital member.

The model of nature which Burke and Marx constructed forms the foundation of their empirical social science. Within a general context of order, they assume three modes of activity within the universe. There is the development in which each being matures into its own form. There is a continuous balancing in the universe between its human and non-human elements. And there is evolution in the physical changes wrought through "co-aptation," the process of adaptation and integration. These three forms of activity occur within the over-all established order of the universe; hence the activity is meaningful, that is, not chaotic, and, therefore understandable. Because Burke and Marx believed that the natural order expresses and fulfills itself through activity, and because activity, as a characteristic of nature, relates to matter, knowledge of the real external world can be obtained only through the empirical method. Thus Marx wrote to Engels in 1866 that "as long as we observe and think, we can never extricate ourselves from materialism."[27]

The real world then for Burke and Marx is the phenomenal (*die sinnliche Welt*) in ordered activity. Were the world static or unchanging order, knowledge of it would be beyond man. There would be no basis for his perceiving the properties of that world. Burke outlines his epistemology in the following excerpt from an essay in his *Notebook* entitled, "Several Scattered Hints Concerning Philosophy and Learning Collected here from my Papers":

> Suppose we divide a Body into many parts; yet each part will have *Length, Breadth, Thickness;* and so will every part of those parts, and so ad infinitum. But those qualities are sensible properties, and when they do not affect the Senses, we cannot be certain that these Qualities exist; since they do not operate; for we know of their Existence but by their Operation. If it be said that they grow too small for the sense, I believe these words are not well understood;

27. Marx and Engels, *Briefwechsel, op. cit.*, 439. (Letter of December 12, 1866).

for small and great are only in reference to the Impression made on the Sensory; and if there is no Impression I don't see how anything can be *great* or *small*. So that if they exist, they must have other Properties, Since those they have are not sensible Qualities. Again all bodies being composed originally of Minute parts, they may in that Separate State have qualities different from what they have in the aggregate: and may be otherwise coloured, figured etc.[28]

Even attributes like color cannot be known without the activity of light rays. The sensory perception of the external world depends not only upon the activity within the object but also upon the interaction of the object, its environment and the sensory receiver.

Marx applied this same concept in *The German Ideology* to the social world, when he emphasized that a "true" (*wirkliche*) social science, i.e., one that is empirically based, must concentrate upon observing and comprehending the "active process of life" (*tätiger Lebensprozess*).[29] Observations "must demonstrate in each case the connection of the social and political structure with production."[30] It must seek to understand individuals "as they really are, i.e., as they produce."[31]

Burke, too, put forth the idea that man—as part of the physical world—can be comprehended only as activity of a particular sort. Thus he claimed that "as God has made all his Creatures active, He has made Man principally so."[32] Similar to studies made about the natural world, Burke and Marx underscore the fact that to com-

28. Somerset, *op. cit.*, p. 93.

29. Marx and Engels, *Die Deutsche Ideologie, op. cit.*, p. 23.

30. *Ibid.*, p.22.

31. *Ibid.* Marx uses the phrase "wie sie wirklich sind, d.h. wie sie wirken" in connecting "real," i.e., active, individuals with the production process. The German verb "wirken," meaning "to work" (or any English verb meaning to effect, operate, produce) has the same root as the noun "Wirklichkeit" (reality) and the adjective-adverb "wirklich" (real or really). As Marx uses the adverb and verb, he is conveying the notion, similar to Burke's, that Reality is substance in operation. The same linguistic meaning can best be found in the noun "actuality," derived from the past participle of the Latin verb "agere," meaning "to do."

32. Somerset, *op. cit.*, p. 69.

prehend the human being one must look to the effects of his active nature. Reality is to both propertied matter in motion.[32]*

The empirical method to Burke and Marx transmits knowledge of this external "real" world. But every sentient being "experiences" and is indeed dependent upon its environment. Hence every individual observes and forms impressions of the active world about him. Can such "empirically-gathered" images be considered *ipso facto* scientific knowledge? To this question Burke and Marx answer categorically in the negative. Reality to them is not merely activity but *ordered* activity. Were the world mere random activity, there could still be experience of this activity. But there would be no comprehension of it and hence no science. Science must account for the manner in which the multifaceted activity of the universe assumes an order (or integration). Thus empirical observations to qualify as the groundwork for scientific knowledge must be made by the trained eye and fitted into a conceptual framework by reflective reasoning.

32*. As Aristotle puts it, "We physicists, on the other hand, must take for granted that the things that exist by nature are, either all or some of them, in motion—which is indeed made plain by induction." Aristotle. *Physics. Works of Aristotle*, Vol. I. *op. cit.*, p. 259.

Chapter III
Historical Empiricism: Its Social Application

Emphasizing order as a vital characteristic of reality, Burke and Marx lean heavily upon historicism as a necessary supplement to direct observation. They consider it self-evident that human beings, insofar as they are active participants in a universal order, are also developmental. Nothing is static in the universe; everything is always in the process of changing and fulfilling itself. To recall Aristotle's example, to describe the properties of an acorn without accounting for its interaction with the environment and subsequent growth into the oak tree would be to miss the point of its existence. Similarly, descriptions of isolated social phenomena taken as *faits accomplis* in and of themselves approach more a crude empiricism than genuine science. Rather social events must be understood in their over-all inter-relationships and historical (or timed) development. Burke and Marx understood society to be the total relations of inter-active individuals operating out of and building upon the accumulated knowledge and habits of generations. As society thereby represents a group experience, history records the development of that experience. Thus historicism was to them the logical adjunct of the empirical method.

It is important to note the word order in "historical empiricism." Why not use the term "empirical historicism"? Both employed history in the selective sense of the broad trends of social development rather than all the myriad events of the past. The study of history is essential to find the order and "scheme of things" in observable reality. By contrast, empirical historicism connotes the attempt to reconstruct the past through empirical evidence, such as is the intent of archaeology. The German archaeologist, Heinrich Schliemann, for example, tested out Homer's description of the ancient site of Troy by using empirical methods. In this respect empiricism becomes the tool for verifying historical situations. Burke and Marx, however, as historical empiricists, used history as the precedent for perceiving the "logic" of "living" experience.

Their emphasis upon history differentiates them from the contemporary empiricists ("behavioralists") in the social sciences. We mentioned previously that contemporary empiricists would most likely not regard either Burke or Marx as scientific. Much of this ostracism by contemporary empiricists is due to the behavioralist's aversion to historicism. Within political science, "behavioralists" have charged that the "traditionalist" approach to studying political life has been primarily historical and legalistic. And they have criticized the "traditionalists" for contributing little through the years to a general theoretical framework of scientific caliber concerning political behavior. As self-conscious "young Turks" in the discipline, "behavioralists" assert they are now building up a science of politics on the basis of empirical methods and evidence.[1] In this vein Peter H. Odegard, former President of the American Political Science Association, makes the following division between the "behavioralist" and "traditionalist" approaches:

1. David Easton, "The Current Meaning of 'Behavioralism' in Political Science," *The Limits of Behavioralism in Political Science*, ed. James C. Charlesworth (Philadelphia: The American Academy of Political and Social Science, October 1962), p. 1. Easton writes: "The now not-so-young Turks who a decade ago were speaking in loud, strident, and sometimes rude voices about the dire need for scientific method in political research have begun to feel that they have finally acquired the garments of legitimacy." "Behavioralism," utilizing empirical methods such as participant-observer techniques, interviews and polls in order to describe more accurately and hence better understand human behavior, began as a movement in political science in the 1920's and 1930's. For this development, see Harold D. Lasswell, *The Future of Political Science* (New York: Atherton Press, 1964), especially Chapter II.

There is a new look in the study of politics; an increasing awareness of the baffling complexity of what since Aristotle has been called the queen of the sciences—the science of politics. No longer a hostage to history, and freed at last from its bondage to the lawyers as well as from the arid schemation of the political taxonomists, political science is in the process of becoming one of the central unifying forces for understanding why we behave like human beings.[2]

Odegard implies that the "old" methods in political science are not only repugnant to the "new" but indeed that they are incapable of permitting a scientific construction of political life. History, in the sense of documentary sources about the past, is considered "subjective" and thus beyond the pale of scientific requirements for "objectivity." Historical events are also not instructive since they do not admit the kind of empirical verification specified by the "behavioralists." While Burke and Marx share the concern for studying the *behavior* of individuals (a concern which has a centuries-long tradition in Western political analysis), they demand that such studies have a historical base. Human behavior is, after all, conditioned by time or historical forces.

Although one can *describe* the human being in non-historical terms, Burke and Marx claimed it is impossible to explain or evaluate his behavior without any understanding of the historical conditioning behind it. In other words Burke and Marx upheld a concept of *Homo historicus*; it would have been inconceivable to either of them to treat

2. Peter H. Odegard, "A New Look at Leviathan," *Frontiers of Knowledge in the Study of Man*, ed. Lynn T. White (New York: Harper and Bros., 1956), p. 94. In its stress upon objective description of observable phenomena, behavioralism is an archenemy of the academic "New Lefters" who seek to commit social science and social scientists to political lobbying. This push for academic trade unionism must be stimulated by ideology, as C. Wright Mills expressed it to the New Left: "It is a kindergarten fact that any political reflection that is of possible public significance is *ideological*: in its terms, policies, institutions, men of power are criticized or approved." Mills describes the contemporary "fetishism of empiricism" as a "pretentious methodology used to state the trivialities about unimportant social areas. . . ." C. Wright Mills, in Long, *op. cit.*, p. 18 The empiricism accepted by the New Left, as described previously by Carl Oglesby, is based upon "critical thought with historical structure." Oglesby, *op. cit.*, p. 5. The crucial word here is "critical" which stems from Marx's description in his *Theses on Feuerbach* of the function of philosophy being to change the world not merely to interpret (or describe) it. According to the New Left, the behavioralists seek merely to describe but lack a historical vantage point to understand even what they describe.

human existence in a time vacuum. And they would have looked upon
the so-called "time studies" made by current-day "behavioralists" on
such phenomena as elections and attitudinal trends as inconclusive
since the scope of such studies tends to be limited at best to several
years and cannot be considered a historical perspective. The period of
time chosen in such studies, being extracted from surrounding
historical situations, would be more apt to represent an artificial
universe deliberately constructed as complete in itself for analytical
purposes. More importantly, such studies do not take into account the
total sweep of forces operating in a society and hence can be only
partial descriptions of isolated events. But Burke and Marx entertained *Weltblicke*; they tried to acquire the "feeling" for broad
historical developments in *whole* societies.

Such inclusive perspectives seemed to come naturally to them.
No doubt they reflected to a large extent their particular intellectual
personalities. But some account must also be made of the European
educational system which, in stressing humanistic learning, concentrated upon historical and philosophical studies. Scientific
scholarship, therefore, did not mean to them duplicating the methods
of the natural and physical sciences in the social sciences. Instead it
meant the acquisition of a breadth of knowledge concerning human
existence and its problems. It meant precision in concepts (not their
translation into mathematical symbols, as is now the intellectual
fashion).

Contemporary "behavioralists" urge what they call interdisciplinary approaches to human behavior, organized around the
alleged "core sciences" of psychology, sociology and anthropology,
but incorporating political science and economics as well.[3] Burke and
Marx also considered a unified social science approach necessary to
the full understanding of social phenomena. Indeed it was Burke who
argued, very much in the contemporary manner, that "one of the
Strongest reasons" he had "for admitting great variety into our

---

3. Easton, *loc. cit.*, p. 18. Easton writes in this article about the interdisciplinary approach: "In
   part, this turn towards empirical theory has been related to a hope that has never been
   completely lost from sight in the whole history of increasing specialization of knowledge and
   which appeared again in particularly strong form in the 1930's and 1940's. This was the idea
   that the understanding of man in society would be immeasurably enriched if some way
   could be found to draw the social sciences together into a basic unity." (p. 15).

Studies, and a passing in a pretty Quick Succession from one to another, is that it helps to form that *versatile ingenium* which is of very great use in life."[4] By being "learned *about* Sciences" rather than *in* them, Burke meant mastering "those principles that govern almost all of them" so as to "extend our views much more considerably . . . and prevent that littleness and narrowness that almost inevitably attends a confined commerce with any Art or Science however noble in itself."[5]

From Marx's own intellectual pursuits into all manner of scientific endeavors, it becomes clear that he appreciated the well-rounded, unobsessive intellect of which Burke speaks. In his own theory that all human relations and ideas about those relations are conditioned by the economic means of production, Marx sought a unifying principle in human activity as well as in intellectual endeavors. At one point in *The German Ideology*, Marx asks, "Where would natural science be without industry and commerce?"[6] Like Burke, Marx recognized that knowledge itself proceeds apace with epochal developments, which for Marx, unlike Burke, meant primarily in the economic realm.

It was self-evident to Marx that to understand "wirkliche Menschen" (real men), a historical method had to be employed which placed man in his total social context. "As soon as this active process of life becomes represented, then history ceases to be a collection of dead facts, as for the abstract empiricists, or an imaginery action of imaginery subjects, as for the idealists."[7] To Marx this is the beginning of what he called the true, positive science.[8]

4. Somerset, *op. cit.*, p. 86.

5. Somerset, *op. cit.*, p. 84.

6. Marx and Engels, *Die Deutsche Ideologie, op. cit.*, p. 42.

7. *Ibid.*, p. 23.

8. *Ibid.* Marx equated empiricism with genuine science: "Da, wo die Speculation aufhört, beim wirklichen Leben, beginnet also die wirkliche, positive Wissenschaft, ..." By a "positive science" Marx did not mean Positivism as represented by Auguste Comte. He had mostly negative words for this, feeling that it was a shallow endeavor and, even though it was concerned with practical phenomena, in its speculations about such phenomena it was idealistic. Marx thought Hegel had more substance. He once remarked to Engels that it was not surprising Positivism appeared in 1832—the year the middle class was enfranchised in England.

A necessary consequence of their integrative, developmental historicism is the emphasis on the group rather than the individual. This is not to say that neither of them recognized the role of the "great men," the outstanding individuals, in the making of history. As mentioned previously, they took political battles seriously and in confronting their opponents fully realized that individual actions can be decisive in history. They never succumbed to the idea of a fated history. Questioning "whoever dreamt of Voltaire and Rousseau as legislators?" despite whatever intellectual merits they had, Burke amazedly confirmed their roles in stimulating the 1789 French Revolution.[9]And Burke took into account the Cromwells, Guises, Condes, Colignis and Richelieus who, as "instruments" of history, were "men of great civil, and great military talents, and if the terror, the ornament of their age."[10]

Marx also considered the maneuvers of individuals historically pertinent. Writing at the time of the Third French Republic, Marx, in a letter of July 15, 1874, to Engels, analyzed the consequences for MacMahon, then Premier, of a pending dissolution of the legislature. At the end of this letter Marx quipped, "Has anything so comical ever been experienced in world history as this collision and its heroes?"[11] In *The German Ideology* Marx explicitly elaborated upon the role of individuals in building up new lands, such as colonial settlements:

> Such lands have no other indigenous pre-requisites outside of the individuals who settle themselves there and moreover who in their necessities become motivated by the inadequate commercial forms of the old lands. They begin, therefore, with the most advanced individuals of the old lands and thus with the accordingly most

9. *The Correspondence of Edmund Burke*, ed. Cobban and Smith, *op. cit.*, p. 81. (Letter of January 1790 to an Unknown Person) Parenthetically, it is interesting to note Burke's remarks about Voltaire and Rousseau in their entirety: "Whoever dreamt of Voltaire and Rousseau as legislators? The first has the merit of writing agreeably; and nobody has ever united blasphemy and obscenity so happily together. The other was not a little deranged in his intellects, to my almost certain knowledge. But he saw things in bold and uncommon lights, and he was very eloquent—But as to the rest!—I have read long since the *Contrat Social*. It has left very few traces upon my mind. I thought it a performance of little or no merit; and little did I conceive that it could ever make revolutions, and give law to nations. But so it is."

10. Burke, *Reflections*, Arlington House, *op. cit.*, p. 60.

11. Marx and Engels, *Briefwechsel, op. cit.*, IV, p. 498.

developed commercial form of these individuals, still before this commercial form can be accomplished in the old lands.[12]

Yet since Burke and Marx underscored the concept of *Homo historicus*, they firmly believed that all individuals, although they might exert unusual influence and demonstrate perspectives above and beyond the "average," are, nevertheless, social products operating under historically-engendered and inherited conditions and frames of reference. This commitment differentiates them from the liberal in the strict Rationalist tradition who assumed that reason can defy history (and thus social conditioning). While the Rationalist claimed it is reason (or "consciousness," as Marx puts it) which determines human existence, Marx maintained that "consciousness is from the very beginning a social product and so it will remain as long as men exist."[13] Burke concurred with Marx on this, stipulating that "those things which appear to depend wholly on reason" have their support in man's "native constitution and complexion," which he understood to be social.[14] Burke and Marx, being in the Aristotalian tradition, considered it absurd to speak of man as anything but a social or political animal—a *zoon politikon*: it is the social existence, not just the individual existence, of man which is of utmost importance. Indeed, as Burke and Marx knew, the individual is dependent upon society for his very well-being (or lack thereof). The "right" society facilitates the development of the "right" individual.[15] Applying the argument of Aristotle, we can say that society, as the end of the individual, exists

12. Marx and Engels, *Die Deutsche Ideologie, op. cit.*, pp. 74-75. Marx had a marginal note at the end of this sentence in the original manuscript referring to "personal energy of the individuals of single nations" ("persönlicher Energie der Individuen einzelner Nationen").

13. *Ibid.*, p. 27.

14. Somerset, *op. cit.*, p. 108.

15. This is not to imply the Rationalists do not adhere to this connection between the right society and the right individual. The difference lies in the fact that the Rationalist accepts society as convention, the product of rational agreement, while Burke and Marx accept it as a natural necessity (instinctual). What is conventional can be changed or obliterated entirely by convention. It is no wonder then that anarchism is a logical extreme off-shoot of Rationalism since it claims man can in fact live asocially. Rationalism, as expressed in modern Liberalism (since the seventeenth century), has tended to define the right society as that which allows the sovereign individual to come forth as clearly as possible.

logically, and we might add, experientially prior to the individual rather than the other way around as the social contract theorists postulated.

This concentration upon social man brings Burke and Marx closer than the Rationalists to the domain of social science. The commitment in much of Enlightenment thinking was that "right" reason in tune with the natural law could deduce those precepts necessary to construct the perfect society. Burke and Marx considered this utopianism. As Burke maintained, to define man only as a "rational being" is to strip him of his other characteristic properties and hence through over-simplication to distort and confuse the nature of his existence. This kind of over-simplification to Burke and Marx is not science but metaphysical illusion. Science demands knowledge of human nature by which, according to R. R. Fennessy, Burke meant "the full complete nature of man, taking into account all his faculties, all his feelings and instincts, his social as well as his individual existence, his full development as well as his initial potentialities."[16] This is a description to which Marx would have added no reservations.

To them, therefore, the Rationalist offers no clues to explaining human behavior. Scientific explanations must be predicated upon generalizations concerning a class of phenomena or species. Although the Rationalist unites men on the basis of shared rational capacities and fits them thereby into the universal scheme of things, he still surmises that each individual, operating on his own conscience and interests, represents his own particular mode of behavior. It is also assumed that the free interplay of such particular individuals generates social well-being and harmony.[17] This strictly in-

---

16. R.R. Fennessy, *Burke, Paine and the Rights of Man* (The Hague: Martinus Nijhoff, 1963), p. 134.

17. In this respect Adam Smith wrote from the economic liberal's perspective that the individual ". . . generally, indeed, neither intends to promote the public interest nor knows how much he is promoting it." In acting upon his own interest he is ". . . led by an invisible hand to promote an end which was no part of his intention, ... By pursuing his own interest he more frequently promotes that of society more effectively than when he really intends to promote it." (Adam Smith, *An Inquiry Into The Nature and Causes of the Wealth of Nations* Chicago: Encyclopaedia Britannica, Inc., 1952), p. 194.

dividualistic approach works against scientific calculations. It becomes virtually impossible to accept the presence of a "type" without likewise assuming that the non-individualistic, i.e., social, characteristics also influence individual behavior. By tearing the individual theoretically out of the social context, Rationalism absolves itself of scientific claims. Insofar too as emphasis is laid upon speculative or deductive truths which bear no necessary correlation to observable "reality," Rationalism can not meet the standards of scientific verification through the inductive procedures of testing and reasoning.

To understand and explain human behavior, no matter how extraordinary, Burke and Marx claim one must assume that the individual is a social and socially-conditioned being rather than an atomistic unit complete in himself. It is the task of the social scientist to analyze the social context from which individuals emerge. As it is impractical to study single individuals and their behavior, so it is likewise impractical for the social scientist to concern himself with single, isolated events or phenomena in society. But what is society? Burke and Marx answer that it is that complex in which the variety of relations individuals enter into with others are stabilized, routinized and integrated. To understand society it must be appraised as a functioning unit.

Although they accept the idea of a "uni-verse," Burke and Marx were fully aware of the fact that man forms a special part in that universe and hence studies of man must be based on investigatory techniques suitable to the human environment. While they sought to apply the acquired knowledge of the natural and physical sciences to human existence, they knew it fruitless to expect social analyses to duplicate the methods of these sciences. Marx talked about "sovereign man," meaning thereby that even though he is a biological entity, man is by virtue of his ability to make his own history supreme in the universe. Burke, too, made a similar claim on behalf of man "whose prerogative it is, to be in a great degree a creature of his own making, and who, when made as he ought to be made, is destined to hold no trivial place in the creation."[18] The tools for inquiry into human affairs have to be fashioned according to the special position of mankind in

18. Burke, *Reflections*, Beaconsfield Edition, *op. cit.*, p. 353.

the natural world and to the particular nature of his social existence.

This special position of man derives from the species as such rather than from isolated individuals. It is inter-human activity which gives shape to historical forces and enables man to realise his inventive potentialities. The individual isolated from a social complex, compelled to grow up without human contact, never fulfills himself as a human being. He cannot through imitation acquire those sophisticated modes of activity (like language) which distinguish the socially-developed individual. But it would be a distortion to posit the individual according to Burke and Marx as little more than a social automaton. They do not abrogate the existence of individual personality traits but merely insist that the development of these traits comes about through the socialization process. (The notion of co-aptation is again relevant here to denote the mutual give-and-take of society and the individual). It is indeed the social environment then which allows the individual to be truly his own individualistic self.

Importantly, Burke and Marx warn against those specialized techniques which would break-up society into its alleged component units for the sake of analysis. If society is the matrix of human activities, then all analyses of human affairs must concentrate upon society as an organism, a system, in itself. It becomes therefore impossible to conduct studies of isolated social phenomena as the chemist would conduct highly specialized experiments on fragments of the physical world under the controlled conditions of the laboratory. Human relations can not be so fragmented for experimental purposes nor can the requisite social context in which these relations occur be duplicated conditionally in a laboratory. The social analyst must accept as his laboratory the "naturally-conditioned" environment of society itself.

In what way, however, is this perspective scientific? The human mind conceives of the whole in terms of its parts. Thus while Burke and Marx discarded those intellectual endeavors which would disjoint society through specialized disciplinary studies, they themselves did seek to find the central organizing principle of society around which to construct analytical studies. For both of them, this organizing principle was the class structure of society. Burke and Marx observed that every society is composed of classes which are functionally interdependent and which are the means by which each individual is absorbed and integrated into society. It is the interdependence of functions which holds men together in a historically perpetuated framework. Men need each other to fulfill their own basic interests and wants. Society is, therefore, that organization which regularizes and coordinates the ways in which these interests are met. The class society, in fact, is a functional unit analogous to other organic entities in the natural world. *Functionalism for Burke and Marx represents the method of social inquiry replicating the natural world rather than the methods of the natural sciences.* As the functioning individual corresponds to the activity and change in the universe, so the interrelated network of multitudinous functions constitutes social order much as in the integrated universe.

In this way Burke and Marx arrive not only at a social perspective but an important analytical tool for understanding all societies in their simplest and most complex forms. The functional approach necessarily leads to an analysis of the entire social system, for no function is meaningful or viable save in its relations with other functioning elements in the society. Thus Burke and Marx argue that empirical studies must be *relational* ones, i.e., studies which establish correlations of existing social relations to the preceding historical relations. On this basis Marx contested the methods of Feuerbach:

> He [Feuerbach] does not see that the surrounding material world is not directly delivered of eternity as a perpetually given thing but the product of industry and social conditions and indeed in the sense that it is a social product, the result of the activity of a whole stream of generations, each of which stands on the shoulders of the preceding generation, developing further its industry and commerce, modifying its social order according to changed needs.[19]

Marx importantly points out here that progressive social history is engendered primarily by the changes wrought in the manner in which basic functions are performed and refined. In the *Economic and Philosophical Manuscripts* of 1844 Marx stipulates that the process of civilization entails the development of new tastes and desires along with the developments in technology and consumer goods. Hence through invention, basic needs are supplemented with luxury "needs," the fulfillment of which requires ever more complex modes of

19. Marx and Engels, *Die Deutsche Ideologie, op. cit.*, p. 41.

functional organization. Marx claims, however, that under capitalism this increasing complexity means also increasing exploitation:

> We have seen what importance should be attributed, in a socialist perspective, to the *wealth of* human needs, and consequently also to a *new mode of production* and to a new *object* of production. A new manifestation of *human* powers and a new enrichment of the human being. Within the system of private property it has the opposite meaning. Every man speculates upon creating a *new* need in another in order to force him to a new sacrifice, to place him in a new dependence, and to entice him into a new kind of pleasure and thereby into economic ruin.[20]

Like Marx, Burke accepted the idea of the historical foundation of all social functions. Through experience and gradual reform, according to Burke, man is able to improve the effects of institutions. Speculations about the proper social organization were to him (and to Marx) but useless hypotheses until they were combined with functioning social institutions and put into practice. Burke in the *Reflections* stated that he must suspend all congratulations to revolutionary France until "the first effervescence is a little subsided, till the liquor is cleared" and it can be observed how the "new liberty" in France has been "combined with government, with public force, with the discipline and obedience of armies, with the collection of an effective and well-distributed revenue, with morality and religion, with solidity and property, with peace and order, with civil and social manners."[21]

Is the proliferation of individual actions to be considered completely functional? Must a differentiation be made between those actions which can be categorized as fulfilling social functions and those which have no bearing on any relevant social interest? Marx is much clearer than Burke in answering this question. The compactness with which he does so probably accounts for the fact that his theoretical system has lent itself more readily to political ideological

---

20. Karl Marx, *Economic and Philosophical Manuscripts*, trans. T.B. Bottomore, reprinted in Erich Fromm, *Marx's Concept of Man* (New York: Frederick Ungar Publishing Co., 1961), pp. 140-141. This selection has been taken from the Third Manuscript (there are four manuscripts altogether) entitled, "Needs, Production, and Division of Labor."

21. Burke, *Reflections*, Beaconsfield Edition, *op. cit.*, p. 243 and p. 241.

movements. Marx assumed that man's most basic function is the economic one. Before the individual can worry about anything else, he must produce food to eat and clothing to wear. In tracing historically the changes due to technological inventions in the modes by which such economic production is conducted, Marx believed he detected accompanying changes in the social and political character of society. He recognized the various changes in economic production as producing historical epochs, each epoch being defined by the particular predominant mode of production.

Out of this historical analysis, Marx hypothesized that all socio-political ideas, mores and life styles are generated by the class relations established under a given economic system within a historical epoch. While economics constitutes the "infrastructure" of social relations, all else is but the "superstructure" built upon the economic system. Marx could thereby argue that all individuals act out of their class positions and that the dominant social mores and "climate of opinion" in any age would be dependent upon the dominant economic class itself. Class is for Marx that economic group which on the basis of its social functions establishes the range of possibilities (as well as the limitations) of particular human actions and thought.

Burke put great emphasis, too, upon the class structure. He considered it to be a "natural" outgrowth of human needs and capabilities. (Marx also took a "naturalistic" approach to classes in the "pre-history" stages before the communist classless society. In this pre-history period classes stemmed from the necessary division of labor in society.) Burke, unlike Marx, did not characterize classes in terms of their built-in antagonisms to each other within a particular epoch, probably because he did not experience the onslaught of large-scale industrialism with the exploitative ventures of the owning classes vis-à-vis the working class.

Burke's concept of a class corresponds more closely to the modern idea of an "interest," i.e., a broad functional grouping, such as the commercial interest, within a society. As an "Old Whig," he considered society to be composed of stable, intricate, "legitimate" interests. To Burke (and the Whigs) such interests "were not shifting groups of individuals who happened to share similar opinions and wishes, as was the case with the great pressure groups formed as voluntary associations in the nineteenth century."[22] It was the "natural" or inherent economic interests in a society which Burke felt had to be represented in Parliament. Hence, as Samuel Beer points out, "Burke attacked the philosophy of natural rights because, among other things, it proposed 'personal representation' and failed to recognize 'corporate personality.' "[23]

It is important to note that Burke as a Whig held a more sociological concept of class than did his Tory counterparts. The class structure, as far as the Tory was concerned, reflected the Divine order of things. Although some individuals are "by nature" suited to govern and others to be governed, the Tory thought this ordained by God. He accepted it virtually as an *a priori* fact in social existence. Hence he did not venture much—if at all—into historical justifications or explanations. By contrast, the Whigs did not tend to place a Divine stamp upon classes, even though they held such classes to be the inevitable expression of naturally unequal and unique individuals. Indeed Burke—in his argumentation against Dr. Price—accused those like Price who urged the election of governors (e.g., the monarch), to be the reverse extreme of "those exploded fanatics of slavery who formerly maintained, what I believe no creature now maintains, 'that the crown is held by divine, hereditary, and indefeasible right.' "[24] (It must be remembered that the Whigs, particularly in the eighteenth century, advocated parliamentarism and sought to limit thereby the authority of the Crown.) Although Burke accepted a hereditary monarch (primarily because the principle of succession had been established in Britain by Parliament itself after the Glorious Revolution in the Act of Settlement), he did not consider monarchy to have a divine ordination. By the same token, he did not hold that any class is secured in its position by Divine sanction. Classes are rather for him merely the various interests which perform necessary functions in a society.

Burke was too much aware of the force of historical circumstances which creates certain classes to succumb to the Tory

22. Beer, Samuel H., *British Politics in the Collectivist Age* (New York: Alfred A. Knopf, 1966), p. 17.

23. *Ibid.*

24. Burke, *Reflections*, Arlington House, *op. cit.*, p. 38.

viewpoint. Like Marx, he accepted the idea that classes, far from being mystically empowered groupings, represent the different sub-divisions in the functional society. Conscious as he was of the tendency of all individuals to habitualize their modes of living, to engross themselves in the routines of their various occupations, Burke comes very close to Marx in assuming that virtually all actions of the human being in some way or another reflect his class position within the society. Indeed it is this assumption which bolsters his support for the landed gentry. He felt that the *genuine* aristocrat had routinized those qualities and actions—that *noblesse oblige*—required for public leadership.[25] Through generations the aristocracy had trained itself for this function. Interests combined into hierarchically-ordered classes signify to Burke the parceling out of social responsibilities and obligations. With the differences in these responsibilities, Burke did not believe it possible to create a classless society: ". . . those who attempt to level never equalize. The levellers, therefore, only change and pervert the natural order of things: they load the edifice of the society by setting up in the air what the solidity of the structure requires to be on the ground."[26]

Marx considered the legal structure of a society to be that social mechanism by which the dominant class secures its position. Law and changes therein must always be figured into the class struggle. But for Burke, steeped as he was in the English legal perspective, law is the integrating force in society. To Burke the common law is not "made"

25. Although Burke claimed that the real source of oppression in pre-revolutionary France had not been the nobility but the "men of the sword," he was not without criticism of the French aristocracy who he felt did not measure up to the English: "A foolish imitation of the worst part of the manners of England, which impaired their natural character without substituting in its place what perhaps they meant to copy, has certainly rendered them worse than formerly they were. Habitual dissoluteness of manner continued beyond the pardonable period of life, was more common amongst them than it is with us; and it reigned with the less hope of remedy, though possibly with something of less mischief, by being covered with more exterior decorum. They countenanced too much that licentious philosophy which has helped to bring on their ruin. There was another error amongst them more fatal. Those of the commons, who approached to or exceeded many of the nobility in point of wealth, were not fully admitted to the rank and estimation which wealth, in reason and good policy, ought to bestow in every country; though I think not equally with that of other nobility." (Burke, *Reflections*, Arlington House, *op. cit.*,) pp. 152-53.

26. Burke, *Reflections*, Beaconsfield Edition, *op. cit.*, p. 295.

in a calculated fashion but rather flows from and hence reflects composite social relations. Since the common law verifies the observable social milieu in which it operates, its legal principles represent a form of "inductive" reasoning. In this respect the law recognizes not only the "natural rights" and "civil rights" of each individual but establishes the relationship and balance among the Monarchy, Parliament and the Church, each institution in itself representing basic class or interest configurations within English society. Rather than re-enforcing an inherent antagonism between classes, as stipulated by Marx, the common law to Burke created the foundations of the entire Constitution and the possibility for order and equilibrium among classes. But Burke recognized that the equity of the law depended upon the willingness of the various interests to accept their responsibilities:

> The constituent parts of a state are obliged to hold their public faith with each other, and with all those who derive any serious interests under their engagements, as much as the whole state is bound to keep its faith with separate communities. Otherwise competence and power would soon be confounded, and no law be left but the will of a prevailing force.[27]

Marx argued that "competence and power" are always confounded in the class society and that it is the economically strongest "prevailing force" which will subordinate all other sections or classes of society to its demands. But Burke was an ardent parliamentarian and had faith that through the historical Constitution the balancing and even reconciliation of various classes is a distinct possibility.

Aside from their differing evaluation and conclusions regarding the role of classes, it is noteworthy that Burke and Marx accepted a similar organizing principle in their analytical methods. Their scientific contribution to social science is the assumption that human actions are organized for the fulfillment of specified functions and that social structures and ideologies reflect and re-enforce these functional divisions.

One of the merits of the functional approach is its universality.[28] It assumes that within every society certain functions must be

27. Burke, *Reflections*, Arlington House, *op. cit.*, p. 32.

28. In contemporary political science "structural-functionalists" such as Gabriel A. Almond and James S. Coleman have discussed the universal application of the approach in the book

performed if the society is to maintain itself and yet it takes into account the historically-produced dispositions and cultures of societies, being predicated upon the supposition that social structures grow out of particular circumstances. Burke and Marx, although concerning themselves first and foremost with Europe, also delved into non-Western cultures and applied their basic analytical methods to these cultures. Burke moved into the non-Western areas as a parliamentarian having to deal with the problems of the British Empire. As noted previously, he versed himself in the Indian legal codes and customs in order to answer the defense of Warren Hastings. Marx, too, was interested in India, writing various articles on the subject for the *New York Tribune* as well as some sections in *Capital*. Thus Karl A. Wittfogel in his *Oriental Despotism* has written about Marx's interest in Asia.

> In the 1850's the notion of a specific Asian society struck Marx with the force of a discovery. Temporarily abandoning party politics, he applied himself intensely to the study of industrial capitalism as a distinct socio-economic and historical phenomenon. His writings during this period—among others, the first draft of *Das Kapital* which he set down in 1857-58—show him greatly stimulated by the Asiatic concept. In this first draft as well as in the final version of his magnum opus, he systematically compared certain institutional features in the three major types of agrarian society ("Asia," classical antiquity, feudalism) and in modern industrial society.[29]

which they edited, *The Politics of Developing Areas* (Princeton: Princeton University Press, 1960). Almond and Coleman argued that a parochialism was characteristic of the comparative government field prior to World War II insofar as emphasis was put primarily on Europe. Since the War, however, when non-Western areas, due largely to the decolonization processes and the subsequent emergence of new nation-states, assumed an important role in the international community, Western political scientists now take a more active interest in these areas. Since most of the new states do not resemble the European states in their sociological make-up, there was the need to devise new methods for studying non-western political processes. Assuming every society has certain "requisite" functions, Almond and Coleman demonstrate that it is the similarities in functions rather than structures which provides the political scientist with a viable method of analysis. The analytical task then becomes to discover those structures in different societies through which the necessary functions like rule-making, rule-implementing and rule-adjudicating are carried out.

29. Karl A. Wittfogel, *Oriental Despotism* (New Haven: Yale University Press, 1964), p. 373.

In his concept of "Oriental despotism," Marx attempted to account for the revealed differences in human social development. Marx, in comparing the Asiatic system of land tenure, for example, with the European feudalism, Wittfogel further states, "ridiculed the attempt to equate the British-made *zamindar*-landlords with England's landed gentry."[30]

One of the problems which apparently intrigued Marx (as well as Engels) was the "maintenance" or survival power of Oriental despotic states. The perpetuation of states governed in a manner adverse to the general welfare of the population also fascinated Burke:

> It is not to be imagined, because a political system is under certain aspects, very unwise in its contrivance, and very mischievous in its effects, that it therefore can have no long duration. Its very effects may tend to its stability, because they are agreeable to its nature. The very faults in the Constitution of Poland made it last; the *veto* which destroyed all its energy preserved its life. What can be conceived so monstrous as the republic of Algiers, and that no less strange republic of the Mamelukes of Egypt? They are the worst form imaginable, and exercised in the worst manner, yet they existed as a nuisance on the earth for several hundred years.[31]

Although Burke uses eighteenth century terminology when he speaks of the effects of a political system being agreeable to its "nature," he means, like Marx, that political systems acquire differentiation as well as composition through the force of historical circumstances.

As historians, keenly appreciative of the intricacies of human development, Burke and Marx shied away from the over-simplification attending rationalistic political theories. They rejected that kind of universalism which claimed that all men being equal, rational beings, it is possible through "right" reason to devise and implement the perfect society on a world-wide scale. In this vein Burke expressed his basic historical empiricism in a letter to a member of the French National Assembly in 1791.

> What a number of faults have led to this multitude of misfortunes, and almost all from this one source,—that of considering certain

30. *Ibid.*, p. 377.

31. Burke, *Thoughts on French Affairs*, Beaconsfield Edition, *op. cit.*, IV, pp. 353-54.

general maxims, without attending to circumstances, to times, to places, to conjunctures, and to actors: If we do not attend scrupulously to all these, the medicine of today becomes the poison of tomorrow.[32]

We must take into account, claimed Burke and Marx, the differing geophysical conditions in which the various segments of the human race find themselves and which influence the subsequent ways in which they mold their own history.

But Burke and Marx did not accept political systems as completely localized, bearing no analogies or similarities to each other. While both were most aware of the persistence of national existence and national consciousness, they also recognized that national societies tend to group themselves into common civilizational units. It was possible for nations with similar backgrounds to learn from each other. Thus the nationalistic Burke wrote to a member of the French National Assembly:

> When I praised the British Constitution, and wished it to be well studied, I did not mean that its exterior form and positive arrangement should become a model for you or for any people servilely to copy. I meant to recommend the *principles* from which it has grown, and the policy on which it has been progressively improved out of elements common to you and to us.[33]

Marx thought along the same lines in contemplating the proletarian revolution which would be effected in industrialized Europe. The existence of the proletariat as an exploited class cuts across national lines and becomes a principal characteristic of international capitalism. Thus, said Marx, "the proletariat can only exist in a world historical fashion" and its emancipation can only be brought about through international revolution.[34] While Burke and Marx accepted without reservation the possibility of historical

---

32. Burke, "Letter to a Member of the National Assembly in Answer to Some Objections to His Book on French Affairs," *Ibid.*, p. 46.

33. *Ibid.*, p. 47.

34. Marx and Engels, *Die Deutsche Ideologie, op. cit.*, p. 33. By a world historical existence (*weltgeschichtliche Existenz*) Marx meant that the "existence of individuals is immediately coupled with world history." (p. 33).

developments producing similar institutional frameworks, they did
not believe that all men by virtue of their rational nature could,
irrespective of time and circumstances, be housed universally under
the same socio-political system.

Burke and Marx were also leary of those grand theories of history
which attempt to explain the varieties in social developments. Burke,
as already mentioned, did not put any stock in theories ascribing unto
human society the essentially individualistic characteristics of birth,
maturity and death. And he warned against attempts to use historical
examples as guides for dealing with all contemporary political events.
In relationship to revolutionary France, Burke claimed that a British
policy based on historical precedent "would be found dangerously to
mislead us. France has no resemblance to other countries which have
undergone troubles and been purified by them."[35] This posture might
seem unusual for Burke. But he did not subscribe to a cyclical theory
of history and hence did not anticipate repetitive occurences in
historical events. At one point Burke remarked that he did not believe
"a diplomatic measure ought to be, like a parliamentary or judicial
proceeding, according to strict precedent: I hope I am far from that
pedantry."[36] International relations have to be adjusted to the
particular circumstances and actions of the actors concerned. History,
while it conditions those relations, does not bind them to past patterns
or solutions. Burke rejects, therefore, the historical as well as the
abstractionist theories of international relations. International policies
have to be predicated upon constantly changing circumstances,
options and actors; they have to be "pragmatic."[37]

It is interesting to find that Marx, despite all his elaborate
theoretical statements concerning the development of history, also

35. Burke, "Policy of the Allies to France," Beaconsfield Edition, *op. cit.*, IV, p. 426.

36. Burke, "Letters Addressed to a Member of the Present Parliament on the Proposals for
Peace with the Regicide Directory of France," Beaconsfield Edition, *op. cit.*, V, p. 261.

37. Burke often used the term "expedient" and for this reason he has been subjected to the same
kind of misunderstanding and even abuse as the pragmatist philosopher, John Dewey. Like
Dewey, Burke did not mean that "anything, if it works, goes." Their positions were not
amoral ones. What Burke meant to convey (like Dewey) was that principles of action must
find their expression in each situation. The rigid solution, characteristic of some ideologies,
in the end cannot apply to changing social realities. Rather the consistency of the principle
must be found and applied to new and relative contexts.

rejects the building of historical "models." In a letter written from London in November 1877 to the Editorial Board of the Russian newspaper, *Fatherland Notes* (*Otechestvennive Zapiski*), Marx sought to clarify in this connection why the Roman proletarians under conditions of "capital formation" in the society did not become the wage-earners characteristic of the modern capitalist society but became instead a "mob of do-nothings":

> Thus events strikingly analogous but taking place in different historical surroundings led to totally different results. By studying each of these forms of evolution separately and then comparing them one can easily find the clue to this phenomenon, but one will never arrive there by using as one's master key a general historico-philosophical theory, the supreme virtue of which consists in being super-historical.[38]

In what way do Burke and Marx use history in their analyses? It was obvious to no one more than these two thinkers that historical facts constitute a never-ending stream. In order to use history as the basis for socio-political analysis, it becomes necessary to approach the welter of facts with basic questions around which to establish an analytical framework. Burke and Marx approached social history with the fundamental question: "What are the organizational means by which political power is defined and exercised?" We must remember that society for Burke and Marx is first and foremost a unit of energy (power) produced by the interdependent functioning of interests or classes. History is thereby reduced to its fundamentals: the struggle of functional groups for self-aggrandizement. Marx had always argued that ideologies are but the justification of class interests and struggles (such as the liberal creed of the capitalist middle class). Burke advanced this idea to a large extent when he said:

> History consists, for the greater part, of the miseries brought upon the world by pride, ambition, avarice, revenge, lust, sedition hypocrisy, ungoverned zeal, and all the train of disorderly appetites . . . These vices are the *causes* of those storms. Religion, morals, laws, prerogatives, privileges, liberties, rights of men are the *pretexts*. The pretexts are always found in some specious appearance of a real good.

38. Marx, "Letter to the Editorial Board of 'Fatherland Notes,' " *Basic Writings, op. cit.*, p. 441.

It is thus with all those, who, attending only to the shell and husk of history, think they are waging war with intolerance, pride, and cruelty, whilst, under colour of abhorring the ill principles of antiquated parties, they are authorizing and feeding the same odious vices in different factions, and perhaps in worse.[39]

Although Marx tends to regard all such "pretexts" as the flimsy vestments of the class struggle, Burke is perhaps more precise—or optimistic—in recognizing the pretexts as the perversion but not the destruction of the general principle to which they make recourse. He assumes that what is done in the *name* of religion or morals or law is not necessarily the legitimate embodiment of what is truly religious, moral or legal. Acknowledging the role of chicanery in the world, Burke is not at the same time led into believing the impossibility of genuine human moral expression and development. Nor, for that matter, is Marx. Despite his bitterness about existing society, Marx reveals a deep-seated trust in the morally-competent future of mankind. But, identifying as he does the "superstructure" of society with the dominant class, Marx equates the substance of religion, law and other institutions with their forms. As long as classes exist, Marx could not accept that any institution could be genuinely "social," i.e., concerned with social well-being rather than class well-being.

By looking at history through a functional analysis, Burke and Marx are able to give expression to the order as well as the activity in human society. Functional man is socially directed and active. Changes in society are thus functional ones. As society advances in technical and organizational sophistication, its methods for fulfilling these functions become necessarily more complex and more efficient. It is for this reason that Burke could not fathom the actions of the French revolutionaries, which, to him at least, were directed toward reducing France (and Europe) to a *de novo,* primitive state of existence. The revolutionaries were bent upon destroying the historical attainments of the French nation. Rather than improving and progressing, they seemed to Burke interested in destroying and regressing. To him, therefore, the Revolution was an "escape from civilization."[40]

39. Burke, *Reflections,* Arlington House, *op. cit.,* pp. 156-57.

40. In a sense Burke was justified in his criticism. Following in the philosophical footsteps of Rousseau, the French revolutionary leaders sought the "natural" man. But, as Carl Becker

With a very different outlook from Burke's regarding social change, Marx, the revolutionary, nevertheless conceives of historical change as the process by which civilization is built. He would, therefore, agree with Burke that those anarchistic actions which destroy and uproot man from his social accomplishments can only be noxious to developmental man.

To Burke and Marx historical empiricism verifies *real* existence. As a method of social analysis, it is able to reduce society to its functioning components and to relate them as an ordered yet dynamic whole. As a critique, it is able to pierce areas of dysfunctionalism in society. And as a general theory, it is able to explain and state probabilities about human actions. It is on these three levels that Burke and Marx are to be considered contributors to social science. Their initial questions come not only from the social environment itself but from the natural universe of which man is an intimate part. Rather than confining themselves to mere "descriptive" science—to which many contemporary empiricists are prone—Burke and Marx tried to grasp the very *raison d'être* of historically active and productive man. Not indulging in escapist speculations or concocting an abstracted "essence" of the human being, they sought to "experience" and to "know" man as he appears and operates in concrete situations within specified periods of time. In understanding

---

has stated, "the error of Rousseau was to confound the 'natural' with the 'primitive.' The true nature of a thing is not found in its origin but in its end: the natural state is therefore a state of development, of accomplishment, of perfection." (Carl Becker, *The Declaration of Independence* New York: Vintage Books, 1942, pp. 260-61). This is an essentially Aristotelian argument which Burke accepted and which, evidently, Becker does also. Burke, however, had enough perspective to realize that a differentiation had to be made between the "master" and his disciples. He recognized that much in the Revolution had its source in Rousseau who in some respect was a "philosophical technician": "Mr. Hume told me, that he had from Rousseau himself the secret of his principle of composition. That acute, though eccentric, observer had perceived, that to strike and interest the public, the marvellous must be produced: that the marvellous of the heathen mythology had long since lost its effect; that giants, magicians, fairies, and heroes of romance which succeeded, had exhausted the portion of credulity which belonged to their age; that now nothing was left to a writer but that species of the marvellous, which might still be produced, and with as great an effect as ever, though in another way; that is, the marvellous in life, in manners, in characters, and in extraordinary situations, giving rise to new and unlooked-for strokes in politics and morals. I believe, that were Rousseau alive, and in one of his lucid intervals, he would be shocked at the practical frenzy of his scholars, who in their paradoxes are servile imitators; . . . ." (Burke, *Reflections*, Arlington House, *op. cit.*,) pp. 186-87.

the interaction of man and his social and physical environment, Burke and Marx come to the important conclusion that while possible alternatives of action present themselves for human decision within the given situational context, whatever choice is made not only affects the immediate social context itself but engenders a "condition" for future actions. Not crude determinists (*"rohe Empiriker,"* as Marx called men like Feuerbach who claimed that "man is what he eats"), Burke and Marx have a conception of man's volition in making his own history.

Disagreeing vehemently with the Rationalist's "free man" who is unbound by time or circumstance, Burke and Marx define freedom as man's capacity in the course of history to clarify and promote his ultimate social *telos* through choice, work and organization. Thus Marx argues that capitalism will not automatically become a world-wide phenomenon. If Russia, for example, desires a capitalist system as the necessary prelude to communism, it must first *create* the conditions for it, namely, the transformation of the peasants into á proletarian class.[41] Similarly, Burke in his various analyses claimed that actions based on certain principles under given conditions must produce specified results. All the results of the French Revolution were for Burke the necessary effects of certain "first causes." Once the revolutionaries had proceeded upon a definite course of action there was let loose, so to speak, an inner momentum in that course toward its own "logical" end. And so Burke claimed:

> In all speculations upon men and human affairs, it is of no small moment to distinguish things of accident from permanent causes and from effects that cannot be altered. It is not every irregularity in our movement that is a total deviation from our course.[42]

This approach, as well as the conclusions drawn from history, brought Burke and Marx face-to-face with political *issues*. Politics for both is essentially a process of decision-making. They were more concerned with the broad, general issues of politics than with localized,

41. Marx, "Letter to the Editorial Board of 'Fatherland Notes,' " *loc. cit., p. 440.*

42. Burke, "Proposals for Peace with the Regicide Directory of France," Beaconsfield Edition, *op. cit.*, p. 234.

isolated events, for it is the former which are historically relevant. This to them is the "politics of reality." Historical empiricism to Burke and Marx is not only an analytical method for *understanding* politics; it is a method for *making* politics.

Chapter IV
Historical Empiricism:
The Politics of Reality

Empiricists with strong historical leanings, Burke and Marx in their own partisan political activities always urged that political policy and action be geared to existing social conditions. Only in relating itself to social reality could politics be "creative," contributing to man's social development. This concept of creative politics differs from that found in the Enlightenment. Enlightenment thinkers like Condorcet or Comte considered "right reason" the source and implementer of creative action. Sidney Hook has described this commitment of the Enlightenment as follows:

> Just as men on the basis of their knowledge of laws and the ways of things could rebuild the houses in which they lived to let in the light and air and pleasing prospect required for a healthy and happy life, so they could shatter and rebuild the institutions of a society to make them fit or worthy for men. Only ignorance, religious superstition and selfishness stood in the way of the needed resolution and reconstruction.[1]

1. Sidney Hook, "The Enlightenment and Marxism," *loc, cit.*, p. 95.

Reason in its purest form, constituted for them the only necessary intermediary between the order of nature and its human reflection. Both Burke and Marx took serious issue with this position.

To them politics is the result of complex social relations which are conditioned by many factors—the natural environment, the pressures of historical precedents and traditions and the changing perspectives of the generations. Politics and the natural law are not static phenomena as posited by the Rationalist. Instead, for Burke and Marx, the natural law is the conditioning factor of order and change under which the universe operates. It is the moving force behind *natura naturata*, the universe in a given hypothetical moment, and *natura naturans*, nature in its dynamic development, to use Spinozistic terms.[2] Burke considered self-preservation or equilibrium the first law, and change the most powerful law of nature. Marx (in a revision of Hegel) recognized the dialectical process as the law of nature. Marx's dialectic—like Hegel's theory of a "thesis" producing and interacting with its "antithesis" and their momentary resolution into a "synthesis"—is fundamentally an explanation of order and change.

This appreciation of the natural law as a *conditioner* differs markedly from the Rationalist's concept of the law as an *absolute*. It provides not only the foundations of Burke's and Marx's empiricism but also of their political perspectives. Accepting a conditional (i.e., relative) world, they emphasize similar qualities in political action. Both shied away from political dogmatism or ideology which by definition must present a *Weltblick* in rigidified, simplified form. Marx made the well-known remark, "I am not a Marxist," and, despite the publicity interests of Engels, he generally withdrew from any endeavor to become an ideological prime mover. In his political activities devoted to organizing the proletariat, Marx sincerely believed he was instructing the industrial workers in their historical mission as spelled out by the realities of a deteriorating capitalist system; he did not think he was providing the proletariat with an ideology or a particularized *viewpoint* of that reality. Indeed it was the elevation of systems of thought into self-contained statements about

---

2. cf., Joseph Dunner, *Baruch Spinoza and Western Democracy* (New York: Philosophical Library, 1955), p. 42.

social relations which Marx criticized so much in the orthodox followers of Hegel and the "utopian" socialists. It is noteworthy that in his later years the only true political tract, the *Communist Manifesto*, with which Marx established an ideological framework, seemed to fade in importance for him.

Likewise, Burke always claimed that politics, that process of continuous compromise and barter, has no room for rigid ideologies. In this respect he pointed out that the Constitutional framework of England—which he thought had proven its merits over time—had not been the work of theoreticians and ideologues. Instead it had resulted from gradual adjustments to changing social realities through the actions of each generation.[3] Thus both Burke and Marx believed that ideological politics loses touch with the society which it is supposed to represent.[4]

Stressing instead a sociological approach to politics, Burke and Marx possessed a keen appreciation for the plasticity of politics or what today is called the process of politics. Marx, who has frequently been viewed as little more than a destructive revolutionary, reveals himself in his correspondence with Engels to have been not only very much aware of contemporary events in their finest details but also extremely sensitive to the course and inter-relationship of these events. He was interested, for example, in the Chartist movement (which among other liberal reforms pushed for universal manhood suffrage in

3. It must be remarked here that Burke gave vent to that typical British prejudice against hard and fast "ideological" rules. This most likely stems from the common law tradition in Britain which, expressed largely in the unwritten Constitution, militates against "theoretical" codification. In contemporary Britain it can be seen that the Labour Party, which is considered more ideological than the Conservative Party due to its socialist background, has displayed great political flexibility. R. McKenzie's work, *British Political Parties* (London: William Heineman, Ltd., 1955), is excellent in its appraisal of the modifying influence parliamentary government has had on the Labour Party and its ideology. Another example of British ideological flexibility is that of the Fabians who embrace a very "pragmatic" socialism and reject rigid, sweeping ideological viewpoints. The ideological mold into which Marxism has fallen, as described by Sidney Hook previously cited in this study, has been generally considered anathema to British outlooks and approaches.

4. This was the kind of criticism made of traditional liberalism by revisionists like John Dewey who argued that such liberalism in its conception of the natural law as absolute and ahistorical had in fact failed to keep pace with social changes. Dewey, therefore, urged a more "pragmatic" liberalism, i.e., one geared to the social and historical relativity of man.

England) and wrote to Engels in 1856 that the politically-active group
of immigrants in London had convinced themselves "that we are the
only 'intimate' allies of the Chartists and that if we hold ourselves
back from public demonstrations and let the Frenchmen flirt openly
with Chartism, we have it in our power at any time to recapture our
befitting historical position."[5] Concerning Chartist strategy, Marx
took issue with Ernest Jones about compromising with the entrepreneurial class. In this connection Marx wrote to Engels that Jones
"should first *organize* a party with which he must go into the industrial
districts. Then the radical burghers will come to him for compromises."[6] Marx was not interested in building utopian political
movements. He wanted to establish a political organization which,
even though it opposed itself to the existing socio-political structure,
nevertheless related itself in its opposition to the prevailing social
framework. This attitude came out clearly again in a letter to Engels
written December 14, 1867, concerning the "Irish question," in which
Marx lamented the political exploits of the Fenian Brotherhood, a
revolutionary group founded in 1858 in New York to secure Irish
independence. The following quotation from this letter gives an
insight into Marx's political perspectives:

> This last Fenian exploit in Clerkenwell is a great stupidity. The
> London masses, which have shown much sympathy with Ireland,
> have been made wild by it and thrown into the arms of the
> Government party. One cannot expect the London proletarians to
> jump in the air in honor of the Fenian emissaries. Such a secret,
> melodramatic, conspiratorial technique is altogether fatal.[7]

5. Karl Marx and Friedrich Engels, *Briefwechsel op. cit.,* II, p. 165. (Letter of April 16, 1856.)
   Marx also notes in this letter that a small celebration had taken place commemorating the
   one year's anniversary of the *People's Paper* of the Chartists. He received an invitation to attend, whick he did (the more so since he was the only one from the "immigrant group" to be
   invited) and received the first toast and was asked to speak on the sovereignty of the
   proletariat.

6. *Ibid.,* p. 307 (Letter of November 24, 1857.)

7. Marx and Engels, *Briefwechsel, op. cit.,* III, p. 550. Marx made no further reference to the
   specific details on the Clerkenwell incident. In this year, however, the Fenians staged an
   unsuccessful uprising in Ireland and exploded a bomb in a Manchester prison in England,
   ostensibly to release two Irishmen but which killed or injured 132 persons. See Walter
   Phelps Hall, Robert Greenhalgh Albion, and Jennie Barnes Pope, *A History of England and the
   Empire-Commonwealth* (New York: Blaisdell Publishing Co., 1965), p. 468.

It is significant here that Marx stresses not only political action in consonance with social conditions—and even "sympathies"—but that he also rejects conspiratorial politics. As will be shown in the next chapter, Marx had a particular concept of revolution which admitted neither anarchism nor social conspiracy.

Burke's entire philosophico-political outlook was predicated upon social continuity. In his speeches concerning reconciliation with the American colonies, for example, he charged the British government with basing its policy on sheer fantasy. In its insistence on taxing the colonies, the Government was contradicting the traditional imperial policy which rejected the taxation of any colony for revenue purposes. Hence over the issue of the tea tax, Burke argued that Parliament was "in the awkward position of fighting for a phantom,—a quiddity,—a thing that wants, not only a substance, but even a name,—for a thing which is neither abstract right nor profitable enjoyment."[8] Karl Polanyi implies that Burke evaluated the American colonies more in financial terms than on the basis of their "rights."[9] This analysis is contradicted by Burke's warning to Parliament about the results of its quixotic behavior: "If that sovereignty [of Britain] and their freedom [the American colonies] cannot be reconciled, which will they take? They will cast your sovereignty in your face. Nobody will be argued into slavery."[10] For Burke a "right" must always be discussed in tangible, not abstract, terms. He considered, therefore, the issue of taxation to be in fact a discussion of basic rights.

Burke could not possibly accept a political approach ignorant of the society for which it was meant. He called political reasoning a "computing principle" by which social demands are coordinated into a just and effective social policy. He was by temperament and background too solidly grounded in what he called the "practical" to make out of politics virtually an esoteric profession and enterprise.

8. Burke, "Speech on American Taxation," Beaconsfield Edition, *op. cit.*, II, p. 18.

9. Polanyi writes: "In eighteenth century, prefederation America, cheap money was the equivalent to Speenhamland, that is, an economically demoralizing concession made by government to popular clamor. . . . Burke identified American democracy with currency troubles and Hamilton feared not only factions but also inflation." (Karl Polanyi, *The Great Transformation, op. cit.*, p. 227).

10. Burke, "Speech on American Taxation," *op. cit.*, p. 73.

Sounding in this vein very much like Burke, Marx in his *Theses on Feuerbach* wrote that "social life is essentially *practical*. All mysteries which mislead theory to mysticism find their rational solution in human practice and in the comprehension of this practice."[11] (It might be suggested that although Marx had from the beginning of his intellectual career rebelled against the idealism of German philosophy, his concern for the forces operating in the real material world (*die sinnliche Welt*), for the existent and for the limits and possibilities of political action at varying times was perhaps even re-enforced by his long London residence.)

Since politics *must* operate through the social medium, it is very much bound, according to Burke and Marx, to the immediate level of development in society. From the Rationalist's point of view (i.e., that "rational" politics can break through the bonds of social precedent and conditions), it might be said they thereby qualified the creative potentials of politics and deprived politics of its spontaneous character in fashioning society. To some extent Marx seems to share this belief that history impedes social creativity. He expressed this in the *Eighteenth Brumaire of Louis Napoleon:*

> Men make their own history, but they do not make it just as they please; they do not make it under circumstances chosen by themselves, but under circumstances directly encountered, given and transmitted from the past. The tradition of all the dead generations weighs like a nightmare on the brain of the living. And just when they seem engaged in revolutionizing themselves and things, in creating something that has never existed, precisely in such periods of revolutionary crisis they anxiously conjure up the spirits of the past to their service and borrow from them names, battle cries, and costumes in order to present the new scene of world history in this time-honored disguise and this borrowed language.[12]

The difference between Marx and the Rationalist is important. For Marx, freedom from history or spontaneous politics is a preference or value-judgment, whereas for the Rationalist it is an axiom of pure

11. Marx, "Theses on Feuerbach," *Basic Writings, op. cit.* p. 245.

12. *Ibid.*, p. 320.

human reason. Marx, the scientist, knew that history is the necessary precondition of human action and that *Homo historicus* is, therefore, not a completely free, rational agent. When Marx repeats in the *Eighteenth Brumaire* that "the social revolution of the nineteenth century cannot draw its poetry from the past, but only from the future," he is venting human inclination.[13] The contradictions here demonstrate in Marx the tension between scientific and utopian thinking.

While admitting the possibility of revolution in history (and certainly advocating revolutionary activity), Marx realized that historical and environmental factors present a powerful brake on human initiative and change, not to speak of total social transformation (revolution). These factors are particularly influential because of the habitual tendency in man's behavior. Like Burke, Marx saw, of course, that this tendency has its positive side; habit cements historical accomplishments and thus makes the civilizing process possible. He knew that a species bent upon anarchism cannot flourish. All this, however, did not prevent him from decrying "habitualism" as an "opiate" which impedes the creative potentials of politics, identified by him as revolutionary change. Thoroughly immersed in the fast-paced tempo of his times and overcome by the idea that the proletarian revolution was close at hand, he resented the strictures of history as barriers against the inauguration of the Communist society and its concomitant, the beginning of real human creativity and freedom.

There are interesting and important implications in this impatience with history. It is reminiscent of those Jacobin revolutionaries who, believing 1789 to be the starting point for a new humanity, charted a calendar starting with the year one to coincide with the revolution itself. In the Enlightenment tradition this reflected the deep-seated, though naive, belief that man could begin *de novo*. Marx was not that utopian, and the similarities between the Jacobins and him on this point should not be exaggerated so as to diminish their real differences. Marx fully realized that Communism would be the direct product of historical growth—that it, in fact, could not be otherwise. But it must be stated that he and the Enlightenment thinkers were not outside of Western tradition in their beliefs that

13. *Ibid.*, p. 323.

man can start afresh in history. For the historian, history starts with those events which mark the dawn of historical memories (or "consciousness"). The entire religious tradition of the West supports this kind of historicism. As the historical memory of the Hebrews as a people commences with Abraham, so Christians have dated their historical experience from the birth of Christ, marking the year one (Anno Domini). The Christian chronological division of "B. C." amounts for them to "pre-history" or the necessary preparatory stage for the first coming of Christ. Similarly, Marx wanted to signify that with the unity of the species in the Communist society—the achievement of a truly humanized consciousness—a "new" human being would emerge and hence the starting of a new historical experience, called by Marx man's real history. The fact that Marx shared in this characteristic Western optimism has led some writers to equate his anticipation of the Communist society with an apocalyptic vision:

> Instead of simply analyzing the suffering of the world, he made men feel that they themselves could transmute the suffering into joy; that indeed, the entire course of history had demonstrated this process being carried out group by group; that history was to culminate in the emergence of a utopia.[14]

But Marx did not believe in or, therefore, describe the Communist society as the apocalypse. If the multitudes have been "inspired" by Marx, it is because he offers not only the concept of meaningful history but because he pictures man as the maker of that history. History has meaning not merely because of what men *impose* in their own lifetimes on the historical process; history acquires meaning because of what is imparted unto developmental man, namely, the achievements and energies of past generations. Thus Marx wrote: "The bourgeoisie itself, therefore, supplies the proletariat with its own elements of political and general education: in other words, it furnishes the proletariat with weapons for fighting the bourgeoisie."[15]

Marx combines pessimism with optimism in his historical perspective. On the one hand, he looks upon history as a millstone

---

14. Phyllis Arora, "Marx: Utopian or Scientist?", *The Political Science Quarterly.* XXXVIII (July-September 1967), p. 312.

15. Marx and Engels, "Manifesto of the Communist Party," *Basic Writings, op. cit.*, p. 17.

around the neck of man. Characterized by class struggles and exploitation—men pitted against men—history signifies human imperfection. On the other hand, Marx recognizes that history presents to man the opportunity to develop his inner potentials for eventual harmonious social living. But Marx was aware of the fact that the kind of revolutionary history he described in Western Europe did not pertain to the rest of the world. He believed that once countries outside Western Europe developed industrial capitalism, then these same countries would necessarily follow the route of Western Europe with all its trials and tribulations toward the proletarian revolution. "The country that is more developed industrially only shows, to the less developed," Marx wrote, "the image of its own future."[15]* Without, however, the world-wide development of industrial capitalism, there would not be the world-wide communist revolution. Lenin understood this problem but wanted anyway the revolution in the name of communism without the capitalist conditions. By insinuating that states can opt to become modern or remain, for one reason or another, non-modern, Marx preserves a concept of historical indeterminism.

> . . . idyllic village communities, inoffensive though they may appear, had always been the solid foundation of Oriental despotism, that they restrained the human mind within the smallest possible compass, making it the unresisting tool of superstition, enslaving it beneath traditional rules, depriving it of all grandeur and historical energies. We must not forget the barbarian egotism which, concentrating on some miserable patch of land, had quietly witnessed the ruin of empires, the perpetuation of unspeakable cruelties, the massacre of the population of large towns, with no other consideration bestowed upon them than on natural events, itself the helpless prey of any aggressor who deigned to notice it at all.[16]

While groping for the "scientific" explanation of Eastern autocracy, Marx could not hold back his non-scientific sense of detestation for such regimes. Again the tension between the two Marxs surfaces here. As Karl A. Wittfogel has importantly demonstrated, the contest

---

15*. Marx, *Capital*, Preface to the First Edition, *Basic Writings, op. cit.*, p. 135.

16. Marx, "The British Rule in India," *loc. cit.*

resulted in Marx's undermining his own scientific standards for the "concept of Oriental despotism contained elements that paralyzed his search for truth," since Marx "could scarcely help recognizing some disturbing similarities between Oriental despotism and that state of his program."[17]

Permitting his hatred of traditionalism full rein, Marx came amazingly to assert that the introduction of the industrial revolution into India by the British engendered the "greatest and, to speak the truth, the only *social* revolution ever heard of in Asia."[18] Although Marx considered imperialism generally noxious, he claimed that if mankind cannot fulfill "its destiny without a fundamental revolution in the social state of Asia," then "whatever may have been the crimes of England, she was the unconscious tool of history in bringing about that revolution."[19]

On the basis of this conclusion, Marx's dialectic as a tool of analysis seems to break down in evaluating Asian society. The dialectic, as applied to Europe, was supposed to explain the forces behind change, and Marx, upon his dialectical analysis, claimed that change, at least in Europe, was "progressive." But Asian society appeared "stagnant"; whatever change did occur was not developmental but tended to re-enforce traditional forms of living. Marx acknowledges on several occasions this quality particularly with regard to India (with which he seemed most familiar probably due to his English experience). He attributes this traditionalism in India in large part to the caste system, especially as it operated in the small villages, which "transformed a self-developing social state into never changing natural destiny . . . ." Implicit in this statement is the assumption that societies can follow the *wrong* organizational path and therewith prevent their potential for progressive development from coming into its own. Thus in the Preface to the First Edition of *Capital* Marx wrote: "One nation should and can learn from another. Even if a society has come on the right track to the natural law of its movement,—. . . —it can neither leap over its natural phases of

17. Wittfogel, *op. cit.*, p. 387.

18. Marx, "The British Rule in India," *loc. cit.*

19. *Ibid.*, p. 480-81.

development nor decree them away. But it can shorten and lessen the birthpangs."[20]

Marx suggestively dichotomizes the deadening effects of a caste system and the creative characteristics of a class system, as in Europe, which, in establishing class antagonisms, provides the economic stimulus for social change. According to Marx, it is necessary in any developing society to have an opposition of interests. By common economic *activity* men develop common economic interests in *relationship* to the economic activity and interests of others in the society. He asserted this relationship to be inherently an antagonistic one, since each class attempts to consolidate and promote its own particular interests at the expense of other classes.

A caste system differs markedly from this, since it is much less an economic than a religious-ethnic stratification. While the various levels of caste correspond to broad occupational categories, the justification of the caste break-down is to be found in religious—and even quasi-racial—dicta. Since caste positions are inherited, the mobility from one caste position to another is kept to a minimum. (Marx claimed that the members of the working class, oppressed in the capitalist system, could not move out of their class and into a higher or capital-owning class. But Marx, of course, did not advocate this "ascendance" in class for the worker who was historically ordained to establish the classless society. The lack of class mobility has not been historically substantiated in democratic industrialized states. While there is a "maintenance" of class positions, this is quite different from the social, religious, ethnic and superstitious underpinnings of castes.)

Marx, however, counted on a descending social mobility in his anticipation of the proletarian revolution. With the increasing monopolization of capital in the hands of the ever-fewer "monopoly capitalists," many, if not most, of the former entrepreneurs would sink down and join the ranks of the proletariat:

> The lower strata of the middle class—the small tradespeople, shopkeepers, and retired tradesmen generally, the handicraftsmen and peasants—all these sink gradually into the proletariat, partly because their diminutive capital does not suffice for the scale on which modern industry is carried on, and is swamped in the

20. Marx, *Das Kapital*, Otto Meissners Verlag, *op. cit.*, p. viii.

competition with the large capitalists, partly because their specialized skill is rendered worthless by new methods of production. Thus the proletariat is recruited from all classes of the population.[21]

This enlargement of the proletariat as well as its increasing pauperization would allegedly exaggerate the antagonism it had with the capital-owning class and hence spark the revolution. Marx envisioned the historical movements of a class as similar to a bell curve—the oppressed class would rise eventually to dominance through revolution, maintain its control over other classes for a while and then gradually sink as a new class moved up to take its place of dominance on the threshold of a new revolution. Class mobility meant essentially to Marx the continuous process of class substitution.

Marx always assumed the interconnection of classes. One of his sharpest criticisms of Indian village life was that it fostered *isolation*. As he had criticized the small landholding peasants in Europe for their isolation which fostered a sense of independence rather than a group or class consciousness of shared interests, so he lamented the Indian village stratifications for similar reasons.[22] Because of the economic diversity within a caste, no shared interests based upon common economic activity could come to the fore. It was possible, for example, for a shopkeeper and a shopworker to be of the same caste. The diversity of each caste was further complicated by the caste's subdivision into myriad, separate groupings. Superstition and social mores entrenched the various caste divisions, keeping each caste member "in his social place." The assignment of caste was considered part of the "fate" of the individual out of which there was no wordly escape. The case of the so-called "untouchables" is a particularly tragic one of

---

21. Marx and Engels, "Manifesto of the Communist Party," *Basic Writings, op. cit.*, p. 15.

22. In the *Eighteenth Brumaire* Marx describes the small holder peasant in Europe as isolated and self-sufficient. He did not consider these peasants a class because "the identity of their interests begets no community, no national bond, and no political organization among them. . . ." Not being a class, the peasants, incapable of representing their own interests, require an authority. "They cannot represent themselves, they must be represented. Their representative must at the same time appear as their master, as an authority over them, as an unlimited government power that protects them against the other classes and sends them rain and sunshine from above. The political influence of the small-holding peasants, therefore, finds its final expression in the executive power subordinating society to itself." (*Ibid.*, p. 339).

such fate-ridden individuals who were isolated as completely as possible from the rest of society. Superstition and the isolation of one caste from another rather than the economic inter-action, interdependence and alleged antagonism characteristic of classes hampered any chance according to Marx's perspective for social change. And, importantly for Marx's thinking, caste remained a distinct expression of particular societies. There existed no transnational identity among caste members as Marx depicted at least in the classes under capitalism. While the *Communist Manifesto* could call upon the workers of the world to unite, castes were isolated from such international consciousness.

In view of these facts, Marx was virtually forced to concede to European imperialism, at least that of Britain, the role of a catalyst in world social change. Although Engels had asserted that "nature is the proof of dialectics," it would appear that in human society dialectical developments seemed more properly a part of European social dynamism.[23] Marx was certainly correct in assigning to the technological inventiveness of Europe at least a substantial share of the responsibility for concomitant social change. But the reasons behind Europe's distinctive aptitude for innovation Marx failed to explain. The dialectical method is ultimately good only for particular societies and even there only as a secondary analysis and explanation.

To justify the catalytic role Marx assigned to Britain in revolutionizing India, it would have been necessary for him to establish a dialectical relationship between the two societies. But this would have led him back to Hegel with his stress on national cultures and a de-emphasizing of the class struggle. And in alluding to Russia, in his time still a largely agrarian society, Marx does not accept this kind of "national" dialectics:

> If Russia is tending to become a capitalist nation after the example of the West European countries—and during the last few years she has been taking a lot of trouble in this direction—she will not succeed without having first transformed a good part of her peasants into proletarians; and after that, once taken to the bosom of the capitalist regime, she will experience its pitiless laws like other profane peoples.[24]

23. Engels, *Socialism: Utopian and Scientific*, *op. cit.*, p. 48.

24. Marx, "Letter to the Editorial Board of the 'Fatherland Notes,' " *Basic Writings, op. cit.*, p. 440.

The implications of this passage are important. Firstly, Marx clearly stipulates here the necessity of systematic internal development in states. Rather than dialectical relationship, Marx describes one of imitation. Secondly, this imitative quality again suggests an element of historical *choice* as we saw already mentioned in the Preface to *Capital*. Although Marx tried to construct a concept of totally conditioned thought ("superstructure"), he obviously did not believe in it completely himself. Otherwise how is learning even possible? Karl Mannheim and Lenin tried to adjust this apparent Marxist dead-end by the déclassé "freischwebende Intelligenz" (free-floating thought) of the intellectual element. But Marx hints at a broader, national "freischwebende Intelligenz" and enters by the back door into a virtually metaphysical form of argument (à la Hegel). Russia, says Marx, must *self-consciously* transform itself if it is to succeed in its capitalistic tendency. Peasants must become proletarians. Factories must be built. Land must be freed from feudal rights and placed on the market. In other words, Marx really admits that it is essentially human ingenuity and effort which create the conditions for social development. Claiming each social economic system has its own organizational momentum or "logic" (e.g., capitalism encourages the accumulation of private capital, private investment and a consumer-oriented economy), Marx in no way proved that each economic system represents the necessary, conditioned outgrowth of its predecessor. He did show forces which created the changes in European history. He did not consider that history could have been otherwise in Europe. And yet in looking at Asia he bewilderingly acknowledges the function of deliberate imitation and assigns to Europe the role of the messenger of change and progress. What Marx is fervently seeking is the merger of freedom and necessity. He describes the "right track" of a society as the one leading to the "natural law of its movement" in which convention (or rational choice) combines with the non-conventional (or "natural" givenness).

By observation it appeared to Marx, however, that one could not assume each society would have the motive power (or "historical energies") necessary to generate its own internal development. It might become imperative for more advanced states to act as the energizing agents in bringing the more slothful into the mainstream of historical progression. Britain's introduction of the industrial revolution into India seemed to him a most important and necessary step in facilitating social growth in Asia. Yet the "destiny of mankind," of which Marx wrote as the objective of world revolution, appears to be but a euphemistic statement, and Marx *nolens volens* only reveals his ethnocentricity when confronted with traditional societies. But there is still the inconsistency in Marx's thinking. The dialectic—far from explaining all societies as he seemed to believe—emerges essentially as an analytical tool solely suitable for advanced technological societies. Marx implicitly admits this qualification in *Capital*, stating that " . . . the end purpose of this work is to expose the economic law of movement of modern society. . . . "[25]

In calling England a possible "unconscious tool of history," Marx sank back into a rhetoric which he used as a shorthand version for his concept of historically conditioned human action. But the phraseology, which imparts in Hegelian fashion a "mystique" to history, obscures the major stress of all his writings that man, the maker of his own history, must become in the end the master rather than the slave of circumstances. It indicates again the ambivalence—the pessimism and optimism—with which he viewed *Homo historicus*.

As Marx, perhaps in his less guarded moments, seemed to lapse into a desire for the rationally fabricated politics advocated by the Enlightenment thinkers, Burke too reveals some indecision regarding the role of "pure" reason in political creativity. Too frequently analysts of Burke's writings classify him as an unequivocal anti-rationalist. Unfortunately, very few venture to read more of Burke than his *Reflections* and hence do not understand the context in which it was written. But also this image of Burke has been fervently nurtured for political reasons either to support ideological vendettas against him or against others. In this vein Geoffrey Butler tries to make a Tory out of Burke:

> The Burke of 1788 is a different person from the Burke of two years later. The Revolution worked as clear a turning point for him as did the vision on the road to Damascus for St. Paul. Therefore, it is possible to disregard his views upon Parliamentary, colonial, and Imperial Government, and to concentrate upon his opposition to the Revolution. To leave out the rest, and to talk alone of this, is to

25. Marx, *Das Kapital*, Otto Meissner Verlag, *op. cit.*, p. viii.

do what is most useful in a systemic study of the growth of Tory doctrine. It would be superfluous to take up any other line.[26]

Butler's approach has the same merit in Burkean scholarship as an evaluation solely of the *Communist Manifesto* would have in Marxist scholarship. The *Reflections* is primarily political propaganda and must be used with caution. A total concentration on this work is not only unfair to Burke but must lead to a serious distortion of his ideas.

Burke did not put himself entirely outside the Enlightenment. He was not anti-intellectual but very concerned to keep himself well-versed in current intellectual movements. He did not embrace such movements helter-skelter as a pseudo-intellectual faddist might but instead judged seriously each idea by the moral principles he held. In this way Burke achieved an integrated understanding and knowledge, the hallmark of his special genius. Thus while he did not accept any idea because it was new, he did not *ipso facto* reject it for the same reason. In a November 1769 letter to Charles-Jean-Francois Depont, Burke wrote: "You will however be so good as to receive my very few hints with your usual indulgence, tho' some of them I confess are not in the taste of this enlighten'd age, and indeed are no better than the late ripe fruit of mere experience."[27] The *Reflections*, therefore, must not be understood from the vantage point of Burke's unequivocable rejection of *all* ideas coming out of the Enlightenment, although, like Marx, he did reject the major rationalist approach of its thinkers. Rather Burke felt that in *some* areas his ideas were not in consonance with the age.

In writing the *Reflections* Burke was acting out of a variety of motives. Foremost among them was his fear of subversion by what he termed the "armed doctrine." He clearly saw that the slogans and deeds of the Jacobins were fashioned not only for France but were the rallying cries for aggression, war and intended French domination over Europe. He was anxious about the social dissolution going on about him in England—the willingness of leaders like Dr. Price and Charles Fox to accept the revolutionaries at face value. He was alarmed by the fluctuation and appeasement in British policy toward

26. Geoffrey G. Butler, *The Tory Tradition* (London: John Murray, 1914), p. 34.

27. *The Correspondence of Edmund Burke*, ed. Cobban and Smith, *op. cit.*, p. 47.

the "new" France. For Burke, the French Revolution figured as the initial step in what he anticipated would be protracted warfare. To appreciate what Burke meant, it is worthwhile to cite the following lengthy quotation from Burke's well-known speech on "Proposals for Peace with the Regicide Directory of France":

> We are in a war of a *peculiar* nature. It is not with an ordinary community, which is hostile or friendly as passion or as interest may veer about,—not with a state which makes war through wantonness, and abandons it through lassitude. We are at war with a system which by its essence is inimical to all other governments, and which makes peace or war as peace and war may best contribute to their subversion. It is with an *armed doctrine* that we are at war. It has, by its essence, a faction of opinion and of interest and of enthusiasm in every country. It has one foot on a foreign shore, the other upon British soil. Thus advantaged, if it can at all exist, it must finally prevail. Nothing can so completely ruin any of the old governments, ours in particular, as the acknowledgement, directly or by implication, of any kind of superiority in this new power. This acknowledgement we make, if, in a bad or doubtful situation of our affairs, we solicit peace, or if we yield to the modes of new humiliation in which alone she is content to give us an hearing. By that means the terms cannot be of our choosing,—no, not in any part.[28]

Burke was fully aware of the fact that he was witnessing in the French Revolution a historical turning point, that a new sophistication had come about in the shape of ideological politics. But he also understood that ideology is frequently the pretext for the accumulation of greater power. From the Jacobin activities he concluded that the revolutionaries were not the social altruists they claimed to be. They had ransacked French society out of ulterior motives, namely, their own special interests. Marx, too, made this same evaluation of the Revolution's descendants. He claimed the "bourgeois republicans" who came out of the Revolution holding the reins of governmental power did not include in their republican concepts all social groupings but set out "to convince the working class that 'social' republic meant the republic ensuring their social subjection and . . . to convince the

---

28. Burke, "Proposals for Peace with the Regicide Directory of France," Beaconsfield Edition, *op. cit.*, V, p. 250.

royalist bulk of the bourgeois and landlord class that they might safely leave the cares and emoluments of government to the bourgeois 'republicans.' "[29] Although Marx was "in favor" of the Revolution since it swept France out of the feudal era and brought to the fore the capitalist middle class, he and Burke were in agreement that the Revolution constituted the aggression of particularized interests. As Burke had opposed absolute power in its Divine Right or mystical justification, so he opposed absolute power in its revolutionary ideological justification.

Burke's critique of the Revolution is by far more complicated and profound than the often alleged semi-hysterical reaction of an "Old" Whig. He agreed France was in need of changes, and he felt that some theorizing about the manner in which to effect such changes was required. He did not take issue with the revolutionaries vis-à-vis their *reasoning* about politics, for Burke considered himself too much in the basic Lockean tradition for that kind of stance. In a speech to Parliament Burke said, "I do not vilify theory and speculation: no, because that would be to vilify reason itself."[30] What he objected to in the revolutionaries, aside from their clandestine behavior, was the "unrealistic" qualities of their theories. And the only way Burke knew to test the correctness of reason was through its implementation in society:

> Whenever I speak against theory, I mean always a weak, erroneous, fallacious, unfounded or imperfect theory: and one of the ways of discovering that it is a false theory is by comparing it with practice. This is the true touchstone of all theories which regard man and the affairs of men,—Does it suit his nature in general?—Does it suit his nature as modified by his habits?[31]

The *Reflections* is Burke's attempt to correlate the revolutionary ideology with the social realities of France.

Because the Jacobins indulged themselves in speculative or abstract theory, they were to Burke irrational—they had lost touch

29. Marx, "The Civil War in France," *Basic Writings, op. cit.*, pp. 363-64.

30. Burke, "Speech on a Motion made in the House of Commons, May 7, 1782, for a Committee to inquire into the State of the Representation of the Commons in Parliament," Beaconsfield Edition, *op. cit.*, VII, p. 97.

31. *Ibid.*

with the "real." He feared such irrationalism since "of all things, wisdom is the most terrified with epidemical fanaticism, because of all enemies it is that against which she is the least able to furnish any kind of resource."[32] It might be said that he tried to confront the fanaticism of irrationality with the fanaticism of the existing, "experienceable" world. (In this contest between the "reall" and the "unreal" are resemblances to the basic elements of Hegel's dialectic.) This was an obligation he felt bound to fulfill, especially as a parliamentarian. All human actions have their source in ideas. Burke expressed his belief in the interdependence of thought and action in his *Notebook:*

> ... Action is influenced by Opinion—and our Notion of things, and nothing but strong and confirmed Opinion can lead to resolute Action. Therefore doubt and skepticism were no more made for Man than Pride and Positiveness: for no Action, or but feeble and imperfect essays toward action, can arise from dubious Notions and fluctuating Principles.[33]

Political ideas must be especially sound, since political actions carry with them wide social repercussions. Burke separates himself from thinkers like Hume who doubt the ability of man to perceive accurately the world about him and hence to engage in scientific endeavors. And he also rejects those of the Enlightenment who claimed that man can perfectly understand the natural law through "intuition." Man can and must come to know the world in which he lives by the application of "right" reason to his experiences.

As mentioned previously, Burke, like Marx, did not consider "reason" to be a faculty independent of man's general physical and emotional state or capable of separating itself from environmental influences. Conditioned by numerous factors, reason can reflect upon the external environment and bring it into a conceptualized order. Indeed for Burke, only in understanding this order can man act "rationally" or with intention. He uses this idea to support political policies based upon a commitment to social evolution rather than revolution. In preserving historical continuity, the individual is surrounded with an ordered social environment in which he can act

32. Burke, *Reflections*, Beaconsfield Edition, *op. cit.*, p. 435.

33. Somerset, *op. cit.*, p. 69.

with regularity and a sense of expectancy. To Burke habit is thus the most important mechanism by which the individual comes to know and understand the world about him. He called this continuity of *valued* experience "prejudice" and claimed:

> . . . prejudice, with its reason, has a motive to give action to that reason, and an affection which will give it permanence. Prejudice is of ready application in the emergency; it previously engages the mind in a steady course of wisdom and virtue, and does not leave the man hesitating in a moment of decision, skeptical, puzzled, and unresolved. Prejudice renders a man's virtue his habit, and not a series of unconnected acts. Through just prejudice, his duty becomes part of his nature.[34]

In contemporary parlance we talk about "political socialization" rather than "prejudice." For example, the value of voting must be taught to a child growing up in a democratic society. When eventually able to vote, that child must understand what he is supposed to do and why he is doing it, that is, he must appreciate the act of voting as significant to his relationship to the society about him. Voting becomes a value or prejudice. If, on the other hand, voting were used only sporadically at the arbitrary decision of government and then only for fixed referenda or elections, the individual would not put any value on voting nor would the action have any inherent rationality—perhaps just fear of the consequences of not voting. Burke tries to convey to us the notion that the lawful orderliness of society (its devotion to constitutionalism) allows individuals to plan and to carry out their plans. We must be able to make certain assumptions about the perpetuity of social values and the routines which give concrete expression to those values (as voting in a democratic state concretizes individual freedom and choice) if we are to have any truly personalized life at all. Otherwise we become the victims of social dictates and manipulations.

Marx was not in serious disagreement with this concept. He knew that only through common habitual actions are class interests formed, consolidated and made conscious. As such classes play necessary historical roles for Marx, it might be said that within his theoretical system their habitual actions are part of historical "reason." But Marx did not place the same emphasis Burke did on

34. Burke, *Reflections*, Beaconsfield Edition, *op. cit.*, p. 346.

habit since he was interested in revolutionizing history. To both, however, political action could be "rational" only if the ideas behind it respected the ordered activity of society. The "salon theoreticians" could not produce socially meaningful ideas. As Marx decried the "utopian socialists," the Fenian "exploits" and various other groups and events he considered politically irrelevant, so Burke considered the French revolutionaries irrational and, as the controllers of political power, dangerous.

Like Marx, then, Burke rejected the major premise of the Enlightenment—the spontaneous creativity of reason. But he was more consistent in this rejection than Marx. Burke, the politiciam, philosopher and social scientist, remained thoroughly committed to the historicist viewpoint. Ironically enough, Burke's historical posture results from the fact that he was much less sure of the historical process than Marx. To Marx history virtually has its own motive power. Its traditions and basic perspectives are such an intimate part of the human social personality that man, for all intents and purposes, can not easily separate himself from the demands and momentum of the historical process. Only through the final proletarian revolution can man sever his umbilical cord and achieve independence and self-mastery. Burke was much less convinced about the durability of historical traditions and even about their tendency to permeate individual lives. He demonstrated that same curious mixture of pessimism and optimism about history, though for different reasons than Marx.

Marx viewed history through the perspective of the changing modes of economic production. Since he tied the historical process to the interplay of vested economic interests, he could be more certain about the tendency of history to change itself progressively. Stability comes from the dominant class attempting to consolidate and promote its position in society, for ". . . in order to oppress a class certain conditions must be assured to it under which it can, at least, continue its slavish existence."[35] Change results from the struggles of a new class against the old. Marx assumed that each rising class, bringing with it new modes of production, builds a progressive step in history. In other words, since technological knowledge, as im-

35. Marx and Engels, "The Manifesto of the Communist Party," *Basic Writings, op. cit.*, p. 19.

plemented in the modes of production, is cumulative, the social relations built around such ever-advancing technology would also become subsequently more sophisticated and refined. In his *Critique of Political Economy*, Marx expressed this in the following manner:

> No social order ever disappears before all the productive forces for which there is room in it have been developed, and new, higher relations never appear before the material conditions of their existence have matured in the womb of the old society. Therefore mankind always takes up only such problems as it can solve, since, looking at the matter more closely, we will always find that the problem itself arises only when the material conditions necessary for its solution already exist or are at least in the process of formation.[36]

Thus the communist society, supposed to be the most advanced economic organization, becomes at the same time the most advanced stage of human social existence. (The difficulty in Marx's thinking here is that he envisioned Communism to be actually the perfection of human social life and organization even though he probably assumed that human technological inventiveness would continue.)

In this sense Marx is very much in the Enlightenment tradition. Condorcet and Comte had expressed abounding optimism in the moral progress accompanying accumulated knowledge. Marx, in concentrating upon the technological, narrowed the scope of Enlightenment thinking but kept its essential meaning. To him all other areas of knowledge would develop in accordance with the increase in technological knowledge.[37]

Burke did not connect moral development in history with technological achievements. Although he had a personal interest in pure and applied science and fully appreciated the worth of science to society, he considered it but one area of human knowledge and certainly not the *prima causa* of human moral progress. He agreed that

36. Marx, "A Contribution to the Critique of Political Economy," *Basic Writings, op. cit.*, p. 44.

37. It is interesting to note that in the United States, the most technologically advanced and innovative society today, there is a tendency to make the same equation Marx did between technological improvements and human improvements. This approach was particularly evident in former President John F. Kennedy's "New Frontiers" Program which stressed the material and physical development of the country as the necessary requirement for fulfilling the society's moral obligation to the individual.

knowledge in general facilitates human refinement and development. To maintain otherwise, he asserted, would be to assign virtue to ignorance:

> Where science flourishes, Vice flies before it; who then is so audacious as to affirm knowledge begets Vice? what opinion can be more senseless? if so, its Opposite Quality, Ignorance should be the parent of Virtue. But so false is this Assertion, that we may venture to say, where Ignorance sways, there can scarce be any true Virtue. But Men who look with an envious Eye on Talents they can never hope to equal, are willing to bring everything to their own Level; and thus many decry the Arts, not that they think them hurtful, but that they despair of ever coming to any excellence in them.[38]

In stressing the importance general social knowledge, Burke was very much a man of the Enlightenment.

But while the Rationalist tended to speak in terms of individual reason, perception and morality, Burke talked about social reason, comprehension and morality. Although he considered it self-evident that each individual possesses the capacity to think and be moral, Burke argued that the individual could not possibly equal the storehouse of knowledge built up by generations. Thus to Burke it was foolishness to suggest and arrogance to assume that the individual can disassociate himself from the mainstream of historical society and on his own accord acquire supreme moral insight. In his classic statement on the issue, Burke stated:

> Because a nation is not an idea only of local extent and individual momentary aggregation, but it is an idea of continuity which extends in time as well as in numbers and space. And this is a choice not of one day or one set of people, not a tumultary and giddy choice; it is a deliberate election of ages and of generations; it is a constitution made by what is ten thousand times better than choice; it is made by the peculiar circumstances, occasions, tempers, dispositions, and moral, civil, and social habitudes of the people, which disclose themselves only in a long space of time. It is a vestment which accomodates itself to the body. Nor is prescription of government formed upon blind, unmeaning prejudice. For man is a most unwise and a most wise being. The individual is foolish, the multitude, for the moment, is foolish, when they act

38. Burke, *The Reformer*, No. 1 (28 January 1747-48), reprinted in Samuels, *op. cit.*, p. 298.

without deliberation; but the species is wise and, when time is given to it, as a species it almost always acts right.[39]

This passage has been sometimes interpreted to signify that Burke denigrated individual reason and tended toward social mysticism. Harold Laski said that Burke "has an angry distrust of reason" and "puts his confidence, not in the deliberate acts of men, but in those vast, impersonal and secular forces, which change institutions in the same unseen, but remoreseless way, as the tides change the contours of a coastline."[40] But this verdict distorts Burke's intention.

What Burke (in the Aristotelian tradition) was trying to emphasize is that society engenders civilization and refined, rational behavior. To consider the individual sufficient unto himself is in actuality to force him back into primitivism. Since progress connotes relative achievement, the individual can participate in and contribute to what has already been accomplished. But to Burke the civilizational veneer of man is thin, and it is possible to destroy rashly the achievements of generations, plummeting man back into a barbaric, confused existence. How is social development, therefore, to be achieved?

Burke considers it the task of politics and law to anchor the individual within a social and civilizing context. Politics to him is the amalgam of diverse group interests; it channels the separate group energies into a common social purpose. To perform this task of integration, politics must take advantage of and protect "social reason." Burke thus assigns to politics the role of a social regulator. But unlike technological achievements, political knowledge does not express itself in a tangible, concrete form. Nor is it necessarily cumulative. The political process *can* break down, scattering chaos and destruction in society. Hence faith in social progress through political regulation rests on a more precarious footing than that of changing economic production.

This is not to say that Burke did not appreciate the economic motivation of individuals. As mentioned in the previous chapter, he shared with Marx a central concern for classes. And while he granted

39. Burke, "Speech on Representation," Beaconsfield Edition, *op. cit.*, p. 95.

40. Laski, *Edmund Burke, op. cit.*, p. 4.

the possible antagonisms between classes, he, nevertheless, believed that through creative political action all classes could be included in a general scheme of social justice. There were many historical examples in England which led him to assume that political institutions and policies could bring classes together. As the English Parliament, for example, took its bicameral form in the thirteenth century, there had notably occurred the banding together of the knights and burgesses into the House of Commons (the greater aristocracy in the tradition of the previous Greater Council withdrew itself into the emerging House of Lords). The Coalition of Knights and Burgesses (a watermark in English Constitutionalism) set an important precedent in the constitutional framework regarding the cooperation of classes. Thus Parliament, the Crown, and the Church have been, according to English political tradition, not only symbols of class interests, but, more importantly, co-participants in national sovereignty. England at a very early time had worked out a mode of interest equilibrium through its institutional framework. Burke was, therefore, very much in this tradition when he addressed himself to the possibility of social harmony through the political process.

He was also in the tradition of his predecessor, John Locke, when he wrote that "Government is a contrivance of human wisdom to provide for human *wants*" and that "men have a right that those wants should be provided for by this wisdom."[41] Burke admits that political government, unlike society, is the deliberate creation of human reason. Commonwealths are "artificial combinations, and, in their proximate efficient cause, the arbitrary productions of the human mind."[42] Insofar as government is the product of reason, it has the social responsibility in providing for human wants to manifest the "highest reason":

> I have ever abhorred, since the first dawn of my understanding to this its obscure twilight, all the operations of opinion, fancy, inclination, and will, in the affairs of government, where only a sovereign reason, paramount to all forms of legislation and administration, should dictate. Government is made for the very purpose of opposing that reason to will and caprice, in the

41. Burke, *Reflections*, Beaconsfield Edition, *op. cit.*, p. 310.

42. Burke, "Proposals for Peace with the Regicide Directory of France," *op. cit.*, p. 234.

reformers, or in the reformed, in the governors or in the governed, in kings, in senates, or in people.[43]

Thus politics is to Burke the most creative of all social instruments. (Marx took a similar standpoint—despite his "economic determinism"—in claiming that all class struggles are at the same time political struggles, that it is "the legal, political, religious, aesthetic, or philosophic—in short, ideological—forms in which men become conscious of this conflict and fight it out.")[44] Politics is that artifact which facilitates and engenders social integration and which permits the evolution of society toward ever higher civilizational planes. Rational, progressive politics coalesces the partial (and selfish) views of classes into the broader social perspective.

Since Burke conceived of political institutions as the products and transmitters of reason, it becomes clear that for him their preservation does not mean that the "tradition of all dead generations weighs like a nightmare on the brain of the living," as Marx put it. Burke generally did not consider history a millstone around the neck of man. An institution is the regularity in human behavior established to accomplish specified goals; the preservation of this regularity means the stabilization of reason in society. But Burke's respect for history did not blind him to the negative aspects of some traditions; he did not believe that institutions are "good" and legitimate *simply because they are old*. He could roundly chastise Algiers, the Mamelukes of Egypt, Poland and Turkey for their time-worn but depraved political existences. Writing to Charles-Jean-Francois Depont in 1789 (at a time when some analysts claim it was fear which propelled Burke into political reaction), Burke made the following comment:

> One form of Government may be better than another; and this difference may be worth a struggle. I think so. A positively vicious and abusive Government ought to be chang'd, and if necessary by violence, if it cannot be (as sometimes is the case) Reformed. . . .[45]

---

43. Burke, "A Letter to a Noble Lord on the Attacks made upon Mr. Burke and His Pension, in the House of Lords," Beaconsfield Edition, *op. cit.*, V, p. 189.

44. Marx, "Critique of Political Economy," *Basic Writings, op. cit.*, p. 44.

45. *The Correspondence of Edmund Burke*, ed. Cobban and Smith, *op. cit.*, p. 48.

Government to be sustained must be reasonable. By "reasonable," Burke meant that it must not sacrifice "any part to the ideal good of the whole. The object of the state is (as far as may be) the happiness of the whole. Whatever makes multitudes of men utterly miserable can never answer that object: indeed, it contradicts it wholly and entirely; and the happiness and misery of mankind, estimated by their feelings and sentiments, and not by any theories of their rights, is, and ought to be, the standard for the conduct of legislators towards the people."[46] This concept of government places Burke squarely in the ancient Greek tradition which regarded political organization as the chance for the "Good Life." According to Burke, therefore, the wise legislator in order to fulfill his social trust will involve himself in the social sentiments and conditions about him. He will ask the question, "How and in what circumstances do you find the society?" and act legislatively in accordance with the empirical assessment of social circumstances rather than on the basis of some speculative theory remote from actual social conditions.[47]

In Burke's view, government, when reasonable, is moral. Very much like Marx, in the final analysis he defines political creativity as moral creativity. Moral creativity means for both the harmonization and integration of society which is effected through time. Burke, however, attributes to politics a more dynamic role than Marx (although Marx in his views of the proletarian revolution imparts unto politics a broader, more immediate goal of social transformation). In assigning to politics the task of bringing together and harmonizing diverse social groups, Burke is not encumbered with Marx's idea that the political arena is *ipso facto* "controlled" by dominant classes. Having convinced himself that there is no reconcilability of classes, Marx viewed all political action in terms of its function within the class struggle.

Politics to Marx was creative to the extent that it accentuated class antagonisms and thereby facilitated change. In this respect he accepts politics as strict partisanship and, therefore, socially divisive.

---

46. Burke, "Speech on a Bill for the Relief of Protestant Dissenters," Beaconsfield Edition, *op. cit.*, VII, p. 45.

47. *Ibid.*

In his contemplated Communist society, politics will cease to exist since it loses its *raison d'être*, namely, class existence: "When, in the course of development, class distinctions have disappeared and all production has been concentrated in the hands of a vast association of the whole nation, the public power will lose its political character."[48] What follows in the communist society is the "simple administration of things" or management. What Marx did not anticipate, however, is that the "managerial class", as described by the American, James Burnham, and the Yugoslav, Milovan Djilas, may become a new source of political activity and dominance. Focusing on the private ownership of the means of production, Marx did not envision a new controlling force, the bureaucratic management of the means of production, and the continued politicization of society. He did expect that the proletarian revolution would be the last spurt of political creativity. It would usher in a stage during which the working class would perhaps be forced to establish its own class dominance through the "dictatorship of the proletariat" and inaugurate sweeping political reforms, as outlined in the *Communist Manifesto*.[49] Society would be so totally transformed through these reforms that the proletariat would undermine its own class rule and, in so doing, the state would wither away. The socialist economy would then create the apolitical existence of man. *Hence the ultimate in creative politics for Marx is political self-destruction.*

Marx, the revolutionary, took for granted those historical forces which would push political activity through to this necessary end. For, as Sidney Hook has pointed out, he believed that the historical process "had an immanent *progressive* direction or *telos*, so that when we truly understand human history we see not only that it is necessary but also

48. Marx and Engels, "Manifesto of the Communist Party," *Basic Works, op. cit.*, p. 29.

49. In a capsulized form the reforms listed in the *Manifesto* are: abolition of property in land and application of all rents to public purposes; progressive income tax; abolition of right of inheritance; confiscation of emigrants' and rebels' property; centralization of credit in the state; centralization of the means of communication and transportation in the state; extension of factories and instruments of production owned by the state, cultivation of wastelands and improvement of the soil; equal liability of all to work; combination of agriculture with manufacturing industries, abolition of distinction between town and country; free education for all children in public schools, abolition of factory labor for children, combination of education with industrial production. *Ibid.*, pp. 28-29.

reasonable."[50] The need for economic provisions and the increasingly sophisticated technological means by which this need is met constituted for Marx a dependent variable in human social existence, for it is the ". . . material transformation of the economic conditions of production, which can be determined with the precision of natural science. . . ."[51] For Burke, politics does not have any one locus of necessary control in society. Indeed he considered political institutions and processes to be the rational framework for the general social environment.

While Marx considered historical society as the inevitable conditioner of politics, Burke accepted this not as a fact but as a *value-judgment*. That is to say, politics *should* be historically and socially oriented. Burke forces himself into a difficult position for historical analysis because he did not consider politics to be the result of a built-in control mechanism but rather the social controller itself.[52] Although this is the virtue in Burke's concept of creative politics, it is at the same time the weakness in his historical theory. How can one thereby calculate political action? Rather than looking at politics strictly from the vantage point of self-interested dominant classes, Burke makes a moral judgment concerning what politics *should* do rather than what it *necessarily* will do within a given circumstance.

Burke was even unwilling to construct an explicit moral code or guide upon which to evaluate politics. With his "pragmatic" approach he claimed that moral truth had to be ascertained in each specific situation: "The pretended rights of these theorists are all extremes; and in proportion as they are metaphysically true; they are morally and politically false. The rights of man are in a sort of *middle*, incapable of definition, but not impossible to be discerned."[53] Perhaps

---

50. Hook, "The Enlightenment and Marxism," *loc. cit.*, p. 95.

51. Marx, "Critique of Political Economy," *Basic Writings, op. cit.*, p. 44.

52. Marx would certainly agree that politics is a control mechanism. Indeed the control might be exercised in a "rational" manner by the dominant class in order to secure its own class position. But this has quite a different connotation from Burke's concept of politics as the general moral regulator in society.

53. Burke, *Reflections*, Beaconsfield Edition, *op. cit.*, p. 313. Engels sounds like Burke when he writes in *Socialism: Utopian and Scientific*: "The solution of the social problems, which as yet

naively, Burke assumed with the Enlightenment that man has moral knowledge within his very nature; it is virtually the essence of rational man. Hence all individuals are capable of moral actions when given the chance. In contrast to the Enlightenment, however, Burke was dubious about the possibility of absolute morality (and subsequently the perfect society), saying, "the rights of men in governments are their advantages; and these are often in balances between differences of good,—in compromises sometimes between good and evil, and sometimes between evil and evil."[54] And yet because politics is the important balancer in the moral community, Burke stipulated that ". . . whenever man is put over men, as the better nature ought ever to preside, in that case more particularly he should as nearly as possible be approximated to his perfection."[55]

Yet governments frequently tyrannize and neglect general social needs. Although there are many different manifestations of and reasons for tyranny, one of its major sources to Burke is the metaphysician with his blueprint for the perfect society, for "by these theorists the right of the people is almost always sophistically confounded with their power."[56] Burke rejected this equation of "right" with "might." Such blueprint theoreticians also pit individual reason against social reason, claiming the former to be "enlightened" and the latter but blind "prejudice." Upon what ground is this claim

---

lay hidden in undeveloped economic conditions, the utopians attempted to evolve out of the human brain. Society presented nothing but wrongs; to remove these was the task of reason. It was necessary, then, to discover a new and more perfect system of social order and to impose this upon society from without by propaganda, and wherever it was possible, by the example of model experiments. These new social systems were foredoomed as utopian; the more completely they were worked out in detail, the more they could not avoid drifting off into pure phantasies." (Engels, *Socialism: Scientific and Utopian, op. cit.,* p. 36).

54. *Ibid.*

55. *Ibid.,* p. 353.

56. *Ibid.,* p. 313. Blueprint utopianism has an innate determinism which is thus liable to despotic interpretation. In claiming to know the perfect society, the utopian eschews negotiation or the toleration of counter-proposals. Any compromise with conceived perfection must end up with imperfection. When deterministic utopians become social fanatics and strive for the levers of political power, they are capable of implementing tyranny.

made? Burke could only deduce it is self-arrogance and intolerance. Ideological movements which want to destroy the social fabric as it has developed to a given point (rather then reforming and improving it) represent not only irrational but anti-social forces. With regard to revolutionary France, Burke tried to bring out the fallacy in such theoretical political constructions:

> Your legislators, in every thing new, are the very first who have founded a commonwealth upon gaming, and infused the spirit into it as its vital breath. The great object in these politics is to metamorphose France, from a great kingdom into one great play-table; to turn its inhabitants into a nation of gamesters; to make speculation as extensive as life; to mix it with all its concerns; and to divert the whole of the hopes and fears of the people from their usual channels, into the impulses, passions, and superstitions of those who live on chances. . . .But where the law, which in most circumstances forbids, and in none countenances gaming, is itself debauched, so as to reverse its nature and policy, and expressly to force the subject to this destructive table, by bringing the spirit and symbols of gaming into the minutest matters, and engaging every body in it, and in every thing, a more dreadful epidemic distemper of that kind is spread than yet has appeared in the world. With you a man can neither earn nor buy his dinner, without a speculation. What he receives in the morning will not have the same value at night. What he is compelled to take as pay for an old debt, will not be received as the same when he comes to pay a debt contracted by himself; nor will it be the same when by prompt payment he would avoid contracting any debt at all.[57]

Thus an "armed doctrine" can do more than change society; it can drain a society's lifeblood. It is possible—despite centuries of development—for civilization to collapse. Man is not necessarily propelled toward progress, though he is capable of it. No manner of technological achievement can provide the bulwark against possible primitivizing unless there be sufficient means by which a society is held fast to its "inner principles"—its historical personality—and continues to develop them. As an individual can not from day to day assume a new character but rather integrates what he has learned into his basic personality structure, modifying and improving it as he goes along, so Burke asserted that it is foolhardy and vain to try to implant

57. Burke, *Reflections*, Arlington House, pp. 209-10.

upon a social organism a network of operations alien to its personality as developed by the dispositions of its component peoples over generations. Even in his youth, before he was forced to respond to the French Revolution, Burke maintained that "nothing can operate but from its own principles."[58] These "principles of existence" are evidenced in the way a people brings itself together as a working social unit, the methods it has achieved to solve social problems and the moral commitments which define its entire existence.

When dealing with society, Burke gave expression to a concept similar to that of "homeostatic equilibrium" used by natural scientists to describe the maintenance system in living organisms. As internal mechanisms adjust the human body, for instance, to changes in temperature and air pressure, so Burke conceived that societies have similar regulating mechanisms which keep them in balance. In this way society "co-apts" to its external and internal environmental changes by absorbing or otherwise responding to these changes in order to maintain itself. (This is perhaps somewhat similar to Marx's concept that every age possesses the wherewithal to solve the problems presented to it through changing economic modes of production.) Burke knew that such system maintenance does not mean unchanged or static existence; society—like all of nature—is in a continuous state of flux. Rather equilibrium means the gradual and perpetual adjustment to change in such a manner that society, while keeping itself intact, moves on to higher levels of social existence.

Burke did not consider social equilibrium a mechanical response to uncontrollable environmental influences. In all natural organisms there is a strong "will" for life, and each organism has its own adaptive processes enabling it to fight for survival. If a plant, for example, does not receive sunlight, it will wither and die. But adaptive processes within the plant will try to orient its growth in such a way that it achieves the needed nurturing element. In all non-human organisms these adaptive qualities are limited to the organism's physical instinctual capacities and the "congeniality" of the surrounding environment. But social man adjusts himself rationally and not just instinctively to changing circumstances. There is not only a physical adaptation but a moral one. Social existence is, therefore, in-

58. Somerset, *op. cit.*, p. 69.

finitely more complex and profound than "natural" survival.

Considering change the most powerful law of nature, Burke knew that man's skill in manipulating change to his own advantage is crucial not only to survival but to establishing a purposeful existence. Civilization-building depends upon society's correct response to a perpetually changing environment. His question is not, therefore, whether or not society should change but rather in what ways or in what direction it should change.

Since Burke did not accept historical determinism, he tended to view history with caution, perhaps even pessimism. It is not the pessimism, however, of Marx, who chastised history for its restraining force in human existence. Burke urges the conscious cultivation of this restraining force in order to ward off social dissolution and anarchy. It is all too easy for individuals to forget a past they did not make but of which they are the beneficiaries, to take for granted historical achievements and consider the society before them the raw material for their own creative will. This is the sense of self-importance of every generation. It was precisely this attitude which moved Thomas Paine to write that "every age and generation must be as free to act for itself, *in all cases*, as the ages and generations which preceded it."[59] Neither Burke nor Marx could agree with Paine that "man has no property in man; neither has any generation a property in the generations which are to follow."[60] Marx, however, would be more prone to side with Paine when he said that "the vanity and presumption of governing beyond the grave, is the most ridiculous and insolent of all tyrannies."[61]

It is the past, warns Burke, which gives each generation its sense of identity. If the contemporary generation is to be creative at all, it must be cognizant of the contributions of the past in order to see what

59. Thomas Paine, *Rights of Man* (New Rochelle, New York: Thomas Paine National Historical Association, 1925), p. 20.

60. *Ibid.*

61. *Ibid.* Paine implicitly contradicted himself when he later concluded that the governmental authority of Britain over the American continent must come to an end and lamented that "as parents, we can have no joy, knowing, that this government is not sufficiently lasting to insure anything which we may bequeath to posterity." (Thomas Paine, *Common Sense* New Rochelle, New York: Thomas Paine National Historical Association, 1925 , pp. 131-32).

is required for the present and future. Without this kind of perspective—in which the restraining force of history provides a reasonable guide— the generation at hand becomes alienated from the social resources of its own creativity. With this concept Burke "implicitly rejected Locke's *tabula rasa* concept as inadequate to explain the individuation of character and imaginative powers which distinguish man from the animals."[62]

To Marx no generation had been more impudent than that which built capitalist society. Filled with the exuberance of expanding economic power, it erected not only an impressive nation-state but spread its power across the world through imperialistic ventures. Inventive, full of innovation, and, most importantly to Marx, sufficiently revolutionary to create the context out of which the proletarian revolution would come, the bourgeoisie were nevertheless the inheritors of a long line of historical accomplishments making possible their creativity.

How did Burke expect the restraining force of history (i.e., the social conditions established by past actions) to facilitate social progress? Are not social restraints and social progress contradictions? The relationship between these two elements is for Burke admittedly precarious. Identifying, however, progress with increasing moral knowledge and its social implementation. Burke felt that only in our historical experiences can we come to distinguish the right or progressive path from the wrong. By civilizing ourselves, we restrain and repress the barbaric, the immoral. These historical experiences form the "inner principles" of a society and become embodied in social values and patterns like the constitution. By contrast with Paine, a constitution for Burke is more than an organizational outline drawn up for a society. It is the very essence or reason of social existence. It "constitutes" the unfolding historical personality. This concept was repugnant to many in the Age of Reason. Russell Kirk has placed Burke vividly against his *philosophe* adversaries, writing:

> At a time when the world was infatuated with constitution-manufacture, when Abbé Sieyès was drawing up organic documents wholesale, when every coffee-house had its philosopher qualified to revise the statutes of a nation on a rational plan, when

62. Russell Kirk, *The Conservative Mind* (Chicago: Henry Regnery Co., 1960), p. 42.

America had just got up fourteen new constitutions and was thinking of more, Burke declared that men do not make laws, they merely ratify or distort the laws of God. He said that men have no right to what they please: their natural rights are only what may be directly deduced from their human nature. The Whig reformer, the advocate of enlightened expediency, told England that there is indeed an immutable law, and there are indeed inalienable rights, but they are of origins and character profoundly different from what *philosophes* and levellers take them for.[63]

While Paine accused England of having no constitution since it did not appear in the written form acceptable to the Enlightenment constitution-makers, Burke considered such polemics a sheer waste of time.[64]

While Burke believed that occasionally constitutional forms of government could be used as "models" for other states (as his letter to Depont previously cited demonstrates), he did not assume that the social personality behind the form could also be transported. (This idea is somewhat akin to Marx's belief in the necessary internal development of states.) Like Marx, Burke recognized that societies may reach impasses at which their political resources may be inadequate to meet their social challenges. They may require external help and stimulation. But what Burke always stressed was the natural foundations of a constitution: constitutional models are but guides and not, as Abbé Sieyès supposed, of universal substantive application.

Burke and Marx, therefore, both claim that although societies have a potential for growth and creativity, this may be thwarted for one reason or another. In the end, each is committed to international cooperation and instruction in bringing all nations, albeit through their own particular development, into the historical momentum of "species development." But Burke was more pluralistic in his concept. Although moral principles can and should be universal guides, they are expressed differently though nonetheless validly in

63. *Ibid.*, p. 54.

64. Paine was not of Burke's intellectual caliber and could not, therefore, meet Burke in a balanced contest over the issues of the day. But Burke did engage himself in a written debate with Paine, presumably to accentuate the fullness of his own thinking against what he considered the absurdities of Paine's.

the various nations. This idea formed his argument against Warren Hastings. But Marx's universalism was predicated upon the assumption that the social forms of all nations had to be the same (e.g., communistic) for the moral principle to be universally realized.

In view of the way Burke defined a constitution, his insistence upon its prescriptive qualities becomes clear. The historical constitution as developing social reason acts as a restraining force only when it serves as the format for all generations. Prescription militates against the loss and facilitates the growth of social reason. But prescription again did not mean rigidity of form. Remembering his statement that by a "Different co-aptation of Parts, and a different Operation of them one on another" changes are produced so that "they acquire other Qualities they had not before," Burke realized that through the differences in and historical impact of generations, societies change, acquire new qualities and progress. He believed, however, that positive, creative change could occur only if the basic personality of the society was preserved. Like chemical compounds, the social components can not be rearranged at will and still preserve their integrity. Nor can any element be introduced into the "compound" without knowledge of its "compatability" with the other constituent elements. The social personality being the integrated expression of all the corporate bodies existing with the society, the destruction of any one element constructively contributing toward this personality must at the very least hamper the development of a society:

> To destroy any power, growing wild from the rank productive force of the human mind, is almost tantamount, in the moral world, to the destruction of the apparently active properties of bodies in the material. It would be like the attempt to destroy (if it were in our competence to destroy) the expansive force of fixed air in nitre, or the power of steam, or of electricity, or of magnetism. These energies always existed in nature, and they were always discernible. They seemed, some of them unserviceable, some noxious, some no better than a sport to children; until contemplative ability, combining with practic skill, tamed their wild nature, subdued them to use, and rendered them at once the most powerful and the most tractable agents, in subservience to the great views and designs of men.[65]

65. Burke, *Reflections*, Arlington House, *op. cit.*, pp. 173-74. Burke's analogy between the moral and physical worlds signifies his concept of the integrated universe. But it also demonstrates

Burke questioned the French revolutionaries, "Did fifty thousand persons, whose mental, whose bodily labour you might direct, and so many hundred thousand a year of a revenue, which was neither lazy nor superstitious, appear too big for your abilities to wield?" and answered his own question with the lament, "Your politicians do not understand their trade; and therefore they sell their tools."[66] To Burke the historical society is creative potentiality. But once the developing potential is curbed or destroyed by revolution or even conquest, the social structure lapses. In such situations a people is forced back upon its most limited resource, namely, instinct.

With his ideas of social progress, Burke's position on revolutionary politics might seem contradictory. How can a society develop without replacing the old with the new? What Burke rejected was the "armed revolutionary" who through violence *forced* the *spontaneous* and *complete* transformation of society. While he supported the use of force under certain circumstances in removing harmful government, he advocated this as a last resort (and in this respect he was close to Locke's argument on revolution). Burke argued that one must try all peaceful means to reform government and make it socially responsible before using violence.

The glorification of history is as deceitful, however, as its total abnegation. History is complex and can be used to support many different positions:

> We do not draw the moral lessons we might from history. On the contrary, without care it may be used to vitiate our minds and to destroy our happiness. In history a great volume is unrolled for our instruction, drawing the materials of future wisdom from the past errors and infirmities of mankind. It may, in the perversion, serve for a magazine, furnishing offensive and defensive weapons for parties in church and state, and supplying the means of keeping alive, or reviving dissensions and animosities, and adding fuel to civil fury.[67]

---

that he was very much like Marx in upholding the ability of "sovereign man" to master the natural world.

66. *Ibid.*, p. 174.

67. *Ibid.*, pp. 155-56.

Burke simply did not esteem the past as a better way of life. He was not a social reactionary. In his *Abridgement* of English history, for example, he clearly demonstrates the qualitative differences in English society from the time of the roving, semi-barbarian tribes of the Picts, Celts, Scots, Danes and Anglo-Saxons. He could wholeheartedly support the 1688 Revolution since he considered Parliament's new sovereignty a progressive step in Constitutional reform. The human species if it is true to its potential must be progressive, not regressive.

In talking about the historical society, its reason and development, we must mean, according to Burke, the manner in which various groups come together and are in the continuous process of integrating their separate interests into a social whole. Insofar as politics is charged with the responsibility for this integration, it becomes the great exchange house of society.

As a dedicated parliamentarian, Burke assumed that such integration is accomplished by representatives of the various interests through the policy-making process. He took for granted that a Member of Parliament has the obligation to represent the basic interests of his constituency. After his own election in 1774 he outlined this responsibility to the electors of Bristol:

> Certainly, Gentlemen, it ought to be the happiness and glory of a representative to live in the strictest union, the closest correspondence and the most unreserved communication with his constituents. Their wishes ought to have good weight with him; their opinions high respect; their business unremitted attention. It is his duty to sacrifice his repose, his pleasure, his satisfaction to theirs,—and above all, ever, and in all cases, to prefer their interest to his own.[68]

This responsibility notwithstanding, Burke adamantly refused to sacrifice to a constituent (or any one) "his unbiased opinion, his mature judgment, his enlightened conscience."[69] Although this attitude did not endear him to his Bristol constituents, Burke nevertheless adhered to the belief that a representative must be

68. Burke, "Speech to the Electors of Bristol," Beaconsfield Edition, *op. cit.*, II, p. 95.

69. *Ibid.*

allowed to act independently though conscientiously in order to achieve the two objectives of politics, namely, interest representation and interest integration. He rejected *"authoritative* instructions, *mandates* issued, which the member is bound blindly and implicitly to obey, to vote, to argue for, though contrary to the clearest conviction of his judgment and conscience. . . ."[70] Such mandates work against the exercise of reason in favor of inclination and particularistic prejudices. They transform the representative into the passive automaton of the represented group. They rigidify his role and, insofar as this occurs, they convert Parliament into a *"congress* of ambassadors from different and hostile interests, which interests each must maintain, as an agent and advocate, against other agents and advocates. . . ."[71] It can only lead to the breakdown of politics for mandated representatives to come to Parliament as predetermined decision-makers and thus merely reinforce the divisive elements they represent. ". . . What sort of reason is that in which the determination precedes the discussion, in which one set of men deliberate and another decide, and where those who form the conclusions are perhaps three hundred miles distant from those who hear the arguments?"[72] It is this concept of the legislator which most genuine democracies hold today. It is assumed that a representative, while guided by the interests of his constituency, can not be bound by instructions stifling individual judgment, especially in view of the increasing technical preoccupations of legislators. Burke—like contemporary legislators—claims that if the representative abuses the trust put in him by his constituents, he must face the prospect of being defeated at the next election.

Burke firmly believed in the independent, conscientious representative as the means by which separate and even hostile interests can be reconciled and integrated into a policy befitting society as a whole. Burke's representative is the rational spokesman for but not the embodiment of these interests. The politician should approach policy-making with "unbiased opinion." This attitude of Burke is consistent

70. *Ibid.*, p. 96.

71. *Ibid.*

72. *Ibid.*

with his belief in a truly liberal education. Since he expected men of education and experience to be parliamentarians, he assumed they would have this kind of broad political comprehension:

> It cannot escape observation, that when men are too much confined to professional and faculty habits, and, as it were, inveterate in the recurrent employment of that narrow circle, they are rather disabled than qualified for whatever depends on the knowledge of mankind, on experience in mixed affairs, on a comprehensive connected view of the various complicated external and internal interests which go to the formation of that multifarious thing called a state.[73]

To subject representatives to narrow partisanship through mandates would be to undermine Parliament as a *"deliberative* assembly of *one* nation, with *one* interest, that of the whole, where not local purposes, not local prejudices, ought to guide, but the general good, resulting from the general reason of the whole."[74]

How can this position be reconciled with Burke's belief in political parties? It must be remembered that parties in the eighteenth century were informal groupings organized usually around notables (thus Burke belonged to the so-called "Rockingham Whigs") rather than the vast bureaucratic vote-getting machines which began to develop with the extension of the suffrage in nineteenth century England and which dominate democratic politics today. There was no such thing as an extraparliamentary branch of the elected party group in the legislature. Nor had the cabinet taken on the structure or functions found under Gladstone and Disraeli, but it constituted instead a loosely defined body of parliamentary administrators (initially picked by the Crown).[75] Hence when referring to "party," Burke had in mind those more or less informal bands of similarly-minded parliamentarians.

73. Burke, *Reflections*, Arlington House, *op. cit.*, p. 57.

74. Burke, "Speech to the Electors of Bristol," *loc. cit.*, p. 96.

75. The concept of a party in Government and a party in Opposition did not ripen until the nineteenth century in England. General sentiments tended to be against the organization of "Her Majesty's Loyal Opposition," feeling this subversive of a national Parliament. But the extension of the suffrage and the subsequent formation of extra-parliamentary parties mandated the formal contest between parties. It is, however, interesting to note that not until the twentieth century did the leader of the Opposition become a salaried public official.

Like James Madison, Burke felt that through deliberation and compromise varying opinions could be voiced and worked out into an amicable solution. To achieve this kind of compromise it is all the more important that parliamentarians be flexible—freed from constituent mandates as well as party dictates.

Burke, like Locke, believed policies decided by the majority vote of such liberally-educated, free parliamentarians would in the main be just. The process of deliberation required to form a majority-based compromise prevents the "sore evil of harsh, crude, unqualified reformations, and renders all the headlong exertions of arbitrary power, in the few or in the many, forever impracticable."[76] The majority principle forces the general articulation of a national interest rather than purely sectional interests. In his general consideration of those qualities qualifying an individual for Parliament, Burke assumed with Thomas Jefferson that the majority deciding political issues would not be right on the basis of its quantitative strength alone but on its inner integrity.[77] It is this kind of conscientious majority which would not abuse a morally-upright minority (although it might be compelled to discipline a minority having no interest in or intent to promote the general social well-being).

In this concept of the "general reason of the whole," Burke seems to bear some affinity with his contemporary, Jean-Jacques Rousseau. Rousseau, who detested representative government as the factionalization of society, believed the "general will"—which could not be broken up and represented in any parliament—is quite distinct from the "will of all." The latter is but the accumulated inclinations of individuals; as such, it amounts to aggregated selfishness. By contrast,

76. Burke, *Reflections*, Beaconsfield Edition, *op. cit.*, p. 277.

77. Baruch Spinoza expressed most cogently this early liberal commitment to the reasonableness and self-restraint of the majority: "In a democracy, irrational commands are still less to be feared: for it is almost impossible that the majority of a people, especially if it be a large one, should agree in an irrational design: and, moreover, the basis and aim of a democracy is to avoid the desires as irrational, and to bring men as far as possible under the control of reason, so that they may live in peace and harmony: if this basis be removed the whole fabric falls to ruin." Baruch Spinoza, *A Theological-Political Treatise*, Volume I of *The Chief Works of Benedict de Spinoza*, trans. R.H.M. Elwes (New York: Dover Publications, Inc., 1955), p. 206. We can see that a very important, though often largely neglected, assumption implied in traditional liberal thinking is the vital function of the community and its shared values in guaranteeing individual freedom.

the "general will" implies for Rousseau the moral good of society, possessing qualities transcending the ephemeral and spurious desires of the single individual. It is the durable, indisputable, indivisible sovereign morality to which a society directs itself. Heavily influenced by his boyhood life in Geneva, Rousseau believed that the "general will" expresses itself best in the small, intimate and directly democratic community.

Rousseau, in using the term *volonté*, puts forth a romantic concept of the moral impulse of a community. In extolling "natural" man, the primitive innocent, Rousseau leaned in this instance far away from the Enlightenment. Burke, on the other hand, in speaking of "social reason," was in full consonance with those *philosophes* who put their faith in civilized man. But to both Rousseau and Burke, the general social "will" or "reason" constitutes that moral quality resulting from a harmonious, integrated society.

It is important to note that Marx shared areas of agreement with Burke and Rousseau on this issue. Like Rousseau, Marx did not believe a representative assembly could correspond to the general social interest, since representation is *ipso facto* controlled by the dominant class. Since Marx viewed the bourgeois democratic state as class-ridden, he considered the democrat's notion of the "will of the sovereign people" a sham and simple, unadulterated class propaganda used to dupe the working class into submission. In fact every class in ascendance employs the idea of a "general will and its representation" for the sake of political expediency: ". . . it follows that every class which is struggling for mastery, even when its domination, as is the case with the proletariat, postulates the abolition of the old form of society in its entirety and of mastery itself, must first conquer for itself political power in order to represent its interest in turn as the general interest, a step to which in the first moment it is forced."[78] Like Rousseau, Marx resented the political polarization of representative democracy. He also looked for the society in which the "general will" would prevail rather than the will of some, that of the ruling class. The classless society will feature a completely realized communal interest, according to Marx, which will be indestructible, having been determined or "fixed" by the very manner of social organization.

78. Marx and Engels, "The German Ideology," *Basic Writings, op. cit.*, p. 255.

Burke conceived of the "general reason of the whole" in more fluid terms. The political integration process creating this reason is fundamentally pluralistic and in constant adjustment. If one extrapolates from Burke's thinking here, it might be said he envisioned such integration would become proportionately more imperative with the increasing complexity of social existence.[79] Although Burke himself was not a democrat in the contemporary sense of that word, this commitment to interest integration based on compromise contains the seeds of pluralistic democratic thought. The combining of partial views and interests into a social interest is for Burke developing social reason which reflects the moral insight of a people at a given time.

Marx assumed that social morality results not just from the *unity* of society but from its *uniformity*. Indeed Marx confused these two attributes. Although Burke talked of "one nation with one interest," he expected this interest would be the refined product of many separate interests. Marx's concept, however, like Rousseau's, strays away from the idea of social unity and morality based on consensus. Rather he gives vent to the notion that only in the equality of economic status (classlessness) can morality come forth. But what does this mean in a functionally diverse state? The lack of exploitation does not necessarily mean egalitarianism. As Sidney Hook interprets this, Marx is really talking about the *equitable* society: "He is merely saying that given different individuals with different or varying needs, the appreciation of an equal standard will result in treatments that are not identical but which for all their differences are equally just."[80] This sounds like the equity of which Burke spoke. All men have equal rights before the law. But in the diversity of talents, activities and the ways in which persons pursue their rights, equal compensation cannot be expected. Otherwise the indolent and the industrious must therewith be given

---

79. In this respect Burke wrote: "By a slow but well-sustained progress, the effect of each step is watched: the good or ill success of the first, gives light to us in the second: and so, from light to light, we are conducted with safety through the whole series. . . . We compensate, we reconcile, we balance. We are enabled to unite into a consistent whole the various anomalies and contending principles that are found in the minds and affairs of men. From hence arises, not an excellence in simplicity, but one far superior, an excellence in composition." (Burke, *Reflections*, Arlington House, *op. cit.*, p. 185).

80. Hook, "The Enlightenment and Marxism," *loc. cit.*, p. 102.

equal dividends.[81] In practice the Marxist emphasis on classlessness or uniformity of economic status has led to the imposition of a "social interest" as defined by the ruling party clique. It was this same identification of the "general will" with uniformity rather than a pluralistic consensus which, according to J. L. Talmon, sowed in Rousseau's philosophy the "origins of totalitarian democracy."[82]

Marx's acceptance of this kind of "general will" becomes all the more enigmatic because of his faith in civilization-building. While Rousseau contemplated the small community, Marx, like Burke, looked forward to increasing social expansion and complexity. Although he anticipated the ultimate abolition of class existence, he thought that under Communism the individual would assume a variety of roles. This is expressed in *The German Ideology:*

> With the division of labor, each has a definite, exclusive sphere of activity which is forced upon him and from which he cannot escape. He is a hunter, fisherman or shepherd or censoring critic

81. Burke's concept of the equitable society is worthy of a full quotation: "Far am I from denying in theory; full as far is my heart from withholding in practice (if I were of power to give or to withhold) the *real* rights of men. In denying their false claims of right, I do not mean to injure those which are real, and are such as their pretended rights would totally destroy. If civil society be made the advantage of man, all the advantages for which it is made become his right. It is an institution of beneficence; and law itself is only beneficence acting by a rule. Men have a right to live by that rule; they have a right to justice; as between their fellows, whether their fellows are in politic function or in ordinary occupation. They have a right to the fruits of their industry; and to the means of making their industry fruitful. They have a right to the acquisitions of their parents; to the nourishment and improvement of their offspring; to instruction in life, and to consolation in death. Whatever each man can separately do, without trespassing upon others, he has a right to do for himself; and he has a right to a fair portion of all which society, with all its combinations of skill and force, can do in his favour. In this partnership all men have equal rights; but not to equal things. He that has but five shillings in the partnership, has as good a right to it, as he that has five hundred pounds has to his larger proportion. But he has not a right to an equal dividend in the product of the joint stock; and as to the share of power, authority and direction which each individual ought to have in the management of the State, that I must deny to be amongst the direct original rights of man in civil society; for I have in my contemplation the civil social man, and no other. It is a thing to be settled by convention." (Burke, *Reflections*, Arlington House, *op. cit.*, pp. 71-72).

82. J. L. Talmon in his *The Origins of Totalitarian Democracy* (New York: Praeger, 1965), p. 6 writes: "Rousseau's 'general will,' an ambiguous concept, sometimes conceived as valid *a priori*, sometimes as immanent in the will of man, exclusive and implying unanimity, became the driving force of totalitarian democracy, and the source of all its contradictions and antimonies."

(*kritischer Kritiker*) and must so remain if he does not want to lose the means for his own existence. In the communist society, however, each can develop himself in whatever area he desires since the society governs the general production and therefore makes it possible for me to do this today and that tomorrow, afternoons to fish, evenings to tend to cattle raising, after a meal to criticize, whatever I have the inclination to do, without becoming at any time a hunter, fisherman, shepherd or critic.[83]

Hence under Communism the individual will broaden himself and diversify his behavior. Being unrestrained by the limitations of class existence, he will become more sophisticated in his modes of living. Thus the humanistic side of Marx contemplated the full expression of individual personality under Communism. But if individuals become more "individualistic" and self-oriented, how is it that these same individuals will in their mass express themselves more in terms of social unity and morality? Marx's inadequate answer is that through the common ownership of the means of production, the individual and social man will be reconciled, harmonized. Since there will be no class exploitation, the individual will assume a socially-generous and benevolent character. But this is logically too pat. Marx succumbed here to the same naive evaluation of human nature that the Enlightenment had. If the right external conditions can be created, the truly human individual will come into play. It is the "wrong" society which in fact creates the "wrong" human being. But what is the right society? It must be the antithesis of all history—non-political existence.

In the last analysis Marx poses an antagonism between politics and the creative individual. As long as politics remains, individuals live under the restraints of a class system. It is only in loosening and finally dissolving these restraints that the individual supplants the political as the creative force in society. This moment is the penultimate of history. But only through the long stages of historical development will sufficient social complexity be achieved to permit the individual free choice and provide the resources by which to act upon that choice. Hence, importantly, Marx did not adulate primitive societies, since in their simplicity they lack the diverse resources and

---

83. Marx and Engels, *Die Deutsche Ideologie, op. cit.,* p. 30.

opportunities needed for full human expression. Only advanced society increases the opportunity for individuation.[84]

While Burke accepted this point of view, he was convinced that the millennium was not required before the "general reason of the whole" could be obtained. Like Marx, he considered this reason to be part of the historical process in which each generation can participate and thereby develop. For Burke, the evolution of reason is not brought about by changing economic modes but rather by the "deliberate election of generations." Volition and reason are as inseparable for Burke as "right" reason and morality. In this sense he is remarkably a man of the Enlightenment.

By reason, Burke did not mean merely mental exercises, however, but the entire *geistige Existenz* of society. Hegel employed much the same concept when he described the embodiment of the World Idea in different societies through the various epochs of history.[85] Burke lends himself to that kind of mystical interpretation which characterizes Hegel since his national historicism at first glance appears to be founded more on sentimentalism than rationalism. In truth he attempted to combine the two qualities and to posit, therefore, society as the historical integration of the rational and emotional individual. Society must bring out not only the "reasonableness" but the "sociability" in the individual. A prevalent strain in all of Burke's thinking is the interdependence of these two features. He claimed that the individual does not understand through the intellect only but in coordination with the emotions:

84. The reactionary elements of the New Left, i.e., those who desire a return to pre-technological, "natural" existence, differentiate themselves markedly from basic Marxism on this score. Defining as "European" the notion that civilization rests upon man's ability to conquer nature (a notion Engels ably expressed in his *Socialism: Scientific and Utopian*), these New Lefters extol civilization as the co-existence with, not the conquest of, nature. The assumption supporting the coexistence approach is again that only "natural" man—man in communion with his own natural self and environment—is free. There are many difficulties in this idea. First, what is natural man? Is reason not a part of man's nature? Is it unnatural for man to transform his environment to his own advantage? Second, is man freer when forced to contend on a day-to-day basis with the elements of nature about him?

85. Russell Kirk warns against the pairing of Hegel and Burke, stating that "people who think that these two men represent different facets of the same system are in danger of confusing authoritarianism (in the political sense) with conservatism. Marx could draw upon Hegel's magazine; he could find nothing to suit him in Burke." (Kirk, *Conservative Mind, op. cit.*, p. 6).

Now suppose a piece was written describing the Nature and extent of any Vice, suppose that it showed its limits, described its several species, gave Directions about the encrease and furtherance of it;—suppose this done in such a manner as to avoid carefully the Affecting any of our passions, and then see how little the reader shall be incited to profit from the lecture. I believe very little. But then, try what a lascivious Song will do. This is directed at the imagination and in a Moment the desires are raised: and so undoubtedly and much more will it hold in Virtue.[86]

Similarly, the spiritual, emotional qualities of a society—its humanness—foster social reason. Both Burke and Marx seek the common sense of social commitment.

With this emphasis Burke and Marx had a similar dislike for the "socially vapid" individual. In his *Notebook*, in an essay entitled, "Character of a Wise Man," Burke pictured the type of individual that Marx described as the bourgeois:

His way of loving mankind is but an intercourse of business; not of affection. For he neither loves nor hates anybody. When he marries he makes a good choice because he chooses without passion. Family and fortune he secures: and does not neglect those qualities that may make his Wife an useful and agreeable companion. He makes to her a good husband: but she has not a great deal of his attention: and when she dies, he has a loss of which he is not insensible: but not to that degree which may hinder him of reflecting that his eldest Son may have a better match by the removal of her jointure. His children are well educated and well kept; and in general well instructed to make a figure in the world. Far from being a burden to him, they may be considered as instruments of his Ambition. By advancing them he makes them useful to him; advancing thereby his own importance and grandeur . . . in publick life.[87]

For the "prudent man," other individuals become but conveniences, since for him "all is self in the picture," while the "good man" is

86. Somerset, *op. cit.*, p. 96.

87. *Ibid.*, p. 112. The elipsis designates an illegible portion of the original manuscript. In the *Economic and Philosophical Manuscripts*, Marx wrote that the wealthy man of pleasure ". . . acquires a contempt for mankind, expressed in the form of arrogance and the squandering of resources which would support a hundred human lives.. . . . He regards the realization of the *essential powers* of man only as the realization of his own disorderly life. . . ." (Marx, *Manuscripts, loc. cit.*, p. 151).

socially oriented and "exerts his fine understanding rather in making the good more beneficial to the party he would oblige than in guarding against the ill Consequences of his own Benevolence."[88]

Since interest groups are the main vehicle for the social integration of individuals, Burke favored corporate representation in Parliament. He considered representation based upon numerically equal territorial units to be grossly unfair to the individuals represented, since a territorial unit is not necessarily coterminous with the various corporate interests of a society. Corporate bodies, on the other hand, are representatives of functional individuals. As Russell Kirk shows, Burke assumed that corporate representation entailed *ipso facto* the meaningful representation of individual interests:

> The country gentlemen, the farmers, the professional classes, the merchants, the manufacturers, the university graduates, in some constituencies the shopkeepers and prosperous artisans, the forty-shilling free holders: men of these orders had the franchise. Within one or another of these categories, the real interest of every person in England was represented. In good government, the object of voting is not to enable every man to express his ego, but to represent his interest whether or not he casts his vote personally or directly.[89]

Schemes for universal suffrage (such as put forth by the Duke of Richmond) were rejected by Burke, although Kirk asserts correctly that "Burke granted the extension of the suffrage was a question to be determined by prudence and expedience, varying with the character of the age."[90] This was in line with Burke's general thinking that as social obligations are historically conditioned and developed, so too are the corresponding social rights. As groups move up, so to speak, to take their place in added social responsibilities, they are entitled to an increase in social privileges and freedoms.

This seems to Burke the only way to create standards in society and hence in politics. Not all were qualified to have a direct participation in political matters, although everyone had the right to

88. *Ibid.*, p. 117.

89. Kirk, *op. cit.*, p. 19.

90. *Ibid.*

be protected and respected by political action. Progress is rarely, if ever, a perfectly coordinated step forward by all the members of a society. Social development is rather *uneven*, corresponding to the social maturation of diverse groups which through time acquire increased responsibilities and in so doing enlarge the social perspective. Change, for Burke and Marx, is the result of the shifting relations among social groups. The creativity of politics lies in its capacity to consolidate this change. For Burke this did not mean that politics must bow to any group pushing its way into political power. He claimed that "men have no right to what is not reasonable, and to what is not for their benefit. . . ."[91] Thus government must with "highest reason" establish the criteria for equity:

> Society requires not only that the passions of individuals should be subjected, but that even in the mass and body, as well as in the individuals, the inclinations of men should frequently be thwarted, their will controlled and their passions brought into subjection. This can only be done *by a power out of themselves* and not, in the exercise of its functions, subject to that will and to those passions which it is its office to bridle and subdue. In this sense the restraints on men, as well as their liberties, are to be reckoned among their rights. But as liberties and restraints vary with time and circumstances, and admit of infinite modifications, they cannot be settled upon any abstract rule; and nothing is so foolish as to discuss them upon that principle.[92]

Marx had in some way ideas similar to Burke's concerning representation, even though he seemed generally to favor universal suffrage. Yet in an interesting letter to Engels of February 11, 1865 (two years before the enfranchisement of the industrial working class in England), Marx seemed reluctant to give the demand for universal suffrage the top priority Lassalle did. Marx indicated in this letter that suffrage might be just another ruse of the capitalist class. Recognizing that the extension of the suffrage had been an earlier demand of the bourgeoisie, for which, he claimed, it had been too cowardly to fight, Marx felt that the working class would in actuality be waging the battle for the bourgeoisie. He anticipated that the

91. Burke, *Reflections*, Beaconsfield Edition, *op. cit.*, p. 313.

92. *Ibid.*, p. 310.

newly-enfranchised would have a nominal participation in democratic procedures but that without what he called the necessary "attendant conditions," such suffrage would change little the status of the working class in capitalist society.[93] Marx was suspicious of what appeared on the surface to be liberal reform legislation, since he did not really believe that parliamentary or any other democratic procedures could reconcile the basic antagonism and struggle of classes.[94]

It is on this particular point that Burke and Marx remain at crucial variance.

And yet if one puts Burke and Marx into long-range perspective, they both come to the ultimate conclusion that out of discord and antagonism in society can come concord and harmony. For Marx, harmony can never be achieved until exploitative class society is destroyed once and for all. Burke is slightly more complex in this, for, stressing the pluralistic nature of society, he assumes there will always be the competition among interests. His primary interest is to find those social forces which tend toward the integration of all social members. It is for this reason that he emphasized, for example, the role of the Church and religion, maintaining that the Church is "one of the great bonds of society"and has as its "object the supreme good, the ultimate end and object of man himself."[95] All those customs, mores, traditions and institutions which work toward social unity are for Burke of utmost importance and must be preserved. It is the political process, however, which is charged with creating the environment out of which such unity comes. It is politics which orders social activities.

---

93. Marx and Engels, *Briefwechsel, op. cit.*, III, pp. 278-79.

94. Some Marxist scholars, like Sidney Hook, stipulate that Marx felt the socialist-communist era could come about peacefully in democratic states like Britain, Holland and the United States. In *Capital* Marx praised the various factory acts between 1853 and 1860 which "had been wrung step by step after a civil war of half a century" from the capitalist class and after which '. . . the power of resistance of capital gradually weakened, whilst at the same time the power of attack of the working class grew with the number of its allies in the classes of society not immediately interested in the question." Marx, *Capital*, Encyclopedia Britannica, *op. cit.*, p. 143.

95. Burke, "Speech on a Bill for the Relief of Protestant Dissenters," *loc. cit.*, VII, p. 43.

Marx did not put any stock in organized religion which he claim-ed dulls and pacifies the exploited in the promise of a better "afterlife." Religion divides rather than unites men. And he con-sidered historical traditions an enforcement of habitualism and a sen-timental *Sehnsucht* in the masses. While Burke—out of his doubt about the "civilizational imperative"—wanted to root the masses in their past, Marx saw the call for traditional loyalty and unity as a ploy of the ruling class against the exploited underdog class. The historical unity of the class society was to Marx a contradiction in terms. Thus he saw it as the task of the social philosopher to unmask the underly-ing contradictions and tensions endemic in class society in order to hasten the demise of class society by creating a credibility gap between the oppressed and their oppressors and therewith stimulating and inflaming the revolutionary struggle.

Yet Marx argued that the "pre-historical" divisiveness of economic man will eventually be resolved into historical unity. But unity implies classlessness. Thus in the *Communist Manifesto* is written: "Communism deprives no man of the power to appropriate the products of society; all that it does is to deprive him of the power to subjugate the labor of others by means of such appropriation."[96]

The "politics of reality" to Burke and Marx is, however, the prerequisite for social creativity. Politics is the means by which man achieves historical goals. While the creativity of political action is historically conditioned, it is nevertheless born our of the ever-changing and competitive characteristics of society. Indeed political creativity to Burke and Marx is ordered activity. It is creative politics which, as the "superstructure" or framework of society, brings social activity into ordered progression toward the goal of social unity. Thus their concept of creative politics brings them into a concern for social change. Insofar as change emanates from basic social conditions, Burke and Marx in their analyses remain empiricists and scientifically-oriented. Insofar as change, however, is the means by which man develops and achieves his historical purpose of unity, Burke and Marx enter into moral evaluations. Creative politics or ordered change is in the end the moral growth of man.

---

96. Marx and Engels, "Manifesto of the Communist Party," *Basic Writings, op. cit.*, p. 23

Chapter V
Historical Empiricism:
The Politics of Change

Burke and Marx accepted change as in the "nature" of things and instrumental to man in his historical struggle toward social unity. Without the ability to change, human beings would necessarily remain at a low instinctual level. It is indeed human reason and its active implementation that distinguishes the human species from any other. As Burke claimed, "Man is made for speculation and action; and when he pursues his nature he succeeds best in both."[1] Important then to the two thinkers is that man has the built-in capacity not just to go along with the tides of change as they ebb and flow in the natural universe but rather to manipulate, initiate, and even master change for his own advantage. It is in this sense that human activity becomes meaningful and developmental. The "politics of reality" is therefore necessarily the "politics of change."

Both thinkers, however, held that change proceeds within the framework of historical order. Marx based his own concept of historical change on the dialectical process which Engels had asserted was the very method of nature. The dialectic is at once a theory of movement and change in the attraction and repulsion of opposites

1. Somerset, *op. cit.*, p. 86.

(the "thesis" and "antithesis"), and a theory of order in the synthesizing of these opposites and the establishment of a new set of antagonisms. Applying the dialectic to history, Marx contended that every social stage, which is but the domination of the major economic class, engenders its own destruction by creating its antithesis, the hitherto suppressed class. Through the class antagonism, society progressively changes.

Interestingly, Burke too seems to have conceived of the universe in terms similar to Marx. Burke never talked of dialectics nor did he design the sophisticated theory of historical movement that Marx did, who had had, after all, the benefit of Hegel's thinking. But he did base virtually all his thinking on the motive power of opposites. As a university student, Burke jotted the following observation in his *Notebook*:

> In reasoning about abstruse matters and the assent we give to Propositions concerning them, we don't sufficiently distinguish between a contrariety and a contradiction. No man in his senses can agree to a contradiction; but an apparent, nay a real contrariety in things, may not only be proposed and believed, but proved beyond any reasonable doubt. Most of our Enquiries, when carried beyond the very Superficial of things, lead us into the greatest Difficulties and we find qualities repugnant to each other whenever we attempt to dive into the manner of Existence.[2]

By a contradiction, Burke would seem to mean that law in logic which stipulates that a premise may not at the same time be both true and false. Hence in propositions concerning the real world a contradiction cannot exist. But a contrariety, that is, an opposition of facts, he seemed to accept as the "manner of existence." Reality is therefore observable, verifiable contrariness.

This youthful statement remains but description and does not venture into the realm of critical analysis. But there are other indications in his *Notebook* which suggest that Burke was further intrigued by this idea. Thus at another instance he wrote that "the wisdom of nature, or rather providence, is very worthy of admiration in this, as in a thousand other things, by working its ends toward

2. *Ibid.*, p. 92.

means that seem directed to other purposes."[3] And with this thought he put into question the concept of utility. How can one know what is really useful when means often seem to be contrary to assumed ends? As a practical example, the young Burke took the issue of religion and tried to demonstrate that it is of "no efficacy considered as a State Engine."[4] Since the perspectives of the state and religion are different, the latter cannot be made the tool of the former without changing its "principle of operation."[5] Thus, he wrote, ". . . by forcing it against its Nature to become a Political Engine, You make it an Engine of no efficacy at all. It can never operate for the Benefit of human society but when we think it is directed quite another way: because it then only operates from its own principles."[6]

This idea puts him at real variance with Jeremy Bentham, who advocated utility as the standard for governmental policy in establishing the "greatest happiness for the greatest number." Burke, even though he thought of politics as the means by which to satisfy human wants, preferred a moral standard which was not conceived in consideration of its utility alone. Morality is not a subject for a mathematical calculus: "Aristotle, the great master of reasoning, cautions us, and with great weight and propriety, against this species of delusive geometrical accuracy in moral arguments, as the most fallacious of all sophistry."[7]

3. *Ibid.*, p. 91.

4. *Ibid.*, p. 67. Burke even uses the word "utility" in demonstrating his case: "If you attempt to make the end of Religion to be its Utility to human society, . . . you then change its principle of operation. . . ."

5. *Ibid.*

6. *Ibid.*

7. Burke, "Speech on Conciliation with America," *loc. cit.*, p. 169. Bentham was not without his quarrels with Burke. In defending his utilitarianism against Burke's principles as he understood them, he wrote: "Upon this plan, everybody is satisfied; orator and people both: whereas upon the orator's [Burke's] plan, only one of the parties is satisfied, viz. the orator; the orator, who is the agent and spokesman of the *ruling few*; while the other party, viz, we the people, are suffering and grumbling, and in our numbers consists our title to regard; a very unpretending title, but not the less a good and sufficient one." (Jeremy Bentham, "Defense of Economy Against the Late Mr. Burke," *The Pamphleteer*, IX (1817), p. 47 .

It was this bias against strictly utilitarian calculations which Burke expressed again in his later years concerning the right of government to intervene in the economic sphere. He placed himself in the tradition of Adam Smith, which, considering the mercantilist policies of Britain at the time, was most liberal. In his *Thoughts and Details on Scarcity*, Burke stated the Smithian faith in the self-regulating market:

> The balance between consumption and production makes price. The market settles, and alone can settle, that price. Market is the meeting and conference of *consumer* and *producer*, when they mutually discover each other's wants. Nobody, I believe, has observed with any reflection what market is, without being astonished at the truth, the correctness, the celerity, the general equity with which the balance of wants is settled. They who wish the destruction of that balance, and would fain by arbitrary regulation decree that defective production should be compensated by increased price, directly lay their *axe* to the root of production itself.[8]

Burke demonstrates in this passage that the market has an "inner principle" in its operations which cannot, therefore, be made the subject of political "utility" and *arbitrary* regulation. More than this, however, he depicts again the interchange of interests which is in effect the implementation of the market's balancing principle. In the "meeting" of the consumer and producer, opposite though interdependent interests, a median price as well as a quality product is established. The harmony of the market is therewith secured.

Burke's appreciation of a *laissez-faire* policy supported his liberal attitude toward the Empire, and in this respect he was one century ahead of his time. Concerning the American colonies, he wrote that England "should be content to bind America by laws of trade. . . . Do not burden them by taxes. . . ."[9] Although the mercantilist Empire had not, since the seventeenth century, been taxed for the internal revenue of the English mother country, there had been those so-called "external" taxes levied as the means by which to keep the protectionist imperial structure intact. Burke, however, was interested in a

8. Burke, "Thoughts and Details on Scarcity," Beaconsfield Edition, *op. cit.*, V, p. 152.

9. Burke, "Speech on American Taxation," Beaconsfield Edition, *op. cit.*, II, p. 73.

voluntary Empire in which the attraction of trade alone would be the binding force among the component members. Echoing Smith's basic assumption, he argued that "man acts from adequate motives relative to his interest," that if it was enough to the interest of the American colonies to have commercial relations with England, they would do so and hence remain within a general imperial association.[10]

To those who argued on behalf of using force against the colonies, Burke retorted with a line of reasoning based on precedent as well as calculations in state power. Since England, he claimed at that time, had no experience with force as an instrument in colonial rule, it was doubtful whether on that consideration alone, the policy could be successful. But could force *per se* bring recalcitrant colonies into line? In answer to this question, Burke demonstrated his usual preoccupation with weighing opposing interests. While it could be asserted that Britain's superior power could overwhelm the colonies, this would be but a temporary solution. There would be the need to subdue again. And it was a contradictory policy since it would "impair the object by the very endeavor to preserve it."[11] Peace is not achieved by the total destruction of another's interests but rather:

> Peace implies reconciliation; and where there has been a material dispute, reconciliation does in a manner always imply concessions on the part or the other. In this state of things I make no difficulty in affirming that the proposal ought to originate from us. Great and acknowledged force is not impaired, either in effect or in opinion, by an unwillingness to exert itself. The superior power may offer peace with honor and with safety. Such an offer from such a power will be attributed to magnanimity. But the concessions of the weak are the concessions of fear.[12]

10. Burke, "Speech on Conciliation with America," *op. cit.*, p. 170.

11. *Ibid.*, p. 119. Ireland, particularly under Cromwell, had been the target of English imperial-colonial militancy. Burke was, as an Irishman, not only aware of Irish affairs but determined to bring justice to that land. His argument on force again means, therefore, that the English had never been successful in this area, as Ireland, even during Burke's time, proved. The Empire at this time consisted primarily of English settlement colonies (except for India which, however, after Clive's victory in 1756 began to be colonized). Burke probably would have been aghast at the "scramble for Africa" policies in the last decades of the nineteenth century.

12. *Ibid.*, p. 106.

The difficulty in Burke's position is that it anticipates *responsible* power-holders. It takes for granted that a negotiated peace in which there has been a willing compromise of interests will be honored by the participating powers. It assumes, in other words, good faith. And Burke felt that he could be secure in these assumptions because the Americans "are not only devoted to liberty, but liberty according to English ideas and English principles. Abstract liberty, like other mere abstractions, is not to be found. Liberty inheres in some sensible object."[13] This "sensible object," among other things, was to Burke the taxation issue, for, according to English tradition, "the people must in effect themselves, mediately and immediately, possess the power of granting their own money or no shadow of liberty could subsist."[14] He admitted, however, that the right of such taxation as a coveted source of freedom might not be dear to another nation which would perhaps have some other "favourite point, which by way of eminence becomes the criterion of their happiness."[15]

But what about those *irresponsible* power-holders? Those who have no interest in reconciliation but rather in domination? Those who seek peace only on their own terms and consider all concessions signs of weakness? This was precisely the way in which Burke viewed the "new" France:

> If I have reason to conceive that my enemy, who, as such, must have an interest in my destruction, is also a person of discernment and sagacity, then I must be quite sure, that, in a contest, the object he violently pursues is the very thing by which my ruin is likely to be the most perfectly accomplished. Why do the Jacobins cry for peace? Because they know, that, this point gained, the rest will follow of course."[16]

In such a situation there is no other recourse but force. However, Burke again denied that the objective of force in the war with France was to destroy the state as such. Since appeasement only advantaged

13. *Ibid.*, p. 120.

14. *Ibid.*, p. 121.

15. *Ibid.*, p. 120.

16. Burke, "Proposals for Peace with the Regicide Directory," *loc. cit.*, p. 287.

the Jacobins in their expansionist ambitions, Burke argued that Britain, while fighting the Radicals, must simultaneously build up the Royalists as the internal counterforce against the revolutionaries. "Otherwise," he claimed, "everything will move in a preposterous order, and nothing but confusion and destruction will follow."[17]

Due to the fact that the British Government had decided in favor of restoring the monarchy to France, Burke asserted that the conditions for monarchy must also be reestablished. It was not enough "to think of the possibility of the existence of a permanent and hereditary royalty, *where nothing else is hereditary or permanent in point either of personal or corporate dignity*"; and to consider it in any other terms would be but a "ruinous chimera."[18] The interest, therefore, of Britain was to preserve the "natural" forces of France while combatting the "unnatural" Jacobin group in order to maintain the safety of Europe:

> France, the author of the Treaty of Westphalia, is the natural guardian of the independence and balance of Germany. Great Britain. . . has a serious interest in preserving it; but except through the Power of France *acting upon the common old principles of state policy*, in the case we have supposed, she has no sort of means of supporting that interest. It is always the interest of Great Britain that the power of France should be kept within the bounds of moderation. It is not her interest that that power should be wholly annihilated in the system of Europe. Though at one time through France the independence of Europe was endangered, it is, and ever was, through her alone that the common liberty of Germany can be secured against the single or combined ambitions of any other power.[19]

In the case of France, then, Burke did not turn the issue on ideology alone. He entered into a complex computation of the interests affected by the activities and machinations of the revolutionaries. Leaving aside the substantive merits of his international evaluation, it is important for the present purposes to emphasize the organizational modes of Burke's thinking. Political issues for him always involved tangible interests which could be

17. Burke, "Policy of the Allies to France," *loc. cit.*, p. 425.

18. *Ibid.*, p. 414. The emphasis appears in the written text.

19. Burke, "Thoughts on French Affairs," *op. cit.*, pp. 323-33.

calculated in their material as well as moral features. What rights are legitimate? Burke would assert that legitimate rights are those necessary to the very existence of the group and its interests. What rights are illegitimate? Those which impinge upon the rights and existence of others. Hence civil rights become a "sort of middle"—an equilibrium of diverse groups.

Burke used the idea of "contrariety" in a number of ways to bolster his arguments concerning social harmony. He felt, for example, that the "action and counteraction," the "combination" and "opposition of interests" are vital to a society (and he added the natural world to this also). Thus Burke wrote:

> In your old states you possessed that variety of parts correspon-
> ding with the various descriptions of which your community was
> happily composed; you had all that combination, and all that
> opposition of interests, you had that action and counteraction
> which, in the natural world and in the political world, from the
> reciprocal struggle of discordant powers, draws out the harmony
> of the universe.[20]

It is out of the diversity and antagonism of interests that social harmony is created since they "interpose a salutary check in all precipitate resolutions."[21] The presence of such interests "render deliberation a matter, not of choice, but of necessity; they make all change a subject of *compromise*, which naturally begets moderation. . . ."[22] And diversity also protects—even furthers—general social liberty, since to Burke it provides as many securities for freedom as there are separate views.

Yet quite conscious that diversity can lead to chaos, he did not urge the artificial stimulation of antagonism and assigned to the political sphere the role of harmonizing and unifying the separate interests. In order to accomplish this task, it might be necessary for government to outlaw or otherwise restrict the activities of certain groups inimical to the general social well-being:

> It is the interest, and it is the duty, and because it is the interest
> and the duty, it is the right of government to attend much to

20. Burke, *Reflections,* Arlington House, *op. cit.,* p. 47.

21. *Ibid.*

22. *Ibid.*

opinions; because, as opinions soon combine with passions, even when they do not produce them, they have such influence on actions. Factions are formed upon opinions, which factions become in effect bodies corporate in the state; nay, factions generate opinions, in order to become a center of union, and to furnish watchwords to parties; and this may make it expedient for government to forbid things in themselves innocent and neutral. . . . For as self preservation in individuals is the first law of Nature, the same will prevail in societies, who will, right or wrong, make that an object paramount to all other rights whatsoever.[23]

Burke showed a sound appreciation for the ways in which liberty could be abused by irresponsible groups. Although he was enough of a libertarian to advocate civil rights, he realized that along with such rights went certain social duties and obligations. Thus the society which grants privileges and rights has its own right to expect that these privileges be exercised in a constructive manner. Otherwise restraints and sanctions must be applied to the abusing party. He would not have been adverse to a democracy prohibiting political movements which abuse the very liberties of a political democracy for their deliberate destruction. Burke set down no hard and fast rules by which to differentiate the socially responsible from the irresponsible. He always maintained that one had to judge the effects of all groups in the particular circumstances in which they operate and in their relation to the total society.

Aside from discussing oppositions in their tangible form of social interests, Burke applied the same kind of concept to the realm of morals. In his terminology and understanding of "good" and "evil" Burke made recourse to Biblical tradition. Yet insofar as the "good" represented for him "right reason," his approach might be put into more psychological terms. In other words, each individual has the potential for "good" or rationality as well as for "evil" or irrationality. To Burke all of life is divided into these antagonistic worlds. Man through his own free will, so to speak, can decide to which "world" he wants to belong. In his idea of the contractual society, for example, Burke vehemently rejected the right of "municipal corporations" in their activities "to separate and tear asunder the bonds of their subordinate community, and to dissolve it into an unsocial, uncivil,

---

23. Burke, "Speech on a Bill for the Relief of Protestant Dissenters," *loc. cit.*, p. 44.

unconnected chaos of elementary principles."[24] Anarchy cannot be justified by human caprice and choice. In this case where men willfully resort to anarchism, Burke stated: "Nature is disobeyed, and the rebellious are outlawed, cast forth, and exiled, from the world of reason, and order, and peace, and virtue, and fruitful penitence, into the antagonistic world of madness, discord, vice, confusion, and unavailing sorrow."[25]

He creates here the impression of a complete dichotomy between "good" and "evil," rationality and irrationality and, particularly in the *Reflections*, desires to make quite clear that each "world" operates in accordance with an inexorable law. Thus certain courses of action must have virtually determined consequences. Anarchy, for instance, is against the whole social nature of man, the source of his morality, and cannot therefore help but lead straightaway to the "antagonistic world" of madness and discord. On the other hand, while Burke tried to be categorical about the moral imperative, his youthful appreciation of the obscurity of things seeped back into his concept of the moral universe when he wrote at another point in the *Reflections* that:

> . . . The real effects of moral causes are not always immediate, but that which in the first instance is prejudicial may be excellent in its remoter operation, and its excellence may arise even from the ill effects it produces in the beginning. The reverse also happens; and very plausible schemes, with very pleasing commencements, have often shameful and lamentable conclusions.[26]

Burke does not succumb to moral absolutism. This was a position which Sidney Hook criticized in the Enlightenment thinkers: "Once we make an absolute of any human right and under no circumstances justify its modification, then we can't escape the Kantian, otherwordly position: 'Let the right prevail, though the heavens fall.' Morality would then become something too good or exalted for man."[27] While Burke put himself into a readily acknowledged area of uncertainty regarding envisaged moral affects and actual outcomes, he did not

24. Burke, *Reflections*, Beaconsfield Edition, *op. cit.*, p. 359.

25. *Ibid.*

26. *Ibid.*, p. 312.

27. Hook, "The Enlightenment and Marxism," *loc. cit.*, p. 100.

claim that man is beyond either moral knowledge or practice. This knowledge must be gained, however, through the experience of the ages which alone can demonstrate by example the principles in operation. "It requires a deep knowledge of human nature and human necessities, and of the things which facilitate or obstruct the various ends which are to be pursued by the mechanism of civil institutions."[28]

Burke accepted change, therefore, as the product of interacting opposites. He conceived that society is challenged on two interrelated levels. In the composition of society are competing groups which act as agents of change as well as of stability in society. He felt that this competition was normally quite healthy and even imperative because it was through the response of government in balancing the claims of such groups that new moral levels could be attained in social relations. Government, as the regulator of society, represented to Burke a kind of front-line defense against the socially antagonistic world of irrationality and chaos. When government fails in this responsibility, the very social structure is put in moral jeopardy.

If change is the result of social tensions, as asserted by Burke and Marx, then those societies which are complex and highly diversified must be the most susceptible to change. It is only in the highly organized society that individuals carry on a variety of functions and in their separate activities come into conflict in their numerous contacts with others. As the individual loses his ability and opportunity to be self-sufficient and becomes more dependent upon society for the fulfillment of his needs, so he becomes more liable to clash with others upon whom he depends.[29] And as political power becomes more extensive in its authority over this complex social organization,

---

28. Burke, *Reflections, op. cit.*, p. 311.

29. Marx expresses this idea in a variety of ways with particular reference to capitalist society, but he dwells extensively on the problem in the *Manuscripts* in whose first portion he was concerned with alienation. Thus he wrote: "We must bear in mind the above-stated proposition that man's relation to himself only becomes *objective* and *real* for him through his relation to the other man. Thus, if the product of his labour, his labour *objectified*, is for him an *alien*, hostile, powerful object independent of him, then his position towards it is such that someone else is master of this object, someone who is alien, hostile, powerful, and independent of him. If his own activity is to him an unfree activity, then he is treating it as activity performed in the service, under the dominion, the coercion and yoke of another man." (From the *Economic and Political Manuscripts* found in David Caute (ed.), *Essential Writings of Karl Marx* [New York: Collier Books, 1970], pp. 57-58).

so interests will combine in the attempt to participate in this power and wrest it from others. It is in the interplay and opposition of individuals and groups, therefore, that change is forced upon society. By contrast, it must be the simple societies, those which have but minimal organization, which are the *least* susceptible to change. Marx was very clear on this issue in *Capital*:

> The simplicity of organization of production in these self-sufficing communities of India that constantly reproduce themselves in the same form and, when accidentally destroyed, spring up again on the spot and with the same name—this simplicity supplies the key to the secret of the unchangeableness in such striking contrast with the constant dissolution and refounding of Asiatic states, and the never-ceasing changes of dynasty. The structure of the economical elements remains untouched by the storm clouds of the political sky.[30]

Why has the economic structure in such societies failed to develop? Marx answered that due to the "simplicity of the organization of production" there had occurred no "division of labour in the workshop."[31] Thus, he wrote, "the labourer and his means of production remained closely united, like the snail with its shell, and thus there was wanting the principal basis of manufacture, the separation of the labourer from his means of production and the conversion of these means into capital."[32] There was no alienation and no exploitation of the worker under the guild system, since "a merchant could buy every kind of commodity, but labour as a commodity he could not buy."[33] The polarization of classes which assumedly takes place in the capitalist industrial system was nonexistent and hence change through class antagonism was thwarted.

Although Burke did not use the same approach as Marx, he quite explicitly rejected the idea that complex man can progress under simple forms of government:

> The nature of man is intricate; the objects of society are of the greatest possible complexity; and therefore no simple disposition

30. Marx, *Capital*, Encyclopaedia Britannica, *op. cit.*, p. 175.

31. *Ibid.*

32. *Ibid.*, pp. 175-76.

33. *Ibid.*, p. 175.

or direction of power can be suitable either to man's nature, or to the quality of his affairs. When I hear the simplicity of contrivance aimed at and boasted in any new political constitutions, I am at no loss to decide that the artificers are grossly ignorant of their trade, or totally negligent of their duty. The simple governments are fundamentally defective, to say no worse of them. If you were to contemplate society in but one point of view, all these simple modes of polity are infinitely captivating. In effect each would answer its single end much more perfectly than the more complex is able to attain all its complex purposes. But it is better that the whole should be imperfectly and anomalously answered, than that, while some parts are provided for with great exactness, others might be totally neglected, or perhaps materially injured by the over-care of a favourite member.[34]

Burke was, of course, contending here against the political theories of the French revolutionaries. As far as he was concerned, the desire to "simplify" government (though not in the sense of streamlining and making more workable) was tantamount to regression and primitivizing. He equated, however, 1789 France with the Romans who in the name of "freedom" had endeavored "to lay low everything which had lifted its head above the level"—in other words, all the organizational complexity and sophistication which had been built up over the ages.[35]

Simplicity, restricting as it does the multifaceted nature of man to a single denominator, must, according to Burke, limit the diversity of

---

34. Burke, *Reflections,* Arlington House, *op. cit.,* pp. 74-5.

35. *Ibid.,* p. 199. Burke was making reference here to the Roman conquests of Greece and Macedonia. He reveals an interesting bias, for the Romans are generally considered by historians to have been the political organizers *par excellence.* But the Greeks were by far more culturally sophisticated and after their capture, even the Romans succumbed to the Hellenization process. This in addition to the fact that the Roman Empire aimed at universalism and the submerging of all national differences motivated Burke, very much in the Greek tradition, to consider that the Greek societies had been "levelled" by the less developed Romans. Marx, too, understood the effects of social leveling: "The thoughts of every individual private property are *at least* directed against any *wealthier* private property, in the form of envy and the desire to reduce everything to a common level; so that this envy and leveling in fact constitute the essence of competition. Crude communism is only the culmination of such envy and leveling-down on the basis of a *preconceived* minimum. How little this abolition of private property represents a genuine appropriation is shown by the abstract negation of the whole world of culture and civilization and the regression to the *unnatural* simplicity of the poor and wantless individual who has not only not surpassed private property but has not yet even attained to it." (Marx, *Economic and Philosophical Manuscripts,* Found in Fromm, *loc. cit.,* p. 125).

activity in a nation. Development is thus impeded, for growth means the burgeoning of potential parts and talents into an interconnected whole. While Marx argued that economic simplicity engendered "unchangeableness," in considering his general thesis that all social activity depends upon the level of economic development, he would probably agree with Burke that simple political structures by their very nature cannot bring out the complex activities of man needed for progress. No opposition of forces can come into operation. Man becomes like the "snail in its shell."

Burke went further than this, however. Simplicity leads to power monopolization, such as Marx had likewise observed in "oriental despotism." As various interests do not appear as balancing forces in the society, so the "quantum of power [which] must exist in the community, in some hands, and under some appellation" becomes concentrated.[36] Regarding France, Burke asserted that should the revolutionary Constitution continue, power would seep into the hands of the oligarchic town burghers.[37] And, said Burke, "here end all the deceitful dreams and visions of the equality and rights of men. In the 'Serbonian bog' of this base oligarchy they are all absorbed, sunk, and lost forever."[38] In his concept of countervailing powers, Burke demonstrated more political insight than Marx. In contemplating the classless society, Marx, though he also anticipated the multi-roled individual, neglected to draw the conclusion that total power, be it social or oligarchic, must in the end suppress individualism. With his emphasis upon power as the prerogative of dominant classes, Marx always envisioned it as *total*. The problem to him was thus to render such power socially responsible, and his nebulous conclusion was to make it total social power through social ownership. But what is society, Burke would question, but various groups? In what specific hands will such total social power be lodged? Marx could not answer this question within the framework of his "utopian" classless society.

36. Burke, *Reflections*, Arlington House, *op. cit.*, p. 156.

37. Long before Marx, then, Burke had understood the French Revolution as a middle class phenomenon. This demonstrates his perceptive analytical abilities since he did not have the benefit of historical hindsight like Marx.

38. Burke, *Reflections*, Arlington House, *op. cit.*, p. 212.

In the end he succumbed to the abstract society as the Enlightenment had succumbed to the abstract individual.[39] The classless—anonymous—society would be the repository of power. The administrative simplicity of the Communist society, however, is, as Burke would claim, its fundamental defect.

What Burke and Marx both feared was that separation or isolation which attends self-sufficiency and anarchism and hinders social cohesion and progress. Marx talked about the independence of the artisan in the guild system as the major factor which prevented his "alienation" from production as well as his exploitation by the merchant. In a different tone Burke alluded to the manner in which the Romans had severed in the Greeks and Macedonians "the bonds of their union, under colour of providing for the independence of their cities."[40] In France Burke considered Paris particularly fortunate in being spared the territorial disjointing proceeding apace in other areas with the redistricting schemes, for it "has a natural and easy connexion of its parts, which will not be affected by any scheme of a geometrical constitution . . . "[41] As to the "other divisions of the kingdom being hackled and torn to pieces and separated from all their habitual means, and even principles of union," Burke believed that they were being reduced to a condition of "weakness, disconnection, and confusion."[42]

It is perhaps through Burke that Marx became particularly conscious of the individualistic tendencies of the peasants and landed

---

39. The scientific in Marx probably held him back from detailed speculations concerning the communist society. As presented in his writings, however, it remains but an abstraction. Yet, ironically enough, Marx was conscious of the fact that "it is above all necessary to avoid postulating 'society' once again as an abstraction confronting the individual. The individual *is* the *social being.*" Marx, *Economic and Philosophical Manuscripts*, found in Fromm, *loc. cit.*, p. 130. But this was merely to assert in Aristotelian fashion the essentially social nature of man. The utopian-like dilemma into which Marx brought himself is well evidenced in *The German Ideology* (see p. 183 of this study) in which he claimed that social ownership allows the individual diversified behavior.

40. Burke, *Reflections*, Arlington House, *op. cit.*, p. 199.

41. *Ibid.*, p. 213.

42. *Ibid.*

aristocracy.[43] Burke described these in some detail and the analysis is worthy of being quoted in its entirety:

> The very nature of a country life, the very nature of landed property, in all the occupations, and all the pleasures they afford, render combination and arrangement (the sole way of providing and exerting influence) in a manner impossible amongst country people. Combine them by all the art you can, and all the industry, they are always dissolving into individuality. Anything in the nature of corporation is almost impractible amongst them. Hope, fear, alarm, jealousy, the ephemerous tale that does its business and dies in a day, all these things which are the reins and spurs by which leaders check or urge the minds of followers, are not easily employed, or hardly at all, amongst scattered people. They assembly, they arm, they act with utmost difficulty, and at the greatest charge. Their effects, if ever they can be commenced, cannot be sustained. They cannot proceed systematically. If the country gentlemen attempt an influence through the mere income of their property, what is it to that of those who have ten times their income to sell, and who can ruin their property by bringing their plunder to meet it at the market? If the landed man wishes to mortgage, he falls the value of his land, and raises the value of assignats. He augments the power of his enemy by the very means he must take to contend with him. The country gentlemen, therefore, the officer by sea and land, the man of liberal views and habits, attached to no profession, will be as completely excluded from the government of his country as if he were legislatively proscribed.[44]

It was these same individualistic qualities in the European peasant that Marx claimed prevented the development of a class consciousness. And he asserted that since they could not represent their own interests, the peasants fell under the direction of executive power. But the peasant to Marx was conservative (even reactionary) in his attempt to preserve whatever meager existence he might have. While some peasants in the throes of becoming members of the proletariat

---

43. Marx never implied such an influence and yet the similarity of approach is quite evident. The description of the landed gentry appears in the *Reflections*, which Marx does not cite in any of his works.

44. *Ibid.*, p. 211.

might become revolutionary, this was generally not the case among the peasants as a group. Burke, talking about the landed gentry and farmers rather than peasants, considered such country gentlemen to be politically liberal because of their education and personal habits. He expressed here that same faith Thomas Jefferson had in the inherently liberal features of the agrarian way-of-life.

Generally speaking, England did not have the same type of peasantry as continental Europe. Feudalism had had a rather different and shorter history in England. Already in the twelfth century the commutation of labor began, whereby a serf could buy his freedom from feudal tenure and obligations. This was, of course, made possible by the early growth of a money economy in England which gnawed away at the basic feudal structure as it had been refined by the Norman conquerors of 1066. With this commutation process occurred the exodus of peasants into the towns as well as the appearance of the small landowning farmer. (This exodus, though never widespread prior to the twelfth century, had, nevertheless, taken place before, since, according to the common law, a serf who ran away from the land and resided undetected in a town for one year and one day was considered a free man. Since the towns, under their own governmental charters, operated independently from the feudal agrarian sections of the country, the escape of the serf was possible.) And those country squires about whom Burke specifically wrote were remnants of the old knightly class who had paid a monetary tribute in order to be quit of their feudal obligations, foremost among which was their attendance at Parliament. Burke was, therefore, faced more with an independent landowner than with a peasant and, the educational and general backgrounds of these two groups differing, it is understandable that he took the view he did regarding the country gentlemen's libertarianism.

Of special pertinence here, however, is Burke's idea that the landed gentry class does not combine easily and, such combinations being required for governmental influence, was virtually excluded from political activity in France. It was for this reason that Burke felt the landed elements of society should be given special protection by government. Sir Lewis Namier, among others, misjudges Burke's attitude toward the aristocracy. Burke, as he himself stated it, did not think of himself as a special friend of the aristocracy and did not uphold government exclusively by aristocrats.[45] His support of the nobility did not arise from unqualified respect. Thus he wrote:

> ... Though hereditary wealth, and the rank which goes with it, are too much idolized by creeping sycophants, and the blind, abject admirers of power, they are too rashly slighted in shallow speculations of the petulant, assuming, short-sighted coxcombs of philosophy. Some decent, regulated preeminence, some preference (not exclusive appropriation) given to birth, is neither unnatural, nor unjust, nor impolitic.[46]

Burke came to the defense of the landed aristocracy out of a cautious political calculation. Remembering that he claimed government should never sacrifice any part to the whole, Burke knew that without special protection the landed interest—vital to society as a whole—would be overwhelmed. Individualism and lack of political acumen made the gentry susceptible to more active political combinations interested in promoting their own interests at any cost:

> Nothing is a due and adequate representation of a state, that does not represent its ability, as well as its property. But as ability is a vigorous and active principle, and as property is sluggish, inert and timid, it can never be safe from the invasions of ability, unless it be out of all proportions predominant in the representation. It must be represented, too, in great masses of accumulation, or it is not rightly protected.[47]

Considering society in terms of its corporate bodies, Burke realized that the landed interest was atomized and "incorporate." Hence government must give it special attention in the form of added representation. Burke would have been very much against the reapportionment decisions (e.g., *Baker v. Carr; Reynolds v. Sims*) handed down by the United States Supreme Court, in which the farming interests lost their "over-representation." The "one man, one vote"

---

45. Burke did not limit "power, authority, and distinction to blood and names and titles." His qualification for government was "virtue and wisdom." But the road from "obscure condition" to "eminence" should not be made "too easy" or be "too much of course," in order to maintain standards. (Burke, *Reflections*, Beaconsfield Edition, *op. cit.*, p. 297).

46. *Ibid.*, p. 299.

47. *Ibid.*, pp. 297-98.

concept by which the urban and rural interests are reduced to arithmetic equality of representation would have seemed to him a most unjust, inequitable and specious policy. Such tallying cannot, according to Burke, take into account the substantive, but only the numerical, properties of an interest. He considered "the trade of a farmer . . . one of the most precarious in its advantages, the most liable to losses, and the least profitable of any that is carried on. It requires ten times more of labor, of vigilance, of attention, of skill and . . . of good fortune also, to carry on the business of a farmer with success, than what belongs to any other trade."[48]

What are the "active elements of ability" of which Burke spoke as a threat to the landed interest? He considered these to be to a large extent the town dwellers:

> It is obvious, that in the towns, all the things which conspire against the country gentleman, combine in favour of the money manager and director. In towns combination is natural. The habits of burghers, their occupations, their diversion, their business, their idleness, continually bring them into mutual contact. Their virtues and their vices are sociable; they are always in garrison; and they come embodied and half-disciplined into the hands of those who mean to form them for civil, or for military action.[49]

Thus equal representation of landed and town interests meant in effect the concentration of power in the urban centers. By their superior numerical strength and their special "sociable" characteristics, the burghers become the monopoly holders of power. It was this "active" quality in the middle class which Marx described in the *Manifesto*: "it has been the first to show what man's activity can bring about" since the capitalist class "cannot exist without constantly revolutionizing the instruments of production, thereby the relations of production, and with them the whole relations of society."[50] Considering that the proletariat was born out of an urban context, to which, according to Marx, the rural centers had been subjected by the

48. Burke, "Thoughts and Details on Scarcity," *loc. cit.*, p. 152.

49. Burke, *Reflections*, Arlington House, *op. cit.*, pp. 211-12.

50. Marx and Engels, "Manifesto of the Communist Party," *Basic Writings, op. cit.*, p. 10.

bourgeoisie, and that it constituted the numerical majority of those in the cities, it was for Marx (as it would have been for Burke) logical to assume that the working class is the most revolutionary, the most active, and the most powerful class in history.

Thus Burke and Marx agree on a basic "contrariety" or "antagonism" of interests in society, namely, the town versus the country. Behind this concept, however, lies an assumption concerning political change which must again be stressed. The individualistically oriented property interest cannot effect changes but is rather the subject of changes brought about by the more agglomerated urban interests. Extrapolating from this basic premise, we might say that in those societies in which self-sufficiency characterizes the major portion of the population, change does not occur as readily as in those which, for one reason or another, assume complex forms of urban organization and thereby establish an interdependent and active society.

Marx thought the transition from the simple to the complex society had to do with the extent to which man, through his tool-making abilities, had mastered the elements of the natural environment.[51] In his description and analysis of village communities in India, Marx observed that these simplistic communities were compact, self-sufficient units and that in each unit "the law that regulates the division of labour in the community acts with the irresistible authority of a law of nature."[52] Even when over-populated communities split, their fission was amoeba-like, each part carrying on the same basic, simple structure. Marx did not question that such simplistic societies change, but he thought that this change was repetitive (in some cases even regressive) rather than developmental. Burke accepted this same idea when he referred to the "preservatives" which kept "ill-constructed" political systems like Crete and the

---

51. In *Capital* Marx wrote in this connection: "Relics of by-gone instruments of labour possess the same importance for the investigation of extinct economic forms of society as do fossil bones for the determination of extinct species of animals. It is not the articles made, but how they are made, and by what instruments, that enables us to distinguish different economic epochs." Marx, *Capital*, Encyclopaedia Britannica, *op. cit.*, p. 86.

52. *Ibid.*, p. 175.

Polish confederation alive.[53] In drawing out Marx's ideas, however, we find that Marx considered dialectical (progressive) change to be very much dependent upon the adaptation of man to his environment. The scarcity or availability of natural resources becomes a key factor in the development of the human tool-maker and his subsequent ability to bring the physical environment under his control. Thus it might be claimed that Marx would consider traditional societies in their perpetuated, unchanging existences to have established an equilibrium with the environment about them. Such societies developed sufficient skills to meet environmental challenges and changes; they were able to provide adequately for themselves so as to survive. But they had not come to the organizational point of *overcoming* or mastering that environment.[54] Since nature remained an awesome force with which man had to contend, traditional societies tended toward naturalistic superstitions which, as Marx outlined, elevated Hanuman, the monkey, and Sabbala, the cow, rather than man, the true sovereign of the universe.

Burke did not enter extensively into the complications of the problem in developmental differences among states, although he would agree with Marx that simplicity and primitivism militate for one reason or another against change.[55] In the *Reflections* Burke noted in passing the irony of human development:

> To hear some men speak of the late monarchy of France, you would imagine that they were talking of Persia bleeding under the ferocious sword of Tachmas Kouli Khan; or at least describing the barbarous anarchic despotism of Turkey, where the finest countries in the most genial climates in the world are wasted by peace

53. Burke, *Reflections*, Arlington House, *op. cit.*, p. 244.

54. Marx was certainly correct in binding together technological production and socio-political change. The case of the so-called "developing states" gives evidence for this. In economic terms "underdevelopment," as the concept has been employed since World War II, refers to low ratios of capital and modern technology to the available supply of labor and other resources. (cf. Calvin B. Hoover, *Economic Systems of the Commonwealth*, Durham, North Carolina: Duke University Press, 1962). It does not necessarily connote, therefore, the lack of natural resources but rather their lack of development by man. There are obviously social and political repercussions attendant on "underdevelopment" as well as on eventual technological advancements. Thus A. F. K. Ostrogorski has written that what is now termed "national development" is characterized by "increasing economic production, by increasing geographic and social mobility, and by increasing political efficiency in mobilizing the

more than any countries have been worried by war; where arts are unknown, where manufactures languish, where science is extinguished, where agriculture decays, where the human race itself melts away and perishes under the eye of the observer.[56]

Burke comes very close here to the Marxist idea that social as well as environmental struggle is the clue to change and civilization building. But what makes one group struggle to build a civilization and another group content itself with existing simply on a day-to-day balance with the natural environment surrounding it? Is the difference between active and passive groups to be explained, as Montesquieu claimed, by the varying climates and other geographic factors? Do material stimuli alone activate the creative spirit of man? If this is so, are some peoples destined never to be awakened to their potential because of their natural environment? If some peoples of the world will not push beyond the shadow of their own primitive existence, should we believe with Burke that "man" is destined to hold no trivial place in the universe or only that some men are so destined, and should we anticipate with Marx the appearance of the fully "humanized" species? The only solution for this dilemma would seem to be mutual aid, the more knowledgeable helping the less knowledgeable and together helping the species move forward socially and morally.

---

human and material resources of the nation for national goals." (A. F. K. Ostrogorski, *The Stages of Political Development*, New York: Alfred A. Knopf, 1965 p. 6).

55. Aristotle has analyzed this problem in the following manner: "But that which is moved by something that, though it is in motion, is moved directly by the unmoved stands in varying relations to the things that it moves, so that the motion that it causes will not be always the same: by reason of the fact that it occupies contrary positions or assumes contrary forms at different times it will produce contrary motions in each several thing that it moves and will cause it to be at one time at rest and at an another time in motion. The foregoing argument, then, has served to clear up the point about which we raised a difficulty at the outset—why is it that instead of all things being either in motion or at rest, or some things being always in motion and the remainder always at rest, there are things that are sometimes in motion and sometimes not? The cause of this is now plain: it is because, while some things are moved by eternal unmoved movement and are therefore always in motion, other things are moved by a movement that in motion and changing, so that they too must change. But the unmoved movement, as has been said, since it remains permanently simple and unvarying and in the same state, will cause motion that is one and simple." Aristotle. *Physics, op. cit.*, p. 346.

56. Burke, *Reflections*, Arlington House, *op. cit.*, p. 141.

But this is not as simple as it sounds. Mutual aid has been abused by the intent of the stronger to oppress the weaker, of the cleverer to confound the naive, and of the discontented to shatter the tranquility of the peaceful. Burke was alert to the complexities of international mutual aid. Although he did not elaborate upon the "internal causes which necessarily affect the fortune of a state," he did consider the external causes which "tend to raise, to depress and sometimes to overwhelm a community."[57] To him England figured as a very important agent in re-establishing France after the Revolution, since France's internal resources had been so severely weakened by the violence. Burke also understood, however, that in the confrontation of national cultures, the "weaker" society can become "demoralized" by the "stronger" and disintegrate out of its own inability to meet the challenge. The force of arms, therefore, is not the only means of conquest. In his own *Abridgement* of English history, Burke showed his extraordinary sensitivity to clashes between cultures when he depicted the attempted Romanization of the indigenous tribes of the British Isles.

The problem of cultural disintegration has been prevalent throughout history. Today we refer to the state of crisis existing in technological societies, particularly those of the West. We mean by this crisis that many of the values associated with the less in-dustrialized state have given or are giving way and have not been replaced as yet by a new set of commonly-accepted values. This void has bred confusion, violence, and general moral degradation. In another vein, Asian and African societies have been undergoing a largely voluntary Westernization process; the social and political élites of Asia and Africa have, at least superficially, adopted the values associated with the technological and mass political culture of Western Europe and the United States. The obverse side of this Westernization process is the subsequent demise of traditional behavior patterns and norms, a fact not patently accepted by the Asian and African masses. Burke knew that culture is the means by which individuals orient themselves to their environment and by

---

57. Burke, "Proposals for Peace with the Regicide Directory," *loc. cit.*, p. 235. Burke in this section wrote that he doubted that history was yet complete enough to understand the internal causes but he was "far from denying the operation of such causes."

which they order and understand their own existence. Where the cultural milieu falls apart—that is, when the cultural participants come to *doubt* the "truth" or validity of their cultural order—the individual can lose his grip on reality and become a listless, purposeless being. Karl Polanyi directed himself to this problem in writing:

> . . . a social calamity is primarily a cultural not an economic phenomenon that can be measured by income figures or population statistics. . . .Not economic exploitation, as often assumed, but the disintegration of the cultural environment of the victim is then the cause of the degradation. The economic process may, naturally, supply the vehicle of the destruction, and almost invariably economic inferiority will make the weaker yield, but the immediate cause of his undoing is not for that reason economic; it lies in the lethal injury to the institutions in which his social existence is embodied. The result is loss of self-respect and standards, whether the unit is a people or a class, whether the process springs from so-called "culture conflict" or from a change in the position of a class within the confines of a society.[58]

Although Marx did not emphasize the nation and its culture in his theoretical analyses, he showed in his correspondence that he was certainly aware of the impact of culture upon the individual and of the differences in culture as such. In a letter of December 7, 1867 Marx wrote to Engels: "Prussia has long ceased to be the country in which any scientific initiative, especially in the political or historical or sociological discipline, would be possible or forthcoming. It represents now the Russian, not the German spirit."[59] Thus Burke and Marx knew that external cultural or economic forces can indeed influence the direction of a state as surely as the internal cultural and economic factors dispose a society toward "co-aptation" and change. While Burke tended to concentrate on the cultural (including the entire political composition of a society) and Marx on the economic factors, together they offer an integrated view of political change.

What is the relationship, however, between change and the opposition of interests? Do all "contrarieties" beget change? To this Burke and Marx answer, "no." It is not enough that interests be

58. Polanyi, *op. cit.*, p. 157.

59. Marx and Engels, *Briefwechsel, op. cit.*, III, p. 546.

active combinations; they must *relate* directly to an opposite interest upon which they are *dependent*. It is this interdependence which creates the focal point, so to speak, of the opposition and against which the activity of the antagonistic interests becomes meaningful. Thus Marx argued that the class antagonisms of the capitalist and the worker revolved around the "cash nexus," the common denominator of the opposition. The significance of the capitalist epoch to Marx was that it had reduced social antagonisms to two primary interdependent classes and hence clarified the opposition itself. Burke stated that the town and country interests met at the market and in the political arena. The interplay of vested interests, therefore, has an inherent order. Interests need each other, contest each other, and change on the basis of their mutual relationship. In this way change can be calculated by the survey of active, related though opposite interests in a society.[60]

But there lay behind their concept of change an apparently fundamental difference. Marx assumed that the antithetical interests would be the progenitors of social change and hence they constituted for him the "wave of the future." Since classes cannot be reconciled (in the sense in which Burke meant it), the "old" must give way to the "new." Marx identified *en bloc* the revolutionary class with "right" since it represents the hitherto oppressed. Since history (or pre-history, as Marx called it) is the successive advance of revolutionary classes, history must be the increasing realization of "right." By stressing class morality rather than individual morality, Marx supplied the ammunition for modern political demagogues to destroy wherever they could a fundamental tenet of Western civilization, that of individual conscience and responsibility. It is this very formula of group morality which has enabled Fascism past and present to speak of racial superiority, contemporary Communism to uphold the party's superiority, and the New Left to sanctify the so-called counter-culture adherents. According to the formula of group morality, one is denied one's moral personality by being born into the wrong group or by maintaining an independent mind. Marx's moral theory is certainly short-sighted, and its practical effects can be devastating. We might

60. With his dialectical perspective, Marx asserted that the duty of the philosopher is no longer merely to interpret the world but to *change* it.

say that his theory was the hasty product of an emotional reaction to the plight of the nineteenth century working class. Marx's analysis of capitalist economics had caused him to resent the fact that the worker was driven to sell his labor as a commodity, that it was not a sense of social responsibility, reflecting his voluntary contributions to society, but rather the coercion of physical need which caused him to produce goods from which he was alienated and for which he was never fully reimbursed. Probably, as Joseph Dunner contends, Marx would have wanted the kind of moral and humanitarian incentives in the economic process as are found today in Israel's *Kibbutzim*.[61] And probably, Marx would not have endorsed the material incentives of wage differentials based upon the qualitative and quantitative differences in economic performance introduced into the Soviet Union with the New Economic Policy and the subsequent five and seven year plans.

It is impossible to compare, however, the few idealistic pioneers of Israel with the masses of urban and rural workers in the Soviet Union. The point to be made is that Marx's theory of economic determinism is incapable of explaining Marx's own confidence in the moral impetus of history. If all men are economically determined, then morality must become little more than the reflex action of prevailing material stimuli. How is this possible? Are slaves necessarily more righteous than their masters? Are the poor and downtrodden without doubt better than the affluent? Are the subjected always entitled eventually to rule? Must the governors always be exploiters and wrong? Marx was not consistent in this identification of class and morality, as Dunner aptly demonstrates:

> If human attitudes and behavior are determined by nothing but social utility in response to economic needs, what justification has Marx to pass a moral judgment on bourgeois society and call its way of life a sham or 'clap-trap'? What justification is there to explain that the proletariat after its allegedly inevitable assent to political power will introduce a higher morality—except the justification which all Machiavellians throughout history have known and idolized—that might is right. . . .What is it that prompted Marx and Engels to express their righteous indignation

61. Joseph Dunner, "Marxism," in *Handbook of World History: Concepts and Issues*, ed. Joseph Dunner (New York: Philosophical Library, 1967), p. 559.

at social conditions which made it impossible for the proletarians to enjoy a decent family life and to look forward to the dawn of a better day? Being themselves members of the bourgeoisie . . . how could Marx and Engels free themselves from the moral cynicism which they ascribed to their own class, unless a person's thought (and will) is a creative reality, unless man's consciousness is not necessarily determined by his class position, unless morality is more than class-bound utility, unless the moral code transcends all specific kinds of social structure, time and space?[62]

Similarly, Sidney Hook in his critique of Marx's insistence on joining moral with economic development asserts that "if the issue was merely one of power or interest, there is no more reason for one class or party in the social conflict to prevail than another, 'right' should be the synonym of 'might' and 'wrong' of 'weakness', a view which no Marxist can consistently hold when he speaks of exploitation of labor or protests against the suppression of human freedom."[63] Marx could not have foreseen that his theory led in the Machiavellian direction, for, as mentioned, previously, his major criticism of Darwin was that his concept of the "struggle for survival" and the "survival of the fittest" when applied to society merely supported the "might" of the bourgeoisie as "right." He himself, therefore, rejected this kind of moral position. But in his theorizing Marx was left without a moral standard by which to judge change. He assumed that victorious interests necessarily bring with them a new level of moral awareness. Thus, without an autonomous moral standard—independent of economics and politics—"we would be hard put to draw the line

---

62. *Ibid.*, pp. 557-58. Marx approached the problem vaguely, as demonstrated in the following quotation, but never seemed to gather the real implications: "The division of labor becomes a real division from the moment there enters a division between material and spiritual labor. From this moment on consciousness can construct itself as something other than only the consciousness of existing reality [*Praxis*] and really represent something without having to represent something *real*—from this moment on consciousness is able to emancipate itself from the world and to proceed to the formation of 'pure' theory, theology, philosophy, ethics, etc." (Marx und Engels, *Die Deutsche Ideologie, op. cit.*, p. 28). Lenin later rationalized the position of the intellectual by claiming that having consciousness of the integrated whole rather than of only a part of the whole as in the "trade union consciousness" of the worker, the intellectual becomes in effect "declassed" and can sympathize with and bring into fruition the historical revolutionary mission of the proletariat.

63. Hook, "The Enlightenment and Marxism," *loc. cit.*, p. 99.

between responsible and irresponsible social action, or distinguish between social sanity and insanity."[64]

Burke, on the other hand, possessed such a standard. He was as willing to prevent the growth of factions anathema to society as he was to support through governmental protection a weaker, vital interest like that of the landed gentry. While Burke believed that civil rights—the political rights of an individual—are historically conditioned and developed, he held firm to the idea that man *qua* man possesses natural rights. "Government," wrote Burke, "is not made in virtue of natural rights, which may and do exist in total independence of it. . . ."[65] Society requires the balancing of these natural rights with the rights of the citizen. Thus Burke sought to make corporate those social forces he considered essential in order to give them thereby the political influence they needed to fulfill their own natural and civil rights. By connecting and protecting such interests through political action, Burke believed that a harmonious society could be created. The mutual advantages afforded in the interdependent society would be great enough to make any interest hesitant to disrupt it. Where this was not the case, the political arm of the state might have to reestablish order for the sake of general liberty. Where such liberty did not exist, however, Burke (like Locke) claimed that government, if it could not be reformed, had no legitimate authority.

Burke was, as mentioned, generally reluctant to interfere politically with the interplay of interests. Pluralism is constructive in the society whose members are joined together by cultural affinity and ties of good faith. He did not assume that a society in which Hobbes' *bellum omnium contra omnes* existed could long prevail. In the *Reflections* Burke emphasized strongly the role of social manners in this respect and lamented the absence of chivalry and other genteel qualities in the Jacobins. Some would interpret this stance as a hearkening back to medievalism. But to Burke social manners represented an important safety catch for protecting the sanctity of the individual. Manners are a form of discipline to stem the coarseness and brutality of the unrestrained individual. Manners are no iron-clad guarantee of inner

64. *Ibid.*, p. 97.

65. Burke, *Reflections*, Arlington House, *op. cit.*, p. 310.

sincerity or civility; behind the most polished mannered appearance can reside the hypocrite. Burke knew that we shall always find shams in life. Not all who profess religion are truly religious. But shall we, therefore, give up religion altogether? And manners are not to be confused with silly etiquette and proprieties, with stuffy gentlemen and haughty women. These are what Burke would call the vanities of men. No, manners are the way in which we treat each other so as to engender mutual respect, trust, and dignity. Where a society is based, therefore, on civilizing manners, Burke felt sure that opposing interests could be brought into cooperation and fair play with minimal governmental regulations.[66]

Marx would have scorned Burke's plea for social manners, not as undesirable, but as impossible in a class society. All such "niceties" of social living were to him so many class prejudices "behind which lurk an ambush."[67] But Marx certainly decried the brutalization of exploited life. He detested the *Lumpenproletariat* or "social scum, that passively rotting mass thrown off by the lowest layers of the old society."[68] He envisioned that with the socialization of the means of production would come a truly social mode of living in which, as Burke would say, no part would be sacrificed for some alleged ideal of the whole. Insofar as individuals become thus truly socialized, they acquire *ipso facto* for Marx social content and, one might add, social "manners."

66. Burke admitted that the line was not clear as to the area restricted to government and that restricted to individual initiative and "manners" or mores. He realized circumstances would dictate the relationship and hence did not fall victim to the error of the nineteenth century *laissez-faire* advocate, as described by Karl Polanyi: "To the typical utilitarian, economic liberalism was a social project which should be put in effect for the greatest happiness of the greatest number; *laissez-faire* was not a method to achieve a thing, it was the thing to be achieved." (Polanyi, *op. cit.*, p. 139).

67. Marx and Engels, "Manifesto of the Communist Party," *Basic Writings, op. cit.*, p. 18. In his "humanistic" tracts Marx wrote about the humanized social individual: "For it is not only the five senses, but also the so-called spiritual senses, the practical senses (desiring, loving, etc.), in brief, human sensibility and the human character of the senses, which can come into being through the existence of *its* object, through humanized nature." (Marx, *Economic and Philosophical Manuscripts*, found in Fromm, *loc. cit.*, p. 134).

68. *Ibid.*,

Although Marx, the scientist, denied morality as an objective standard, in the final analysis, he was personally motivated by a moral conscience in his writings and daily life. It is interesting to see in his correspondence with Engels his sensitivity in this area. Shy about and anguished by the carbuncles with which he suffered, Marx once wrote to Engels that beside the pain there was the "unpleasant moral impression" of the disease.[69] At another point in which he was depressed by family and financial matters, he asserted: "You see into what particular straits the 'civilized' come under given circumstances."[70] While the theoretical differences are evident between Burke and Marx on this issue, in their social analyses they come around to similar moral positions.

In their general moral perspectives Burke and Marx hold that it is the social involvement of individuals which develops their moral potential.

The most revolutionary or socially active class will, according to Marx, engender moral perfection. In a youthful though illuminating passage from his *Notebook*, Burke defined what he meant by morality:

> We have a relation to other Men.
> We want many things compassable only by the help
>   of other beings like ourselves.
> They want things compassable within our Help.
> We love these beings and have a Sympathy with them.
> If we require help, 'tis reasonable that we should
>   give help.
> If we love, 'tis natural to do good to those whom
>   we love.
> Hence one Branch of our Duties to our fellow Creatures
>   is active—hence Benevolence.
> *This is the foundation of Morality.*[71]

These words of Burke resemble those of Marx who wrote that the Communist society will be "an association in which the free develop-

---

69. Marx and Engels, *Briefwechsel, op. cit.*, III, p. 193 (Letter of December 27, 1863).

70. *Ibid.*, p. 141 (Letter of January 8, 1863).

71. Somerset, *op. cit.*, 70.

ment of each is the condition for the free development of all."[72]
Morality then is not the Thoreau-type withdrawal from society; it is
the active relation of mutual help between men—fully socialized
humanity. But how can men become fully socialized save in a society
which creates interdependence between them? It is for this reason that
Burke and Marx emphasized the civilized individual rather than the
primitive innocent. Although they express it in different ways, both
come to the conclusion that it is through the restraining force of
civilization that individual egotism is transmuted into social responsibility. Interdependence establishes the moral necessity—men must
cooperate or perish. Their actions, therefore, go beyond the impulses
of momentary choice. This is what the social ownership of the means
of production means utlimately in Marx, as for Burke it is the
interconnection of interests through the political regulator.

Interdependent interests indicate the order and activity of human
beings. The activity is important as the means of moral expression. In
the complex society the individual is afforded increased opportunities
for personality development. His talents and hobbies become the basis
of his volition rather than social dictates (as Marx thought was part of
a class existence). And the interdependence of this society requires
cooperation among its members. Thus for Burke and Marx the
individual becomes more moral in his relations with others as society
in general becomes more moral in its treatment of the individual.
Volition and necessity are harmonized.

But interdependence also signifies the order in which this dual
activity of man becomes directed. Morality is positive action and
hence demands the "right situation." Full morality cannot be
achieved where exploitation, chaos and aggression take place. It is
therefore necessary to *create* the moral context. As meaningful change
cannot be effected through haphazard actions, so Burke and Marx
argued that history must provide that continuity through which active
social man can progress. This is the "synthesizing" process Marx
assigned to antagonistic classes, while for Burke it was social
prescription.

Far from having an anarchistic view of social change, Marx in his
concept of revolution stressed the preparation for and establishment of

72. Marx and Engels, "Manifesto of the Communist Party," *Basic Writings, op. cit.*, p. 29.

the propitious moment when such revolution could take place. This he expressed clearly in the *Eighteenth Brumaire of Louis Napoleon:*

> Society now seems to have fallen back behind its point of departure; it has in truth first to create for itself the revolutionary point of departure, the situation, the relations, the conditions under which alone modern revolution becomes serious.[73]

In response to the *coup de main* of February 1848 and the *coup de tête* of December 1851 in France, in which "instead of *society* having conquered a new content for itself, it seems that the *state* only returned to its oldest form," Marx muttered, "easy come, easy go."[74] The antagonism between classes must develop to its fullest expression and exaggeration before the rising class is prepared for its historical task. Thus, as Sidney Hook has maintained, "what the Marxists stressed was not the *willingness*, but the ripeness. The readiness was all."[75] Marx's concept of revolution required the *evolution* of the required context.

It was for this reason that Marx decried the Fenian Brotherhood's "exploits." Not only were they premature but in their conspiratorial nature they did not correspond to social reality. With his idea of inevitable change coming out of the proper preparations, Marx considered conspiracy unwarranted. He really pictured the "open" society in the sense that political activity for him was forthright and unequivocal.[76] The conspirator of the Blanqui type, the subverter, was anthema to him as much as was the grandiose myth-maker like Georges Sorel. Thus he built political parties rather than secret underground movements and stated publicly the claims of the Communist organization. And he hailed the capitalist society for the

---

73. Marx and Engels, "Eighteenth Brumaire of Louis Napoleon," *Basic Writings, op. cit.*, p. 323. (Written by Marx alone.)

74. *Ibid.*

75. Hook, "The Enlightenment and Marxism," *loc. cit.*, p. 96.

76. It is interesting to note again Marx's concern for his own political role. In November 27, 1867 he wrote to Engels: "I must be diplomatic with the Fenians. I cannot completely keep quiet, but I do not wish in any respect that these fellows include in a critique of my book that I am a demagogue." Marx und Engels, *Briefwechsel, op. cit.*, III, p. 538.

clarity with which it brought out the relationship between classes.

In preparing the "revolutionary point of departure," Marx was in favor of political reform. While he did not want the working class, for example, to be soothed by such measures, he, nevertheless, considered reform part of the necessary development toward the final "break." This was demonstrated in his attitude toward the factory legislation in England and, as another example, it can be seen in his attitude toward Ireland.[77] In a letter of November 30, 1867 to Engels, Marx outlined the following reforms which he considered important in settling the "Irish question": (1) home rule and independence from England; (2) agrarian revolution. The English cannot make this revolution for them even out of the best intentions but they can give the Irish the legal means by which to make it for themselves; and (3) a protective tariff against England.[78] Marx spoke often of patience in his letters—one must wait and see how events take shape. Of the

---

77. In *Capital* (Part III, Chapter X), Marx discusses the struggle of labor to shorten the number of daily working hours. As Marx saw it, "capital is reckless of the health or length of life of the labourer, unless under compulsion from society." (Marx, *Capital*, Encyclopaedia Britannica, *op. cit.*, p. 130). In tracing the developments leading up the various factory acts in 19th century England, Marx stipulates that the limitation of child and adult working hours was accomplished after a protracted civil (class) war. One of the purposes of Marx's historical sketch of the regulation of the working day is to demonstrate that "The isolated labourer, the labourer as 'free' vendor of his labour power, when capitalist production has once attained a certain stage, succumbs without any power of resistance." (*Ibid.*, p. 145) Urging unified working class action in the political arena, Marx ends this particular section of *Capital* with a summary of the past struggle and a program for the future: "It must be acknowledged that our labourer comes out of the process of production other than he entered. In the market he stood as owner of the commodity 'labour power,' face to face with owners of commodities, dealer against dealer. The contract by which he sold to the capitalist his labour power proved, so to say, in black and white that he disposed of himself freely. The bargain concluded, it is discovered that he was no 'free agent,' that the time for which he is free to sell his labour power is the time for which he is forced to sell it, that in fact the vampire will not lose its hold on him 'so long as there is a muscle, a nerve, a drop of blood to be exploited.' For 'protection' against the 'serpent of their agonies,' the labourers must put their heads together, and, as a class, compel the passing of a law, an all-powerful social barrier that shall prevent the very workers from selling, by voluntary contract with capital, themselves and their families into slavery and death. In place of the pompous catalogue of the 'inalienable rights of man' comes the modest Magna Charta of a legally limited working day, which shall make clear 'when the time which the worker sells is ended and when his own begins.' *Quantum mutatus ab illo!*" (*Ibid.*, p. 146).

78. *Ibid.*, p. 543.

Germans, Marx wrote on November 2, 1867 that "our people over there do not understand how to agitate. In this respect one must do like the Russians—wait. The core of the Russian diplomacy and success is patience."[79] Reform was of primary strategic importance to Marx in facilitating the gestation of eventual revolution.

In the emphasis upon the "readiness" for change, Burke and Marx bear affinity to one another, although each would justify on different grounds the importance of such "readiness." Marx believed historical necessity and ultimate revolution could be coordinated. Burke saw in what we call the "readiness for change" concept a means for the conservation of the social equilibrium.

Sudden change was ludicrous to Burke. He called this "innovation" and in a well-known passage wrote:

> There is a marked distinction between change and reformation. The former alters the substance of the objects themselves, and gets rid of all their essential good as well as of all the accidental evil annexed to them. Change is novelty. . . .Reform is not a change in the substance or in the primary modification of the object, but a direct application of a remedy to the grievance complained of. . . .To innovate is not to reform.[80]

As Marx felt rude eruptions in society could not accomplish anything positive and durable, so Burke wrote to the Earl of Charlemont in 1791 a similar criticism of the over-all effects of the French Revolution: "I did not think that Europe reforming, or more properly, ameliorating itself, upon its antient principles, which more or less it was throughout all the states almost without exception ought to be disturbed with violent convulsions which would precipitate a premature birth of reformation, and consequently render it distempered and short-lived."[81]

Burke thought that evolutionary reform was the only way in which society could chart its historical course with any certainty and

---

79. *Ibid.*, p. 523.

80. Burke, "Letter to a Noble Lord about the Attacks made upon Mr. Burke and His Pension," *loc. cit.*, pp. 186-87. Burke uses the term "change" in a clearly special sense. Strictly speaking, reform involves change, but in Burke's not always consistent usage, change means a radical overhauling, an uprooting of conventional institutions.

81. *The Correspondence of Edmund Burke*, ed. Cobban and Smith, *op. cit.*, p. 330.

accuracy. In its immediate limitations, reform can be cautiously handled. If a specific reform fails, all is not lost; if it succeeds, society is so much the better. But innovation is contrary to this since "whether it is to operate on any one of the effects of reformation at all, or whether it may not contradict the very principles upon which reformation is desired, cannot be certainly known beforehand."[82]

If evolutionary change is to contribute to the moral harmony of society, it must create an integrated balance between interests, according to Burke. The real merit of reform, therefore, is that one can "proceed by degrees" and, if possible, by "insensible degrees."[83] In this way "everything is provided for as it arrives" without the "inconveniences of mutation" although with "all the benefits which may be in change."[84] In this way, too, one prevents the "unfixing of old interests at once: a thing which is apt to breed a black and sullen discontent in those who are at once dispossessed of all their influence and consideration."[85] But such change affects not only old interests but those new rising interests which ride on the crest of change. Since Burke knew that suddenly acquired liberty means power, he was anxious not to modify that power but to discipline it: "This gradual course, on the other side, will prevent men long under depression from being intoxicated with a large draught of new power, which they always abuse with a licentious insolence."[86] He also realized that there is such a thing as the "credibility" of reform, that groups may become discontented and discouraged should the process be too slow. And thus he added an important caveat: "But, wishing as I do, the change to be gradual and cautious, I would, on my first steps lean rather to the side of enlargement than restriction."[87]

---

82. Burke, "Letter to a Noble Lord," *loc. cit.*, p. 186.

83. Burke, "Letter to Sir Hercules Langrische on the Roman Catholics of Ireland," *loc. cit.*, p. 301.

84. *Ibid.*

85. *Ibid.*

86. *Ibid.*

87. *Ibid.*

Thus both Burke and Marx argued that the careful construction of society is the necessary prerequisite for moral man. A Georges Sorel who considered that a new society would emerge out of the aimless destruction of the old or the anarchism of a Bakunin would be anathema to them both. But the question remains as to what Marx meant then by revolution. Was it armed rebellion? In his letter of November 2, 1867 Marx seemed to suggest that agitation in the physical sense might be required. But he did not make a categorical statement on the nature of revolution for he felt that in some states it might come peacefully while in others the wresting of power by the proletariat from the capitalist class would involve violence. Yet in his concept of evolutionary revolution Marx showed his essentially philosophical orientation. Going back to Aristotle's example, while the *telos* of the seed is the tree, the actualization of the seed's potential involves a number of dramatic changes which finally amount to a transformation of the seed itself.[88] The tree's quantitative and qualitative properties are so dissimilar from those of the seed that the tree becomes its own special existence; it is essence realized.

---

88. In his *Physics* Aristotle explores the process of coming-to-be, of potential transformed into the actual. In the natural world many things which come-to-be do so on the basis of what Aristotle calls conditional necessity. Given the proper conditions, the process of development will begin and complete itself. Seeds need the right kind of soil and the right amount of water and sunlight to grow. And things grow in an expected fashion, for we do not anticipate, for example, that wheat will bring forth olives. Like begets like under satisfactory conditions. But what does the process of coming-to-be involve in itself? On the one hand, that which is changing is susceptible, as Aristotle puts it, through and through to the process of change so that "everything that is changing must have completed an infinite number of changes." (Aristotle, *Physics, op. cit.*, p. 320) On the other hand these infinite number of changes necessarily transform the 'what is not' into the 'what is': "In one sense things come-to-be out of that which has no 'being' without qualification: yet in another sense they come-to-be always out of 'what is.' For coming-to-be necessarily implies the pre-existence of something which *potentially* 'is,' but *actually* 'is not'; and this something is spoken of both as 'being' and as 'not being.'" (Aristotle, *On Generation and Corruption, op. cit.*, 413-414. Compare these ideas of Aristotle with those of Marx who wrote: "The working class did not expect miracles from the Commune. They have no ready-made utopias to introduce *par decret du peuple*. They know that in order to work out their own emancipation, and along with it that higher form to which present society is irresistibly tending by its own economic agencies, they will have to pass through long struggles, through a series of historic processes, transforming circumstances and men. They have no ideals to realize but to set free the elements of the new society with which old collapsing bourgeois society itself is pregnant." (Karl Marx, "The Civil War in France," *Basic Writings, op. cit.*, p. 370)

Analogously, Communist man is totally realized human essence, the potential of "pre-historical" man actualized. Revolution is in Marx's view not merely the destruction of old society but its positive transformation. In his concept of *qualified* revolution, Marx bears little in common with the practical revolutionary in the twentieth century who emphasizes the *unqualified, anarchistic* revolution.

And, conversely, it might be arged *vis-à-vis* Burke that gradual reforms can in the long run amount to a revolution in society.[89] We should not identify as revolutionary simply the use of force in changing society. A palace revolt changes the personnel of government forcefully but does not necessarily signify, in fact rarely signifies, revolution. A revolution is a complete or marked change in the socio-political organization and may or may not involve force and bloodshed. In many respects we could say that the concept and practice of government in the United States were revolutionized in the 1930's and 1940's with the policies of the New Deal; there was a radical departure from the previous *laissez-faire* credo. Accumulated governmental reforms can produce a non-violent but nonetheless thoroughgoing revolution in a constitutional state. Unlike Marx, Burke did not advocate revolution. But Burke used the term "revolution" to denote that which rips historical man from all roots which have nurtured him and aided his development. He equated revolution with destruction and anarchism. Burke accepted, in other words, a highly specific definition of revolution. Believing in the possibility of progress, Burke must have foreseen the transformation of man in society. Otherwise, how is it possible to achieve the better, more civilized society unless the barbaric existence is "revolutionized" or completely changed? Burke knew that eighteenth century England represented a tremendous social improvement over the wild and often warring tribal life of pre-Normanic times, an improvement that had entailed various radical changes in the social organization and political structure of England. Being a Whig, Burke was committed to

89. Under the heading, "Causes of Revolution," in the *Politics*, Aristotle writes that "a great change of the whole system of institutions may come about unperceived if small changes are overlooked. In Ambracia, for example, the property qualification for office—small to begin with—was finally allowed to disappear under the idea that there was little or no difference between having a small qualification and having none at all." Aristotle. *The Politics*. trans. Ernest Barker (Oxford: Clarendon Press, 1946), p. 210.

the principle of parliamentary sovereignty, certainly a marked
change from monarchical sovereignty. He hailed the 1688 Revolution because it brought about the supreme Parliament and constitutional monarchy.[90] While he attempted to justify the crowning of
William and Mary as still within acceptable historical principles,
Burke undoubtedly realized that this so-called bloodless revolution
had set the stage for a dramatic change in the relationship between
Crown and Parliament, a change which was to move England into its
democratic period. The point to be made here is that Burke put a
premium on society's *evolving*, that is, changing under the Rule of Law
toward a better, more humane society. He knew that a society which
does not change must stagnate and decay. Certainly a reformist,
Burke, nevertheless anticipated that in time man, destined to hold "no
trivial place in the universe," would lift himself, if he so chose, out of
the quagmire of the uncivilized. In order for society to attain higher
levels of civilization, Burke fervently believed that the new must
accomodate the *worthwhile* elements of the old. In *general* terms it
cannot be said that Burke had no vision of a revolutionized society; in
his view history *should* be the *gradual transformation* of man. The
Aristotelian sensitivity for the process of and conditions for
developmental change is to be found in Burke and Marx. Marx's
concept of class struggle gives his historical view an abruptness and
radicalism not to be found in Burke's outlook. Yet each believed that
through time and change, man, the "political animal," to use
Aristotle's phrase, can develop his sociability. In the end this
socialization process should create humanity, the realized moral
potential of the political animal.

90. With regard to the Revolution of 1688 Burke wrote: "The ceremony of cashiering kings, of
which these gentlemen sympathizers with the French Revolution talk so much at their
ease, can rarely, if ever, be performed without force. It then becomes a case of war, and not
of constitution. Laws are commanded to hold their tongues against arms; and tribunals fall
to the ground with the peace they are no longer able to uphold. The Revolution of 1688 was
obtained by a just war, in the only case in which any war, and much more a civil war, can be
just. 'Justa bella quibus *necessaria*.' The question of dethroning, or, if these gentlemen like the
phrase better, 'cashiering kings,' will always be, as it has always been, an extraordinary
question of state, and wholly out of the law; a question (like all other questions of state) of
dispositions, and of means, and of probable consequences, rather than of positive rights."
Burke, *Reflections*, Arlington House, *op. cit.*, p. 42.

Conclusion

Edmund Burke and Karl Marx lived in very different times and this fact is clearly reflected in their writings and general social theories. Burke in the eighteenth century had not experienced many of the features and paraphernalia associated with the modern state today—industrialism, political parties as massively organized vote-getting machines, universal suffrage, large-scale bureaucratic government. Marx, coming in the nineteenth century when many of these features were developing, nevertheless did not encounter the increasing democratization process in Western states, particularly the growth of the working class into a significant countervailing power in democracies, the technological revolution and the emergence of the specialized "technocrats." Burke and Marx, therefore, were unaware of many of the organizational features which are a part of the contemporary age.

And yet, despite this, there has been a growing interest among political activists and academicians in the social theories of this eighteenth century Irishman and nineteenth century German. This interest goes beyond historical curiosity—beyond nostalgia or intellectual reconstructionism aimed at discovering how Burke or Marx analyzed the specific issues of their day. There has instead been a deliberate attempt of diverse individuals and groups to apply the principles of either Burke or Marx to the specific issues of today. The assumption can be made, therefore, that Burke and Marx are in some way relevant to contemporary politics. If this is so, do these two "philosopher-politicians," considered the political antagonists *par excellence* in the sense of their approaches to politics, bear some similarity to each other? These questions motivated the present study, whose purpose it was to relate the political philosophies of Burke and Marx to the major characteristics and concerns of contemporary politics and in so doing to compare the essential concepts in the two sets of philosophies themselves.

Such a study had its initial difficulties. The stereotypes which have been drawn to characterize and epitomize each are well established. Thus much of the literature on Burke and Marx has tended merely to give weight to these caricatures, be they negative or positive ones. This has been particularly the case because Burke and Marx are remembered chiefly as controversial political figures. Burke and Marx are in a sense very special types of political philosophers; they were also politicians and hence entered into the thicket of political ideological battles. They represent ideological *standpoints* and thus menace their political opponents in ways which other philosophers have not. To write about Burke or Marx is, therefore, considered to be the equivalent of showing sympathy with or to attacking the one or the other, but only rarely considered as a nonpartisan analysis. And no comprehensive attempt has been made to study them together.

The *clichés* are well known. Burke is a member of the Old Whig faction and the person who more than anyone else established the principles of conservative politics. The nation, the embodiment of all that is right, must be preserved in its historical framework. Thus change should be evolutionary—cautious and sparing. Likewise, the national solidarity must not be disrupted by individualism and democratic procedure. Rather a national parliament should consist of those landed gentry who virtually represent the interests of the nonfranchised. Aristocratic paternalism is just, because society—like nature—moves in a hierarchical order in which the lowliest classes are guided, albeit assumedly for their benefit, by the upper-class "philosopher-kings." More often than not Burke has been represented as a historical romantic and the stubborn opponent of change.

By contrast, Marx has been depicted as that revolutionary determined to destroy middle class society and its capitalist base with the coming proletarian revolution. Since history is "determined" by the economic modes of production, the individual is but the reflection of his class interests which are nothing in turn but the transitory elements in the dialectical struggle toward the classless, egalitarian society of tomorrow. This being so, all political institutions become the tools of the dominant class in its role as general social oppressor and manipulator. Reform, therefore, becomes meaningless in ameliorating the lot of the downtrodden, since the classes of society remain irreconcilable historical combatants. The only solution lies in revolution and the final destruction of class existence.

These stereotypes (like most stereotypes) have not been based just on wishful thinking or sheer illusion, for they derive to some degree from the very texts and language of Burke and Marx. They did have different viewpoints concerning classes. And Burke did contest democracy, particularly the French revolutionary variant, while Marx in the *Communist Manifesto* hailed the proletarian revolution as the final expression of true democracy.

Yet philosophical differences can not be derived from semantics alone. Too little attention has been given to in-depth analyses of language in the categorizing of political philosophers into one tradition or the other. Language has its own historical content, developing with the dispositions and preoccupations of the people who use it. Thus a superficial survey of the language of Burke and Marx would seem to verify their antagonistic approaches to political life. A side endeavor of the present study has been to suggest through example that at least some of the categories by which political philosophers are agglomerated together into various "traditions" within Western civilization would seem to be inadequate either in clarifying the separate philosophies themselves or in piercing the essential philosophical commitments of Western man. The question is whether the *differences* between Burke and Marx, between Plato and Aristotle, between Hobbes and Locke, to select only three pairs of assumed "opposites," are more important than their similarities. Indeed do these very similarities, which in the end identify the Western tradition, become obscured and forgotten in the quest for oppositions?

This study had to probe beyond linguistic surfaces in order to answer the questions previously outlined as its major objective. What were Burke and Marx trying to say that perhaps is still being said today? Where is their connection to contemporary politics? Perhaps the greatest difficulty, therefore, was to cut through the stereotypes and into the substance of dynamic thought. A new organizational perspective was required for this. Rather than examining Burke and Marx on the basis of their own internal logic alone, it was necessary to conceptualize the major characteristics of contemporary politics and to apply the conceptual frameworks of Burke and Marx respectively to these characteristics. What, in other words, do the issues of today demand of political theory and thus of the theories of Burke and Marx? This is a different procedure from asking in what ways Burke and Marx would address themselves to contemporary issues. The former provides a method of analysis; the latter remains but historical guesswork.

Proceeding then from this perspective, three major features were outlined as defining generally the content of contemporary politics. Firstly, there is the scientific orientation of the present age. We are living in the midst of a technological revolution whose impact has been to channel the modern mind into less speculative and more "scientific" considerations. Politics has not been immune to this. With the increasing social responsibilities in such a technological era, legislators, judges, and executives must make decisions based upon highly technical knowledge. And this in turn means that politics *per se* must come to grips with the social confusion engendered by the machine's substitution in many cases for the individual in the working, functional operations of modern society. Social cohesion has suffered in the lessening of traditional bonds and systems of belief within the "scientificized" society.

But the disruptions of war as well as the establishment of many new states since the 1950's have also been sources of strain upon social integration. New states (often the anomalous end products of territorial units haphazardly carved out by former colonial imperialists) have tried to build up "nations" among the diverse populations within their borders as old states have sought to recover from the ravages of war. Above and beyond the outlook of the single state has been the notable striving toward regional organizations, such as the European Economic Community and the world association in the United Nations. All these efforts have been predicated upon the belief that neither national nor international atomism can facilitate harmonious and peaceful social existence.

And yet the factor of change often seems to militate against the attainment of social cohesion. The technological world in which man has encased himself seems to proceed faster in its growing complexity and sophistication than the social forces needed to control it can cement themselves. Revolution and *coup d' état* have been frequent resorts of those who tire of allegedly antiquated regimes and social structures. And "generation gaps" bring into focus the astonishing pace with which society not only renews but transforms and differentiates itself. Change is certainly in the "nature" of contemporary life and the problem remains, particularly under the pending threat of nuclear annihilation, whether or not today's society can come to that level in political skill and moral insight required to meet the challenges of rapid change. Scientific orientations, problems of social integration and the challenge of revolutionary change characterize the contemporary age. Are the ideas of both Burke and Marx relevant to these contemporary emphases and problems?

Science is based upon the belief that knowledge about the "real" world is possible. The external environment is not just a perception, as George Berkeley would say, but a concrete, understandable, objective reality. Burke and Marx both believed wholeheartedly in an independent material world. They emphasized an empirical approach as the means to all knowledge. Man through his sense perception and mental reflection can "experience" and come to know the world about him. Hence they considered experiencing man to be both *responsive* to that reality and *responsible* in his understanding of it. But such knowledge is possible not only because man interacts with and hence absorbs his experience of the external environment but because the universe itself is meaningful. There is an order which renders all activity in the universe "sequential" or "logical" rather than chaotic. "When the objects of an inquiry, in any department," Aristotle wrote in the *Physics*, "have principles, conditions, or elements, it is through acquaintance with these that knowledge, that is to say scientific knowledge is attained."[1] Insofar as Burke and Marx, each in his own way, tried to comprehend the conditions and principles of socio-political life, they were scientific in the Aristotelian sense. In applying their empirical approaches to society, Burke and Marx claimed that it is the order and activity of society which permits progressive historical change. Since society is organization, it imposes regulations upon the activities of its component groups. But, more importantly, as a developmental phenomenon, society is itself conditioned by historical forces. Therefore, all scientific knowledge concerning social relations must entail the results not only of empirical observations but the integrated perspective of broad historical developments and trends. In this way the social scientist comes to understand the social "principles of operation."

In this connection Burke and Marx urged a political approach geared to social realities. How can political action, they asked, have any social relevance if the ideas behind it are but speculation or even illusion? If politics is to be creative, that is, promote social development, it must direct itself toward actual social circumstances and groups. Marx argued that this was necessarily the case since all social institutions become the instruments of control for the dominant class. Hence the "politics of reality" was to him the attempt of the dominant economic class to further its own interests. But with his optimism concerning the historical process, Marx claimed that each historical epoch gives way to a higher level of "reality" until the proletariat through revolution accomplishes its mission of social justice and harmony. Burke was less convinced than Marx that history would progress, although he very much believed it could, since he did not tie the social development to technological changes. Politics, according to Burke, had to be rooted in a social perspective through historical prescription and the corporate representation of vital economic

---

1. Aristotle. *Physics. op. cit.*, p. 259. Aristotle saw the overall task of the scientist as explanatory rather than purely descriptive: "We must explain the 'why' in all the senses of the term, namely, (1) that from this that will necessarily result ('from this' either without qualification or in most cases); (2) that 'this must be so if that is to be so' (as the conclusion presupposes the premises); (3) that this was the essence of the thing; and (4) because it is better thus (not without qualification, but with reference to the essential nature in each case). *Ibid.*, p. 275.

interests in the legislature. It had to assume the role of a social "regulator" in harmonizing all the divergent interests into a social policy in which "no part would be sacrificed for the ideal of the whole." Assigning to politics "highest reason," Burke assumed that correct political action could be creative and protect and foster the harmonious growth of society at large.

But such harmony to Burke and Marx is possible only in complex societies. They did not idolize the "natural" man or primitive innocent. The interdependence of individuals in the complex society makes individuals more aware of the moral imperative; men must acquire social habits and cooperate if they are to survive. But it is only in the complex society, too, that the individual can develop his full personality through diverse functions and activities. In this sense society, potentially at least, offers the individual full opportunity for development and hence becomes "moral" in its treatment of the human being. And by establishing the necessary interdependence of men, it demands and requires the active moral expression of individuals to each other. Society and the individual are reconciled.

Only through change are complex societies produced. Burke and Marx, therefore, considered change vital, a moral necessity. But any kind of change? To this they both responded negatively. Change must grow up out of prepared social situations. The creativity of politics depends upon the direction of change into socially beneficial channels. Thus Marx did not condone destructive anarchism as the proper means by which to spark the proletarian revolution. History rather must be staged and correctly acted out before the "determined" consequences can follow. Similarly, Burke in his concept of evolution argued that social development must be treated artistically. There must be the conception of the objective, the right materials and the blending of all parts. And in depicting a progressive society, Burke, like Marx, assumed that "socialized" man would be in effect the realization of human "essence."

Burke and Marx do fulfill the requirements for contemporary political thought. But what do we really *learn* from them? To begin with each offers an instructive concept of man. Man is not an atom as the proponents of orthodox liberalism conceived of him. Neither Burke nor Marx substantially altered Aristotle's idea that social life is the medium in which man in relationship with his fellow-men fulfills his own nature. Against the basic assumption of Adam Smith that the juxtaposition of free, rational individuals within the framework of minimal legal rules and restraints not only preserves individualism but also—though unintentionally—fosters social harmony, Burke and Marx established man as a variable in an interactive social context. Certainly the liberal model of man as a self-sufficient entity might be appreciated as the reaction of the rising and potentially wealthy English and French bourgeoisies to feudalism with its prescriptive stratification and accompanying class rights and obligations. But the consequent liberal concept of society as a sort of burdensome limitation to human individualism lent itself from the beginning to Social Darwinism, the glorification of individual isolationism and the concomitant apathy toward the weak and poor in society.

Although Marx preferred to explain moral sentiments as mere subjective by-products of an objectively amoral historical development, although he based his prediction of proletarian revolution on the inefficiency of outmoded capitalist conditions of production, distribution, and consumption, rather than on moral indignation, there can be little doubt that it was the contact with the social debris of *laissez-faire* which motivated his search for a more just, ideal society. But however significant his analysis of the *laissez-faire* period is, it must be stated that he had the advantage of an eye witness. Burke, by contrast, must be credited with having anticipated the long-run social outcome of the orthodox liberalism of the Enlightenment. Confronted with such liberalism in France, his critical analysis went far beyond the disposition and perspectives of the Restoration following Napoleon's defeat. John MacCunn is correct in saying that ". . . though Burke's words are often those of the eighteenth century, his thought is that of the nineteenth."[2] Like Marx and John Dewey later on, Burke recognized a fundamental defect in orthodox liberalism, namely, its "lack of perception of historical relativity," to use Dewey's phrase.[3] Changing times and circumstances, Burke argued, require new or adjusted propositions and solutions.

2. John MacCunn, *The Political Philosophy of Edmund Burke* (London: Edward Arnold, 1912), p. 58.

3. John Dewey, "The Future of Liberalism," *Journal of Philosophy*, XXXII (April 25, 1935), p. 226.

In addition to imparting a social perspective based on history, Burke and Marx notably stand forth as normative thinkers. While Burke had a clear commitment to a moral standard, Marx shunned in his official theories any operative moral standard. And yet Marx's writings cannot be read without the reader's being aware that Marx was writing his judgments of things he studied and observed as well as describing and inter-relating his data. The problem in Marx's evaluation of an historical process he considered "determined" has been discussed earlier. In summary the paradox is that while he believed there was a determined historical process, he also felt he could censure history and participate in its improvement. The so-called "humanist" Marx is without question a Marx concerned with normative issues and a Marx having a certain moral vision for the future. After Bernstein's revision of Marx's ideas and predictions and after much of the economic and dialectic theories of Marx has been demonstrated false by events in the Western democratic states (e.g., the increasing affluence of the working class rather than its pauperization) and in present-day Communist states (e.g., the presence of a "new class," as Djilas demonstrates), it is Marx's emphasis upon an egalitarian society free of alienation which continues to be a moral inspiration for Marxists and of interest even to non-Marxists. Marx denounced all organized religion, and so we obviously cannot derive his normative concepts from a specific religious doctrine. But even Burke, a member of the Anglican Church, did not address himself to theological specifics of the Church or appear to attempt to fit socio-political events into a doctrinal religious interpretation. The normative position of each seems to be more generally the product of Western civilization, of which they were so much a part. According to this tradition (in its Aristotelian, Judaic and Christian strains), man is by virtue of his rational capacity "sovereign" in the universe, to use Marx's phrase. Conditioned by time and circumstances, man can nevertheless improve himself and his existence. Were the individual but a repetitively acting creature, were he "unconscious," moral perspectives would be meaningless. One cannot judge the actions of the instinctual where no alternative action lies within the capacity of its nature. But the individual has the opportunity for choice and action upon that choice. Having this free will, the individual also has the responsibility for the consequences of his choice. And, importantly, man as a species has a historical memory which permits learning from the past and building upon the past. Civilization—and not just individual existentialism—is a distinctly human possibility.

As philosopher-politicians, Burke and Marx believed that knowledge of social man is instrumental in the civilizing process; by attempting to comprehend the *raison d'être* of social existence, we clarify the choices before us and we are able to act with assurance. Marx felt sure that his understanding of dialectical development toward the good life, Communism, had crystallized the position of the working class in capitalist society and had mandated the mobilization of this class in preparation for its historical moment, the revolution of the last class-ridden society. And Burke, claiming that circumstances, though variable, do not invalidate certain "basic principles" in human existence, was as equally convinced that on the basis of these principles he could perceive the inner momentum and direction of socio-political events and, as a parliamentarian, could fashion "correct" public policy. With their respective teleological concepts of history, Burke and Marx saw their responsibilities as being the acquisition of historical and empirical knowledge in order to understand the social conditions they confronted and to map out policies which would be relevant to the historical make-up and purpose of the society. Knowledge for them had an essentially practical purpose. This is the reason each denounced so vehemently the "metaphysicians" and "utopians" of his time as individuals who assumed that ideas grounded only in the imagination could be used as references for constructive social action. Burke and Marx took the development of the societies around them extremely seriously; they wanted to understand them and help direct them.

This posture sets Burke and Marx at sharp variance with modern empiricism in the social sciences, represented by the so-called "behavioralists." David Easton has differentiated the "behavioralists" from all those traditional political thinkers who accepted as their responsibility the "analysis of the moral rather than strictly empirical world" and claimed that the "quest for an understanding of the nature of the good life" created a "limiting image" of political theory which is being changed by the empirical theorists:

> In the last decade, however, for the first time this limiting image
> has begun to change decisively and there can be little doubt,

permanently. It now becomes possible for theory to escape the shackles imposed by so narrow a perspective and to broaden its scope to include a serious and systematic concern for descriptive theory. To the extent that theory takes advantage of this opportunity it holds out the promise of sharing the study of political life much more intimately with the rest of political science and of measuring up to the expectations always inherent in the very idea of theoretical research itself.[4]

Mulford Q. Sibley—not without criticism—puts the stated scientific objectives of the "behavioralists" into focus:

> . . . Once we descend to the formulation of scientific hypotheses, the process of verification, it would appear, can in principle proceed without the value judgments coloring the observation. This is not to deny, of course, that the bias of the observer may affect the verification procedure. It is, however, to assert that methods exist in political as well as a natural science investigation to minimize the danger of such bias. Within the wholes, that is to say, whose comprehension in part transcends the scientific process, the parts can be investigated with relative objectivity. He [the behavioralist] will explain *how*, under carefully given and controlled circumstances and conditions, men have in fact acted. He will also be able to suggest how, under previously formulated conditions and circumstances they *would* probably behave in the future, and he will provide us with statements of limits beyond which, under specified controlled environments, they would probably *not* act.[5]

Because Burke and Marx did not seek "objectivity" in the sense of "non-involvement" (although they earnestly sought the "truth" in what they observed), modern "behavioralists" would probably consider them but speculative thinkers of the traditional sort. Regarding the Marxist approach, Sibley writes that "the user of dialectics locates the meaning of his categories in logical relationships of his system and his 'discoveries' can therefore not be empirical."[6] It must be questioned whether the attempt of "behavioralists" to construct

4. David Easton, *A Systems Analysis of Political Life* (New York: John Wiley and Sons, 1965), p. 5.

5. Mulford Q. Sibley, "The Limits of Behavioralism," in *The Limits of Behavioralism, op. cit.*, p. 81.

6. *Ibid.*, p. 72.

theoretical social science does not also involve the establishment of logical categories. How are we to comprehend without such categories? Can they not pertain to the "real" world as Burke and Marx assumed? Burke has not generally been considered systematic or empirical enough to warrant the appellation "scientist," even though he concerned himself all his life with scientific endeavors and forever advocated an empirically based political approach. But this fact has gone largely unnoticed. Burke and Marx would have been shocked had they been called "speculative" thinkers. They were devoted students of history and thought they had in effect made a science of *Homo historicus*.

But how can one reconcile their "science" with their normative approaches? This is a question which a behavioralist would ask, and the basic assumption behind such a question is, of course, that there exists an opposition of forces between science and normativism. According to the behavioralists, one cannot have expressed values and still be scientific because values are *relative* to individuals and groups while science entails statements of allegedly proved universal "facts." Burke and Marx were only too aware of the relativity of norms and human behavior, such relativity being one of the conditions for historical progress. But they also recognized that there are forces of order in the historical process which permit our understanding of the world around us and of our place in history. These elements of order make possible what we call science.

The behavioralist would, however, stress that the scientific endeavor to describe the order or pattern of human behavior does not require the scientist's evaluation of the behavior being analyzed; in fact scientists should not evaluate their findings. While it is proper, for example, for a social scientist to describe the machinery of a political campaign and the various blocs of voters producing the elected official, it is improper for him to assess whether the election was a good one or a bad one on the basis of his own moral judgment. It is equally improper for the social scientist to indulge in any declarative "should" or "ought to" statements—e.g., "the government should follow such a policy" or "there ought to be in society this kind of reform." Statements involving "should" or "ought to" are typical of normative approaches, and the behavioralist wants to confine himself to "what is."

If a social scientist does not want to get involved in normative assessments, that is his right. But to insist that all social scientists if they are to be scientists must never raise normative questions or posit normative conclusions is a restriction fraught with serious problems. In accordance with the idea of "value-free' science, behavioralists must withdraw themselves from the substance of socio-political issues. They can state how the issues came about and perhaps how persons participating in them will behave, but they cannot—on the basis of their own set limitations—participate in the *solution* of issues. Nor can they establish value priorities as guides for action. Since the existence of values "can neither be proved nor disproved by the methods characteristic of behavioral investigation," the behavioral method is, therefore, "powerless to provide us the values upon which those choices depend.'" Stopping short of a value involvement in issues, behavioralists reduce their position as social scientists to one of data collectors and describers and efficiency experts (e.g., under what conditions can policy x be effected?"). Without a moral commitment on the part of the social scientist, the conclusions to be drawn from behavioral studies must be left entirely to the social engineers and politicians. Each in his own way, Burke and Marx declined to leave decisions to others; they stated preferred actions in their personal involvement in political issues. In fact it is questionable whether we can ever be as human beings totally objective and "value-free' and whether, even if we attempt such objectivity, we can truly understand social phenomena which we do not also judge or evaluate. Leo Strauss, in his *What is Political Philosophy?*, has demonstrated succinctly the vital connection between social science and value judgments by showing the absurd position into which "value-free" social science falls:

> It is impossible to study social phenomena, i.e., all important social phenomena, without making value judgments. A man who sees no reason for not despising people whose horizon is limited to their consumption of food and their digestion may be a tolerable econometrist; he cannot say anything relevant about the character of human society. A man who refuses to distinguish between great statesmen, mediocrities, and insane imposters may be a good

7. *Ibid.*, p. 83 and p. 82.

biographer; he cannot say anything relevant about politics and political history. A man who cannot distinguish between a profound religious thought and a languishing superstition may be a good statistician; he cannot say anything relevant about the sociology of religion. Generally speaking, it is impossible to understand thought or action or work without evaluating it. If we are unable to evaluate adequately, as we very frequently are, we have not yet succeeded in understanding adequately. The value judgments which are forbidden to enter through the front door of political science, sociology and economics, enter these disciplines through the back door; they come from that annex of present-day social science which is called psychopathology. Social scientists see themselves compelled to speak of unbalanced, neurotic, malad-justed people. But these value judgments are distinguished from those used by the great historians, not by a greater clarity or certainty, but merely by their poverty: a slick operator is as well adjusted as, he may be better adjusted than, a good man or a good citizen.[8]

Burke and Marx were too involved in the social issues of their time to assume that analysis precluded evaluation. Concerning social science, knowledge to them meant not only understanding physical man but perceiving the manner by which he works toward his own "inner" fulfillment. They appreciated the fullness of life, that it is more than revealed by statistics and attitudes. It is a historical struggle toward all that can be considered truly profound in man's creative, moral nature. Burke and Marx thus offer contemporary social science a less mechanistic and more dynamic approach to the human being in society. They demonstrate that political science and political philosophy are necessary partners in the building of *Homo historicus*.

The differences between Burke and Marx are real, and yet we can see that they shared many outlooks and orientations. Their differences have spawned the ideological splits we witness still today between those supporting constitutional evolution and those favoring class revolution. Their similarities have been obscured in the ideological arena, but these similarities suggest that there is at least some basis for mutual understanding between the two groups and the possibility of dialogue. Ideologists, unfortunately, are usually immune to discussion; this immunity is part of the function of their rigid, even

8. Leo Strauss, *What Is Political Philosophy?* (Illinois: The Free Press of Glencoe, 1959), p. 21.

petrified, outlook. Marx always claimed he abhored ideology ("I am not a Marxist," he said) for ideology implied to him a fixed system of ideas removed from social realities. Burke was the very opposite of an ideologist; he was open-minded but principled. It would be interesting to see how these two thinkers would have reacted to each other had they been able to have a personal encounter in the twentieth century and had been given the opportunity to redefine their terms in language understandable to both. Such an encounter might have smoothed out some areas of apparent discrepancy, but, more importantly, they could have perhaps learned from each other. Marx might have come to realize that Burke was not the "out and out vulgar bourgeois" he thought, eager to entrench existing property relations for the rural gentry. Marx, predicting the ultimate realization of Hegels "Divine Idea" on human egalitarianism (classlessness), the complete merger of all individual interests with those of society as a whole, could have learned from Burke the more sophisticated understanding that a harmonious arrangement of divergent individuals and classes can be accomplished in society through political skill.

Burke, on the other hand, who in his time could not have forseen the negative aspects of the industrial revolution and the exploitation of the working class in what Marx called *Fruehkapitalismus,* might, on the basis of Marx's insights, have become considerably less willing to endorse *laissez-faire* as a policy. His very concern for the nation as the embodiment of culture would have probably led him in the political direction of Benjamin Disraeli who, for the preservation of the nation and to avoid its division into "two nations" (property-owning entrepreneurs and propertyless workers), became an advocate of governmental intervention and government-sponsored labor legislation. As shown throughout this study, Burke had no predilection for inherited titles and wealth *per se* but rather always connected social privilege with social responsibility. He would have abhorred the alienation of the propertyless masses from the state, making the state thereby indeed the instrumentality of the possessing ruling class. But rather than inciting the workers into class war and thus estranging them further from the nation, Burke most likely would have offered efforts for social reform not unlike the Fabians.

Burke could have also contributed to Marx's historical viewpoint. Rather than assuming that social progress would follow

axiomatically from technological advances, Burke was more sensitive
to those factors which cause civilizations to decay and die. Considering man a rational creature capable of willful action, he knew
only too well that such reason, when it escapes into fantasy or when it
does not operate upon principled considerations, can engender
chaotic and destructive social actions. Civilization is a necessity for
moral man but, claimed Burke, not a requirement built into historical
conditions.

Burke, however, was certainly not averse to technological growth.
Rooted as he was in an essentially agrarian way-of-life, he
nevertheless prided himself on the application of scientific.knowledge
to his farming enterprises. But he could not foresee that technology
would create the possibilities for social affluence. For this reason he
did not envision that the laboring masses in all walks of life could be
raised substantially in their economic level. Land, his economic unit,
though it be parcelled out equally, could not provide enough for all to
make a decent living. Thus he argued in his *Thoughts and Details on
Scarcity* that it is useless to plunder the rich and divide the spoils. But
Marx, witnessing large-scale industrialization, saw the over-
production of goods under capitalist property relations and could be
more optimistic about the possibility of the individual gaining the
necessary economic security and leisure to develop his own personality in the industrialized Communist society. And he could see that
such over-production changed the meaning of property from land to
other means of production. Burke could have been shown the
possibility of redistributing wealth in society and thus probably would
have become himself more optimistic concerning the ability of society
to provide a more equalized affluence among all its members.[9]

These thoughts do not detract from the genuine similarities in
Burke and Marx. The interest shown in these men in the twentieth

---

9. It is important to demonstrate that Burke was well aware of and even bitter about the
problem of distribution. He wrote in the *Reformer* about the plight of the cottier: "Gentlemen
perceiving that in *England* Farmers pay heavy Rent, and yet live comfortably, without
considering the Disproportion of Markets and, every thing else, raise their Rent high, and
extort it heavily. Thus none will hold from them but those desperate Creatures who ruin
their land (in vain) to make their Rent; they fly; the Landlord seizes, and to avoid the like
Mischance, takes all into his own hands; which being unable to manage, he turns to
grazing; thus one part of the Nation is starved, and the other deserted." (Burke, *The*

century is not the sign of political indiscrimination. In their historical-empirical method, in their emphasis upon a "politics of reality" and their insistence upon directed, meaningful change, Burke and Marx offer important ideas for contemporary politics. At a time when ideas are strung together into ideological chains, we are cautioned by Burke and Marx to be responsive to changing realities. At a time when violence has been legitimized as a tool of social change by its users, Burke and Marx remind us that irrational political action never accomplishes anything good or permanent in history. At a time when anarchism flowers in the minds of many, Burke and Marx warn us that we are by nature social animals. If we defy that nature, we can only lose in the end our moral identity. And at a time when many despair over our seeming inability to control our technogical environment, Burke and Marx encourage us to remember that it is the problems of social existence which in their challenge sharpen our reason and in their necessary solution refine our awareness of each other. If we are to progress and civilize ourselves further, certainly no mean task but an exhilarating one, we must reflect upon our past, confront our present and envision our future. And with all this we must then get down to work and to creation. Our very ability to create, however, depends upon our willingness to learn from the generation before us. Otherwise, like a whirlwind in a desert, we shall destroy all the footsteps and the outposts before us and the hints of who we are and where we are going.

Reformer, loc. cit. 10 March 1747-48 , p. 316). Sounding very much like Marx, Burke wrote in this same passage that the laborers are the lowest and most numerous class (he was referring to those agrarian laborers having one acre of land) and are forced to work for a "master" most of the year. "Then judge," said Burke, "what Time they have to procure Cloaths and other Necessaries for themselves and their Families; Thus they must labour and that without intermission, for the lowest livlihood. . . ." (*Ibid.*, p. 316). And, finally, Burke expressed his regard for the "gentlemen": "I fancy, many of our fine Gentlemen's Pageantry would be greatly tarnished, were their gilt coaches to be preceded and followed by the miserable wretches, whose labour supports them. That some should live in a more sumptuous manner than others, is very allowable; but sure it is hard, that those who cultivate the soil, should have so small a Part of its fruits; and that among Creatures of the same kind there should be such a Disproportion in their manner of living; it is a kind of blasphemy on Profidence, and seems to shew, as our Motto finely expresses, "the Heavens unjust." (*Ibid.*).

Selected Bibliography

Primary Sources on Burke

Burke, Edmund. *Reflections on the Revolution in France*. New Rochelle, New York: Arlington House, 1966.

Copeland, Thomas W. (ed.) *The Correspondence of Edmund Burke*. 6 vols. Chicago: University of Chicago Press, 1958, 1960, 1961, 1963, 1965, 1967.

Samuels, Arthur P. I. (ed.), *The Early Life, Correspondence and Writings of the Rt. Hon. Edmund Burke Ll.D.* Cambridge: Cambridge University Press, 1923.

Somerset, H. V. F. (ed.). *A Notebook of Edmund Burke*. Cambridge: Cambridge University Press, 1957.

The Writings and Speeches of the Rt. Hon. Edmund Burke. Beaconsfield Edition. 12 vols. Boston: Little, Brown and Co., 1901.

Secondary Sources on Burke

Books

Barry, Liam. *Our Legacy From Burke*. Cork, Ireland: Paramount Printing House, 1952.

Batchelder, J. L. *The Genius of Edmund Burke*. Chicago: J. L. Batchelder, 1866.

Boulton, James T. *The Language of Politics in the Age of Wilkes and Burke.* London: Routledge and Kegan Paul, 1963.

Braune, Friede. *Edmund Burke in Deutschland: Ein Beitrag zur Geschichte des Historisch-politischen Denkens.* Heidelberg: Carl Winters Universitaets-buchhandlung, 1917.

Butler, Geoffrey G. *The Tory Tradition: Bolingbrook, Burke, Disraeli, Salisbury.* London: John Murray Co., 1914.

Canavan, Francis P., S. J. *The Political Reason of Edmund Burke.* Durham, North Carolina: Duke University Press, 1960.

Capadose, I. Edmund Burke: *Overzigt van het Leven en de Schriften van ean Antirevolutionair Staatsman.* Amsterdam: Bij J. H. Gebhard and Co., 1857.

Chapman, Gerald W. *Edmund Burke: The Practical Imagination.* Cambridge, Massachusetts: Harvard University Press, 1967.

Cobban, Alfred. *Edmund Burke and the Revolt against the Eighteenth Century.* London: George Allen and Unwin LTD, 1960.

Cone, Carl B. *Burke and the Nature of Politics: The Age of the French Revolution.* Lexington, Kentucky: University of Kentucky Press, 1964.

Copeland, Thomas W. *Edmund Burke: Six Essays.* London: Jonathan Cape, 1950.

Courtney, C. P. *Montesquieu and Burke.* Oxford: Basil Blackwell, 1963.

Fay, C. A. *Burke and Adam Smith.* Belfast: Marjory Boyd, 1956.

Fennessy, R. R. o.f.m. *Burke, Paine and the Rights of Man.* The Hague: Martinus Nijoff, 1963.

Graubard, Stephen R. *Burke, Disraeli and Churchill: The Politics of Perseverance.* Cambridge, Massachusetts: Harvard University Press, 1961.

Hagberg, Knut. *Burke, Metternich, Disraeli.* Stockholm: P. A. Norstedt and Söners Förlag, 1931.

Kirk, Russell. *The Conservative Mind.* Chicago: Henry Regnery Co., 1960.

——————. *Edmund Burke.* New Rochelle, New York: Arlington House, 1967.

Laski, Harold J. *Edmund Burke.* Dublin: Falconer Press, 1947.

Lennox, Richmond. *Edmund Burke und Sein Politisches Arbeitsfeld in den Jahren 1760 bis 1790.* Muenchen: R. Oldenbourg Verlag, 1923.

Lucas, F. L. *The Art of Living: Four Eighteenth Century Minds.* London: Cassell and Co., Ltd, 1959.

MacCunn, John. *The Political Philosophy of Burke*. London: Edward Arnold, 1913.

Mahoney, Thomas H. D. *Edmund Burke and Ireland*. Cambridge, Massachusetts: Harvard University Press, 1960.

Meusel, Friedrich. *Edmund Burke und die Franzoesische Revolution*. Berlin: Weldmannsche Buchhandlung, 1913.

Montgomery, H. de F. *Gladstone and Burke*. London: P. S. King and Son (Parliamentary Agency), 1886.

Morely, John. "Burke" in *English Men of Letters*, ed. John Morely. New York: John Wurtile Lovell, 1881. pp. 9-135.

Oppenheimer, Felix Frh. von. *Edmund Burke und die Franzoesische Revolution*. Wien: Manzsche Verlag, 1928. pp. 41-71.

Opzoomer, C. W. *Konservatismus und Reform: Eine Abhandlung ueber Edmund Burkes Politik*. Utrecht: W. F. Dannenfelser, 1852.

Osborn, Annie Marion. *Rousseau and Burke*. New York: Russell and Russell, 1964.

Parkin, Charles. *The Moral Basis of Burke's Political Thought*. Cambridge: Cambridge University Press, 1956.

Reynolds, E. E. *Edmund Burke*. London: S. C. M. Press, 1948.

Schumann, Hans-Gerd. *Edmund Burkes Anschauungen vom Gleichgewicht in Staat und Staatensystem*. Meisenheim am Glan: Verlag Anton Hain, 1964.

Skalweit, Stephan. *Edmund Burke und Frankreich*. Koln: Westduetscher Verlag, 1956.

Stanlis, Peter J. *Edmund Burke and the Natural Law*. Ann Arbor: University of Michigan Press, 1965.

_____. (Ed.). *The Revelance of Edmund Burke*. New York: P. J. Kennedy and Sons, 1964.

Underdown, P. T. *Bristol and Burke*. Bristol: University of Bristol, 1961.

Utley, T. E. *Edmund Burke*. London: Longmans, Green and Co., 1957.

Wheare, G. E. *Edmund Burke's Connection with Bristol from 1774 to 1780*. Bristol: William Bennett, 1894.

Willi, Hans Ulrich. *Die Staatsauffassung Edmund Burkes*. Winterthur: Verlag Hans Schellenberg, 1964.

Wyss, Walter von. *Edmund Burke*. Muenchen: Verlag George D. W. Callway, 1966.

Articles

Bentham, Jeremy. "Defense of Economy Against the Late Mr. Burke," *The Pamphleteer*, IX (January 1817), 3-47.

Einaudi, Mario. "The British Background of Burke's Political Philosophy," *Political Science Quarterly*, XLIX (December 1934), 576-98.

Hart, Jeffrey. "Burke and Radical Freedom," *The Review of Politics*, XXIX (April 1967), 221-38.

——————. "Habit and Being in Burke," *The University Bookman*, IV (Autumn 1963), 3-8.

Kirk, Russell, "Edmund Burke and the Philosophy of Prescription," *Journal of the History of Ideas*, IX (June 1953), 365-80.

Rothbard, Murray N. "A Note on Burke's 'Vindication of Natural Society,' " *Journal of the History of Ideas*, XIX (January 1958), 114-18.

Primary Sources on Marx

Beer, Samuel (ed). *The Communist Manifesto*. New York: Appleton-Century-Crofts, 1955.

Caute, David (ed). *Essential Writings of Karl Marx*. New York: Collier Books, 1970.

Feuer, Lewis (ed). *Basic Writings on Politics and Philosophy: Karl Marx and Friedrich Engels*. New York: Doubleday and Co., Inc., 1959.

Marx, Karl and Engels, Friedrich. *Briefwechsel*. 4 vols. Berlin: Dietz Verlag, 1949, 1950.

Marx, Karl. *Capital*. trans. Samuel Moors and Edward Aveling from the Third German Edition. Chicago: Encyclopaedia Britannica, Inc., 1952.

——————. *Das Kapital*. Hamburg: Otto Meisners Verlag, 1922.

Marx, Karl and Friedrich Engels. *Die Deutsche Ideologie*. Berlin: Dietz Verlag, 1960.

Marx, Karl. *Economic and Philosophical Manuscripts,* trans. T. B. Bottomore, in Fromm, Eric. *Marx's Concept of Man*. New York: Frederick Ungar Publishing Co., 1961, pp. 84-260.

Secondary Sources on Marx

Books

Adams, H. F. *Karl Marx in His Earlier Writings*, New York: Russell and Russell, 1965.

Aptheker, Herbert (ed.). *Marxism and Alienation*. New York: Humanities Press, 1965.

Bekker, Konrad. *Marx' Philosophische Entwicklung: Sein Verhaltnis zu Hegel*. Zuerich: Verlag Oprecht, 1940.

Bittel, Karl. *Karl Marx als Geschichtsphilosoph*. Berlin: Paul Gassirer Verlag, 1920.

Cole, G. D. H. *Socialist Thought: The Forerunners 1789-1850*. Vol. I: *A History of Socialist Thought*. London: Macmillan Co., 1965.

_____. *Marxism and Anarchism: 1850-1890*. Vol. 2: *A History of Socialist Thought*. London: Macmillan Co., 1965.

Cornforth, Maurice. *Marxism and the Linguistic Philosophy*. London: Lawrence and Wishart, 1965.

Croce, Bendetto. *Essays on Marx and Russia*, trans. Angelo A. De Gennaro. New York: Frederick Ungar Publishing Co., 1966.

Drachkovitch, Milorad M. (ed.). *Marxism in the Modern World* Stanford: Stanford University Press, 1966.

Dunner, Joseph. "Marxism" in *A Handbook of World History: Concepts and Issues*. ed. Joseph Dunner. New York: Philosophical Library, 1967. pp. 548-59.

Eastman, Max. *Marxism, Is It Science?* New York: W. W. Norton and Co., Inc., 1940.

Glickson, Moshe. *The Jewish Complex of Karl Marx*. New York: Herzl Press, 1961.

Gregor, A. James. *A Survey of Marxism*. New York: Random House, 1965.

Heitzer, Heinz. *Karl Marx als Historiker*. Leipzig: Urania Verlag, 1955.

Hook, Sidney. *From Hegel to Marx: Studies in the Intellectual Development of Karl Marx*. Ann Arbor: University of Michigan Press, 1962.

_____. *Marx and the Marxists*. Princeton: D. Van Nostrand Co., Inc., 1955.

_____. *Towards the Understanding of Karl Marx*. New York: The John Day Co., 1933.

Kamenka, Eugene. *The Ethical Foundations of Marxism*. London: Routledge and Kegan Paul, 1962.

Kiss, Gabor (ed.). *Gibt es eine 'Marxistische' Soziologie?* Koeln: West Westdeutscher Verlag, 1966.

Laski, Harold J. *Marx and Today*. London: Victor Gollancq Ltd, 1953.

Lichtheim, George. *Marxism: An Historical and Critical Study*. New York: Frederick A. Praeger, 1963.

Mehring, Franz. *Karl Marx*. trans. Edward Fitzgerald. Ann Arbor: University of Michigan Press, 1962.

Petersen, Arnold. *Karl Marx and Marxian Science*. New York: New York Labor News Co., 1943.

Popper, Karl. *The High Tide of Prophecy: Hegel, Marx and the Aftermath.* Vol. 2: *The Open Society and Its Enemies.* New York: Harper Torchbooks, 1963.

Somerville, John MacPherson. *Methodology in Social Science: A Critique of Marx and Engels.* New York: Columbia University Press, 1938.

Sultan, Herbert. *Gesellschaft und Staat bei Karl Marx und Friedrich Engels: Ein Beitrag zum Sozialierungs-Problem.* Jena: Verlag von Gustav Fischer, 1922.

Their, Erich. *Das Menschenbild des Jungen Marx.* Goettingen: Vanderbook und Ruprecht, 1957.

Tucker, Robert. *Philosophy and Myth in Karl Marx.* Cambridge: Cambridge University Press, 1961.

Wittfogel, Karl A. *Oriental Despotism.* New Haven: Yale University Press, 1964.

Wolfe, Bertram D. *Three Who Made a Revolution: A Biographical History.* Boston: Beacon Press, 1948.

Articles

Arora, Phyllis. "Marx: Utopian or Scientist?" *The Political Quarterly,* XXXVIII (July-September 1967), 301-14.

Avineri, Schlomo. "Marx and the Intellectuals," *Journal of the History of Ideas,* XXVIII (April-June 1967), 269-78.

Dumas, Andre. "Marxismus, Ideologie und Glaube," *Dokumente,* VI (December 1966), 427-34.

Feuer, Lewis S. "John Stuart Mill and Marxian Socialism," *Journal of the History of Ideas,* X (April 1949), 297-303.

Hook, Sidney, "Karl Marx and Bruno Bauer," *Modern Monthly,* VII (April 1933) 160-74.

_____. "Karl Marx and Max Stirner," *Modern Monthly,* VII (October 1933), 547-55, 569.

_____. "Karl Marx and Moses Hess," *The New International,* I (November 1934), 140-44.

_____. "Marx's Criticism of 'True Socialism,' " *The New International,* II (January 1935), 13-16.

_____. "The Enlightenment and Marxism," *Journal of the History of Ideas,* XXIX (January-March 1968), 93-108.

Johnston, William M. "Karl Marx's Verse of 1836-37 as a Foreshadowing of his Early Philosophy," *Journal of the History of Ideas,* XXVIII (April-June 1967), 259-68.

Krieger, Leonard. "Marx and Engels as Historians," *Journal of the History of Ideas,* XIV (June 1953), 381-403.

Liber, M. "Judaisme et Socialisme: Henri Heine, Karl Marx et le Judaisme," *La Révue de Paris*, IV (Juillet-Août, 1928), 607-28.

"Marx: Unser Zeitgenosse", *Der Spiegel*, June 23, 1969.

Mayer, Jacob Peter, "Alexis de Tocqueville und Karl Marx: Affinitaeten und Gegensaetze," *Zeitschrift fuer Politik*, XIII (Maerz 1966), 1-13.

McFadden, Charles Joseph. "The Metaphysical Foundations of Dialectical Materialism," *Philosophical Studies*, XXXVIII (1938), 11-198.

Régnier, Marcel. "Hegelianism and Marxism," *Social Research*, XXXIV (Spring 1967), 31-46.

Schaeffer, Alfred. "Reichtum und Gewalt: Industrielle und Politische Revolution in den Schriften des Jungen Marx," *Zeitschrift Fuer Politik* XIV (Juni 1967), 130-49.

_____. "Zur Soziologie von Karl Marx," *Die Neue Gesellschaft*, II (Maerz-April 1967), 153-57.

Spargo, John. "The London Residences of Karl Marx," *The Comrade*, II (1903), page numbers illegible.

General Sources

Almond, Gabriel A. and Coleman, James S. *The Politics of Developing Areas*. Princeton: Princeton University Press, 1960.

Aristotle. *Works*. Volume I. Chicago: Encyclopaedia Britannica, Inc., 1952.

Aron, Raymond. *The Industrial Society*. New York: Frederick A. Praeger, 1967.

Barker, Ernest. (trans.) *The Politics of Aristotle*. Oxford: Clarendon Press, 1946.

Becker, Carl. *The Declaration of Independence: A Study in the History of Political Ideas*. New York: Vintage Books, 1942.

Beer, Samuel H. *British Politics in the Collectivist Age*. New York: Alfred A. Knopt, 1966.

Brinton, Crane. *The Shaping of Modern Thought*. Englewood Cliffs, New Jersey: Prentice Hall, Inc. 1963.

Burnham, James. *Congress and the American Tradition*. Chicago: Henry Regnery Co., 1965.

Charlesworth, James C. (ed.). *The Limits of Behavioralism in Political Science*. Philadelphia: The American Academy of Political and Social Science, October 1962.

Dunner, Joseph. *Baruch, Spinoza and Western Democracy*. New York: Philosophical Library, 1955.

Easton, David. *A System Analysis of Political Life*. New York: John Wiley and Sons, 1965.

Engels, Friedrich. *Socialism: Utopian and Scientific*, trans. Edward Aveling. New York: International Publishers, 1935.

Federn, Karl. *The Materialist Conception of History*. London: Macmillan Co., 1939.

Goldman, Peter. *Some Principles of Conservatism*. London: Conservative Political Centre, 1961.

Haldane, John Scott. *The Sciences and Philosophy*. London: Hodder and Staughton, Limited, 1928.

Hall, Walter Phelps; Albion, Robert Greenhalgh and Jennie Barnes Pope. *A History of England and the Empire-Commonwealth*. New York: Blaisdell Publishing Co., 1965. pp. 273-485.

Hook, Sidney. *Political Power and Personal Freedom*. New York: Criterion Books, 1959.

Hoover, Calvin B. *Economic Systems of the Commonwealth*. Durham, North Carolina: Duke University Press, 1962.

Joll, James. *The Second International: 1889-1914*. New York: Harper and Row, Publishers, 1966.

Lasswell, Harold D. *The Future of Political Science*. New York: Atherton Press, 1964.

_____. *Politics: Who Gets What, When, How*. New York: Meridian Books, 1958.

Long, Priscilla (ed.). *The New Left*. Boston: Porter Sergent Publisher, 1962.

Mannheim, Karl. *Ideology and Utopia*. New York: Harcourt, Brace and Co., 1949.

McKenzie, R. *British Political Parties*. London: William Heineman Ltd, 1955.

Namier, Sir Lewis. *The Structure of Politics at the Accession of George III*. London: Macmillan Co., 1960.

Odegard, Peter H. "A New Look at Leviathan" in *Frontiers of Knowledge in the Study of Man*, ed. Lynn T. White. New York: Harper and Bros., 1956, pp. 93-108.

Oglesby, Carl (ed.). *The New Left Reader*. New York: Grove Press, 1969.

Ostrogorski, A. F. K. *The Stages of Political Development*. New York: Alfred A. Knopf, 1965.

Paine, Thomas. *Common Sense*. New Rochelle, New York: Thomas Paine National Historical Association, 1925.

_____. *The Rights of Man*. New Rochelle, New York: Thomas Paine National Historical Association, 1925.

Polanyi, Karl. *The Great Transformation*. New York: Farrar and Rinehart, Inc., 1944.

Rossiter, Clinton. *Conservatism in America*. New York: Random House, 1962.

Sabine, George H. *A History of Political Theory*. New York: Holt Rinehart and Winston, Inc., 1961, pp. 607-67, 755-882.

Smith, Adam. *An Inquiry into the Nature and Causes of the Wealth of Nations*. Chicago: Encyclopaedia Britannica, Inc., 1952.

Smith, Goldwin. *A History of England*. New York: Charles Scribner's Sons, 1957. pp. 445-526.

Spinoza, Baruch. *A Theological-Political Treatise*. Vol. I of *The Chief Works of Benedict de Spinoza*. New York: Dove Publications, 1953.

Strauss, Leo. *What is Political Philosophy?* Glencoe, Illinois: The Free Press of Glencoe, 1959.

Talmon, J. L. *The Origins of Totalitarian Democracy*. New York: Frederick A. Praeger, 1965.

Williams, E. H. *The Eighteenth Century Constitution: 1688-1815*. Cambridge: Cambridge Unviersity Press, 1965.

Wolf, Robert; Moore, Barrington Jr. and Herbert Marcuse. *A Critique of Pure Tolerance*. Boston: Beacon Press, 1969.

Articles

Berlin, Isaiah, "Political Ideas in the Twentieth Century," *Foreign Affairs*, XXVIII (April 1950), 351-85.

Dewey, John. "The Future of Liberalism," *Journal of Philosophy*, XXXII, No. 9, (April 25, 1935), 225-30.

Holborn, Hajo. "Greek and Modern Concepts of History," *Journal of the History of Ideas*, X (January 1949), 3-13.

Johnson, Harold H. "Three Ancient Meanings of Matter: Democritus, Plato and Aristotle," *Journal of the History of Ideas*,XXVIII (January-March 1967), 3-16.

Koerner, S. "Some Relations between Philosophical and Scientific Theories," *The British Journal for the Philosophy of Science*, XVII (February 1967), 265-70.

Ries, Raymond E. "Social Science and Ideology," *Social Research*, XXI (Summer 1964), 234-43.